Just The facts101
Textbook Key Facts

European Union Privatization Programs and Regulations Handbook

by Cram101
Textbook NOT Included

Table of Contents

Title Page

Copyright

Foundations of Business

Management

Business law

Finance

Human resource management

Information systems

Marketing

Manufacturing

Commerce

Business ethics

Accounting

Index: Answers

Just The Facts101

Exam Prep for

European Union Privatization Programs and Regulations Handbook

Just The Facts101 Exam Prep is your link from
the textbook and lecture to your exams.

**Just The Facts101 Exam Preps are unauthorized and comprehensive reviews
of your textbooks.**

All material provided by CTI Publications (c) 2019

Textbook publishers and textbook authors do not participate in or contribute to these reviews.

Just The Facts101 Exam Prep

Copyright © 2019 by CTI Publications. All rights reserved.

eAIN 444722

Foundations of Business

A business, also known as an enterprise, agency or a firm, is an entity involved in the provision of goods and/or services to consumers. Businesses are prevalent in capitalist economies, where most of them are privately owned and provide goods and services to customers in exchange for other goods, services, or money.

:: Land value taxation ::

_____, sometimes referred to as dry _____, is the solid surface of Earth that is not permanently covered by water. The vast majority of human activity throughout history has occurred in _____ areas that support agriculture, habitat, and various natural resources. Some life forms have developed from predecessor species that lived in bodies of water.

Exam Probability: **High**

1. *Answer choices:*

(see index for correct answer)

- a. Land
- b. Land value tax
- c. Georgism
- d. Lands Valuation Appeal Court

Guidance: level 1

:: Finance ::

_____ is a field that is concerned with the allocation of assets and liabilities over space and time, often under conditions of risk or uncertainty. _____ can also be defined as the art of money management. Participants in the market aim to price assets based on their risk level, fundamental value, and their expected rate of return. _____ can be split into three sub-categories: public _____, corporate _____ and personal _____.

Exam Probability: **Low**

2. *Answer choices:*

(see index for correct answer)

- a. Political arbitrage
- b. Finance
- c. Unitax
- d. Putty-putty

Guidance: level 1

:: Workplace ::

_____ is asystematic determination of a subject's merit, worth and significance, using criteria governed by a set of standards. It can assist an organization, program, design, project or any other intervention or initiative to assess any aim, realisable concept/proposal, or any alternative, to help in decision-making; or to ascertain the degree of achievement or value in regard to the aim and objectives and results of any such action that has been completed. The primary purpose of _____ , in addition to gaining insight into prior or existing initiatives, is to enable reflection and assist in the identification of future change.

Exam Probability: **Medium**

3. *Answer choices:*

(see index for correct answer)

- a. 360-degree feedback
- b. Evaluation
- c. Workplace phobia
- d. Staff turnover

Guidance: level 1

:: International trade ::

The law or principle of _____ holds that under free trade, an agent will produce more of and consume less of a good for which they have a _____. _____ is the economic reality describing the work gains from trade for individuals, firms, or nations, which arise from differences in their factor endowments or technological progress. In an economic model, agents have a _____ over others in producing a particular good if they can produce that good at a lower relative opportunity cost or autarky price, i.e. at a lower relative marginal cost prior to trade. One shouldn't compare the monetary costs of production or even the resource costs of production. Instead, one must compare the opportunity costs of producing goods across countries.

Exam Probability: **High**

4. *Answer choices:*
(see index for correct answer)

- a. Trade commissioner
- b. International free trade agreement
- c. Comparative advantage
- d. International monetary systems

Guidance: level 1

:: Business law ::

_____ is where a person's financial liability is limited to a fixed sum, most commonly the value of a person's investment in a company or partnership. If a company with _____ is sued, then the claimants are suing the company, not its owners or investors. A shareholder in a limited company is not personally liable for any of the debts of the company, other than for the amount already invested in the company and for any unpaid amount on the shares in the company, if any. The same is true for the members of a _____ partnership and the limited partners in a limited partnership. By contrast, sole proprietors and partners in general partnerships are each liable for all the debts of the business.

Exam Probability: **Medium**

5. *Answer choices:*
(see index for correct answer)

- a. Ordinary resolution
- b. Secret rebate
- c. Participation
- d. Wrongful trading

Guidance: level 1

:: Consumer theory ::

A _____ is a technical term in psychology, economics and philosophy usually used in relation to choosing between alternatives. For example, someone prefers A over B if they would rather choose A than B.

Exam Probability: **High**

6. *Answer choices:*

(see index for correct answer)

- a. Elasticity of substitution
- b. Delayed gratification
- c. Hicksian demand function
- d. Preference

Guidance: level 1

:: Critical thinking ::

An _____ is a set of statements usually constructed to describe a set of facts which clarifies the causes, context, and consequences of those facts. This description of the facts et cetera may establish rules or laws, and may clarify the existing rules or laws in relation to any objects, or phenomena examined. The components of an _____ can be implicit, and interwoven with one another.

Exam Probability: **Medium**

7. Answer choices:

(see index for correct answer)

- a. Argumentation theory
- b. False equivalence
- c. Explanation
- d. Argument by example

Guidance: level 1

:: Debt ::

_____ is the trust which allows one party to provide money or resources to another party wherein the second party does not reimburse the first party immediately, but promises either to repay or return those resources at a later date. In other words, _____ is a method of making reciprocity formal, legally enforceable, and extensible to a large group of unrelated people.

Exam Probability: **High**

8. Answer choices:

(see index for correct answer)

- a. Credit
- b. Default
- c. Bailout
- d. Bad debt

Guidance: level 1

:: Human resource management ::

> _____ is the corporate management term for the act of reorganizing the legal, ownership, operational, or other structures of a company for the purpose of making it more profitable, or better organized for its present needs. Other reasons for _____ include a change of ownership or ownership structure, demerger, or a response to a crisis or major change in the business such as bankruptcy, repositioning, or buyout. _____ may also be described as corporate _____ , debt _____ and financial _____ .

Exam Probability: **Medium**

9. *Answer choices:*
(see index for correct answer)

- a. Job knowledge
- b. Cross-functional team
- c. Job design
- d. Human resource policies

Guidance: level 1

:: E-commerce ::

_____ is the activity of buying or selling of products on online services or over the Internet. Electronic commerce draws on technologies such as mobile commerce, electronic funds transfer, supply chain management, Internet marketing, online transaction processing, electronic data interchange , inventory management systems, and automated data collection systems.

Exam Probability: **Medium**

10. *Answer choices:*

(see index for correct answer)

- a. Adult Check
- b. Electronic trading
- c. Segundamano
- d. Variable pricing

Guidance: level 1

:: Business models ::

_____ es are privately owned corporations, partnerships, or sole proprietorships that have fewer employees and/or less annual revenue than a regular-sized business or corporation. Businesses are defined as "small" in terms of being able to apply for government support and qualify for preferential tax policy varies depending on the country and industry. _____ es range from fifteen employees under the Australian Fair Work Act 2009, fifty employees according to the definition used by the European Union, and fewer than five hundred employees to qualify for many U.S. _____ Administration programs. While _____ es can also be classified according to other methods, such as annual revenues, shipments, sales, assets, or by annual gross or net revenue or net profits, the number of employees is one of the most widely used measures.

Exam Probability: **High**

11. *Answer choices:*

(see index for correct answer)

- a. Collective business system
- b. Small business
- c. Home business
- d. Praenumeration

Guidance: level 1

:: Statistical terminology ::

_____ is the ability to avoid wasting materials, energy, efforts, money, and time in doing something or in producing a desired result. In a more general sense, it is the ability to do things well, successfully, and without waste. In more mathematical or scientific terms, it is a measure of the extent to which input is well used for an intended task or function. It often specifically comprises the capability of a specific application of effort to produce a specific outcome with a minimum amount or quantity of waste, expense, or unnecessary effort. _____ refers to very different inputs and outputs in different fields and industries.

Exam Probability: **Low**

12. *Answer choices:*

(see index for correct answer)

- a. Efficiency
- b. Geometric standard deviation
- c. Innovations vector
- d. Trend stationary

Guidance: level 1

:: Project management ::

Some scenarios associate "this kind of planning" with learning "life skills". _____ s are necessary, or at least useful, in situations where individuals need to know what time they must be at a specific location to receive a specific service, and where people need to accomplish a set of goals within a set time period.

Exam Probability: **High**

13. *Answer choices:*

(see index for correct answer)

- a. Time limit
- b. Schedule
- c. Management process
- d. Pre-construction services

Guidance: level 1

:: Business ::

The seller, or the provider of the goods or services, completes a sale in response to an acquisition, appropriation, requisition or a direct interaction with the buyer at the point of sale. There is a passing of title of the item, and the settlement of a price, in which agreement is reached on a price for which transfer of ownership of the item will occur. The seller, not the purchaser typically executes the sale and it may be completed prior to the obligation of payment. In the case of indirect interaction, a person who sells goods or service on behalf of the owner is known as a _____ man or _____ woman or _____ person, but this often refers to someone selling goods in a store/shop, in which case other terms are also common, including _____ clerk, shop assistant, and retail clerk.

Exam Probability: **High**

14. *Answer choices:*

(see index for correct answer)

- a. Joint employment
- b. Values scales
- c. Sales
- d. Policy capturing

Guidance: level 1

:: Treaties ::

An _____ is a relationship among people, groups, or states that have joined together for mutual benefit or to achieve some common purpose, whether or not explicit agreement has been worked out among them. Members of an _____ are called allies. _____ s form in many settings, including political _____ s, military _____ s, and business _____ s. When the term is used in the context of war or armed struggle, such associations may also be called allied powers, especially when discussing World War I or World War II.

Exam Probability: **Low**

15. *Answer choices:*

(see index for correct answer)

- a. Treaty
- b. Guillotine clause
- c. Multilateral treaty

- d. Alliance

Guidance: level 1

:: Management ::

> The _____ is a strategy performance management tool – a semi-standard structured report, that can be used by managers to keep track of the execution of activities by the staff within their control and to monitor the consequences arising from these actions.

Exam Probability: **Low**

16. *Answer choices:*

(see index for correct answer)

- a. Goal
- b. Downstream
- c. Balanced scorecard
- d. Coworking

Guidance: level 1

:: ::

_____ is a marketing communication that employs an openly sponsored, non-personal message to promote or sell a product, service or idea. Sponsors of _____ are typically businesses wishing to promote their products or services. _____ is differentiated from public relations in that an advertiser pays for and has control over the message. It differs from personal selling in that the message is non-personal, i.e., not directed to a particular individual. _____ is communicated through various mass media, including traditional media such as newspapers, magazines, television, radio, outdoor _____ or direct mail; and new media such as search results, blogs, social media, websites or text messages. The actual presentation of the message in a medium is referred to as an advertisement, or "ad" or advert for short.

Exam Probability: **High**

17. *Answer choices:*

(see index for correct answer)

- a. Character
- b. corporate values
- c. functional perspective
- d. similarity-attraction theory

Guidance: level 1

:: Fraud ::

In law, _____ is intentional deception to secure unfair or unlawful gain, or to deprive a victim of a legal right. _____ can violate civil law, a criminal law, or it may cause no loss of money, property or legal right but still be an element of another civil or criminal wrong. The purpose of _____ may be monetary gain or other benefits, for example by obtaining a passport, travel document, or driver's license, or mortgage _____, where the perpetrator may attempt to qualify for a mortgage by way of false statements.

Exam Probability: **Medium**

18. *Answer choices:*

(see index for correct answer)

- a. Fraud
- b. Deceptive advertising
- c. Sham marriage
- d. Credit card kiting

Guidance: level 1

:: Alchemical processes ::

In chemistry, a _____ is a special type of homogeneous mixture composed of two or more substances. In such a mixture, a solute is a substance dissolved in another substance, known as a solvent. The mixing process of a _____ happens at a scale where the effects of chemical polarity are involved, resulting in interactions that are specific to solvation. The _____ assumes the phase of the solvent when the solvent is the larger fraction of the mixture, as is commonly the case. The concentration of a solute in a _____ is the mass of that solute expressed as a percentage of the mass of the whole _____ . The term aqueous _____ is when one of the solvents is water.

Exam Probability: **Low**

19. *Answer choices:*

(see index for correct answer)

- a. Digestion
- b. Fixation
- c. Unity of opposites
- d. Solution

Guidance: level 1

:: Data collection ::

A _____ is an utterance which typically functions as a request for information. _____ s can thus be understood as a kind of illocutionary act in the field of pragmatics or as special kinds of propositions in frameworks of formal semantics such as alternative semantics or inquisitive semantics. The information requested is expected to be provided in the form of an answer. _____ s are often conflated with interrogatives, which are the grammatical forms typically used to achieve them. Rhetorical _____ s, for example, are interrogative in form but may not be considered true _____ s as they are not expected to be answered. Conversely, non-interrogative grammatical structures may be considered _____ s as in the case of the imperative sentence "tell me your name".

Exam Probability: **Medium**

20. *Answer choices:*

(see index for correct answer)

- a. Global surveillance
- b. Unstructured data
- c. PISCES
- d. Question

Guidance: level 1

:: Unemployment ::

In economics, a _____ is a business cycle contraction when there is a general decline in economic activity. Macroeconomic indicators such as GDP, investment spending, capacity utilization, household income, business profits, and inflation fall, while bankruptcies and the unemployment rate rise. In the United Kingdom, it is defined as a negative economic growth for two consecutive quarters.

Exam Probability: **Low**

21. *Answer choices:*

(see index for correct answer)

- a. Phillips curve
- b. Recession
- c. Mount Street Club
- d. Discouraged worker

Guidance: level 1

:: Debt ::

_____ is when something, usually money, is owed by one party, the borrower or _____ or, to a second party, the lender or creditor. _____ is a deferred payment, or series of payments, that is owed in the future, which is what differentiates it from an immediate purchase. The _____ may be owed by sovereign state or country, local government, company, or an individual. Commercial _____ is generally subject to contractual terms regarding the amount and timing of repayments of principal and interest. Loans, bonds, notes, and mortgages are all types of _____. The term can also be used metaphorically to cover moral obligations and other interactions not based on economic value. For example, in Western cultures, a person who has been helped by a second person is sometimes said to owe a "_____ of gratitude" to the second person.

Exam Probability: **Medium**

22. *Answer choices:*

(see index for correct answer)

- a. Extendible bond
- b. Borrowing base
- c. Teacher Loan Forgiveness
- d. Interest

Guidance: level 1

:: Generally Accepted Accounting Principles ::

An _____ or profit and loss account is one of the financial statements of a company and shows the company's revenues and expenses during a particular period.

Exam Probability: **High**

23. *Answer choices:*

(see index for correct answer)

- a. Closing entries
- b. Generally accepted accounting principles
- c. Fin 48
- d. Cash method of accounting

Guidance: level 1

:: Industrial design ::

In physics and mathematics, the _____ of a mathematical space is informally defined as the minimum number of coordinates needed to specify any point within it. Thus a line has a _____ of one because only one coordinate is needed to specify a point on it for example, the point at 5 on a number line. A surface such as a plane or the surface of a cylinder or sphere has a _____ of two because two coordinates are needed to specify a point on it for example, both a latitude and longitude are required to locate a point on the surface of a sphere. The inside of a cube, a cylinder or a sphere is three-_____ al because three coordinates are needed to locate a point within these spaces.

Exam Probability: **Medium**

24. *Answer choices:*

(see index for correct answer)

- a. Dimension
- b. Industrial design right
- c. Community design
- d. Danish design

Guidance: level 1

:: Accounting software ::

_____ is any item or verifiable record that is generally accepted as payment for goods and services and repayment of debts, such as taxes, in a particular country or socio-economic context. The main functions of _____ are distinguished as: a medium of exchange, a unit of account, a store of value and sometimes, a standard of deferred payment. Any item or verifiable record that fulfils these functions can be considered as _____ .

Exam Probability: **Low**

25. *Answer choices:*

(see index for correct answer)

- a. Quicken
- b. BIG4books

- c. Invoiceit
- d. Money

Guidance: level 1

:: ::

An _____ is an area of the production, distribution, or trade, and consumption of goods and services by different agents. Understood in its broadest sense, 'The _____ is defined as a social domain that emphasize the practices, discourses, and material expressions associated with the production, use, and management of resources'. Economic agents can be individuals, businesses, organizations, or governments. Economic transactions occur when two parties agree to the value or price of the transacted good or service, commonly expressed in a certain currency. However, monetary transactions only account for a small part of the economic domain.

Exam Probability: **Low**

26. *Answer choices:*
(see index for correct answer)

- a. surface-level diversity
- b. personal values
- c. hierarchical
- d. Economy

Guidance: level 1

:: International relations ::

A _____ is any event that is going to lead to an unstable and dangerous situation affecting an individual, group, community, or whole society. Crises are deemed to be negative changes in the security, economic, political, societal, or environmental affairs, especially when they occur abruptly, with little or no warning. More loosely, it is a term meaning "a testing time" or an "emergency event".

Exam Probability: **Low**

27. *Answer choices:*

(see index for correct answer)

- a. Asialink
- b. Periphery countries
- c. China Institute of International Studies
- d. Crisis

Guidance: level 1

:: Legal terms ::

_____ , a form of alternative dispute resolution , is a way to resolve disputes outside the courts. The dispute will be decided by one or more persons , which renders the " _____ award". An _____ award is legally binding on both sides and enforceable in the courts.

Exam Probability: **High**

28. *Answer choices:*

(see index for correct answer)

- a. Grievous bodily harm
- b. Arbitration
- c. Offer of proof
- d. Querulant

Guidance: level 1

:: Casting (manufacturing) ::

A _____ is a regularity in the world, man-made design, or abstract ideas. As such, the elements of a _____ repeat in a predictable manner. A geometric _____ is a kind of _____ formed of geometric shapes and typically repeated like a wallpaper design.

Exam Probability: **Low**

29. *Answer choices:*

(see index for correct answer)

- a. Semi-steel
- b. Pattern
- c. Tape casting
- d. Plaster mold casting

Guidance: level 1

:: Management ::

In organizational studies, _____ is the efficient and effective development of an organization's resources when they are needed. Such resources may include financial resources, inventory, human skills, production resources, or information technology and natural resources.

Exam Probability: **High**

30. *Answer choices:*

(see index for correct answer)

- a. Empowerment
- b. Resource management
- c. Logistics management
- d. Competitive advantage

Guidance: level 1

:: Classification systems ::

_____ is the practice of comparing business processes and performance metrics to industry bests and best practices from other companies. Dimensions typically measured are quality, time and cost.

Exam Probability: **High**

31. *Answer choices:*

(see index for correct answer)

- a. Ranally city rating system
- b. Benchmarking
- c. International Classification of Diseases for Oncology
- d. Viridiplantae

Guidance: level 1

:: Organizational theory ::

_____ is the process of groups of organisms working or acting together for common, mutual, or some underlying benefit, as opposed to working in competition for selfish benefit. Many animal and plant species cooperate both with other members of their own species and with members of other species.

Exam Probability: **High**

32. *Answer choices:*

(see index for correct answer)

- a. Cooperation
- b. Star Roles Model
- c. Organizational theory
- d. Battlefield promotion

Guidance: level 1

:: Globalization-related theories ::

_____ is an economic system based on the private ownership of the means of production and their operation for profit. Characteristics central to _____ include private property, capital accumulation, wage labor, voluntary exchange, a price system, and competitive markets. In a capitalist market economy, decision-making and investment are determined by every owner of wealth, property or production ability in financial and capital markets, whereas prices and the distribution of goods and services are mainly determined by competition in goods and services markets.

Exam Probability: **Medium**

33. *Answer choices:*

(see index for correct answer)

- a. post-industrial
- b. Capitalism
- c. postmodernism

Guidance: level 1

:: Energy and fuel journals ::

In physics, energy is the quantitative property that must be transferred to an object in order to perform work on, or to heat, the object. Energy is a conserved quantity; the law of conservation of energy states that energy can be converted in form, but not created or destroyed. The SI unit of energy is the joule, which is the energy transferred to an object by the work of moving it a distance of 1 metre against a force of 1 newton.

Exam Probability: **High**

34. *Answer choices:*

(see index for correct answer)

- a. Flow, Turbulence and Combustion
- b. Energies
- c. Heat and Mass Transfer
- d. Advanced Energy Materials

Guidance: level 1

:: Management ::

_____ is the process of thinking about the activities required to achieve a desired goal. It is the first and foremost activity to achieve desired results. It involves the creation and maintenance of a plan, such as psychological aspects that require conceptual skills. There are even a couple of tests to measure someone's capability of _____ well. As such, _____ is a fundamental property of intelligent behavior. An important further meaning, often just called " _____ " is the legal context of permitted building developments.

Exam Probability: **High**

35. *Answer choices:*

(see index for correct answer)

- a. Logistics support analysis
- b. Customer Benefit Package
- c. Planning
- d. DMSMS

Guidance: level 1

:: Stock market ::

A _____, equity market or share market is the aggregation of buyers and sellers of stocks, which represent ownership claims on businesses; these may include securities listed on a public stock exchange, as well as stock that is only traded privately. Examples of the latter include shares of private companies which are sold to investors through equity crowdfunding platforms. Stock exchanges list shares of common equity as well as other security types, e.g. corporate bonds and convertible bonds.

Exam Probability: **Medium**

36. *Answer choices:*

(see index for correct answer)

- a. Stock market
- b. Stop price
- c. Non-voting stock
- d. Intermarket sweep order

Guidance: level 1

:: Market research ::

A _____ is a small, but demographically diverse group of people and whose reactions are studied especially in market research or political analysis in guided or open discussions about a new product or something else to determine the reactions that can be expected from a larger population. It is a form of qualitative research consisting of interviews in which a group of people are asked about their perceptions, opinions, beliefs, and attitudes towards a product, service, concept, advertisement, idea, or packaging. Questions are asked in an interactive group setting where participants are free to talk with other group members. During this process, the researcher either takes notes or records the vital points he or she is getting from the group. Researchers should select members of the _____ carefully for effective and authoritative responses.

Exam Probability: **Medium**

37. *Answer choices:*

(see index for correct answer)

- a. Worm
- b. Cume
- c. Cogent Research
- d. Preference regression

Guidance: level 1

:: Marketing techniques ::

_____ is the activity of dividing a broad consumer or business market, normally consisting of existing and potential customers, into sub-groups of consumers based on some type of shared characteristics. In dividing or segmenting markets, researchers typically look for common characteristics such as shared needs, common interests, similar lifestyles or even similar demographic profiles. The overall aim of segmentation is to identify high yield segments – that is, those segments that are likely to be the most profitable or that have growth potential – so that these can be selected for special attention.

Exam Probability: **Medium**

38. *Answer choices:*

(see index for correct answer)

- a. Angel dusting
- b. Wait marketing
- c. Market segmentation
- d. Marketing co-operation

Guidance: level 1

:: Management ::

A _____ is an idea of the future or desired result that a person or a group of people envisions, plans and commits to achieve. People endeavor to reach _____ s within a finite time by setting deadlines.

Exam Probability: **Low**

39. *Answer choices:*

(see index for correct answer)

- a. Vasa syndrome
- b. Double linking
- c. Goal
- d. Enterprise planning system

Guidance: level 1

:: Financial regulatory authorities of the United States ::

The _____ is the revenue service of the United States federal government. The government agency is a bureau of the Department of the Treasury, and is under the immediate direction of the Commissioner of Internal Revenue, who is appointed to a five-year term by the President of the United States. The IRS is responsible for collecting taxes and administering the Internal Revenue Code, the main body of federal statutory tax law of the United States. The duties of the IRS include providing tax assistance to taxpayers and pursuing and resolving instances of erroneous or fraudulent tax filings. The IRS has also overseen various benefits programs, and enforces portions of the Affordable Care Act.

Exam Probability: **High**

40. *Answer choices:*

(see index for correct answer)

- a. Internal Revenue Service
- b. Consumer Financial Protection Bureau
- c. National Futures Association
- d. Federal Deposit Insurance Corporation

Guidance: level 1

:: Management occupations ::

_____ ship is the process of designing, launching and running a new business, which is often initially a small business. The people who create these businesses are called _____ s.

Exam Probability: **Low**

41. *Answer choices:*
(see index for correct answer)

- a. Ceco
- b. Vorstandsassistent
- c. Entrepreneur
- d. Chief diversity officer

Guidance: level 1

:: Actuarial science ::

_____ is the possibility of losing something of value. Values can be gained or lost when taking _____ resulting from a given action or inaction, foreseen or unforeseen. _____ can also be defined as the intentional interaction with uncertainty. Uncertainty is a potential, unpredictable, and uncontrollable outcome; _____ is a consequence of action taken in spite of uncertainty.

Exam Probability: **Medium**

42. *Answer choices:*

(see index for correct answer)

- a. Force of mortality
- b. Ruin theory
- c. Disease
- d. Actuarial present value

Guidance: level 1

:: Mathematical finance ::

In economics and finance, _____ , also known as present discounted value, is the value of an expected income stream determined as of the date of valuation. The _____ is always less than or equal to the future value because money has interest-earning potential, a characteristic referred to as the time value of money, except during times of negative interest rates, when the _____ will be more than the future value. Time value can be described with the simplified phrase, "A dollar today is worth more than a dollar tomorrow". Here, `worth more` means that its value is greater. A dollar today is worth more than a dollar tomorrow because the dollar can be invested and earn a day`s worth of interest, making the total accumulate to a value more than a dollar by tomorrow. Interest can be compared to rent. Just as rent is paid to a landlord by a tenant without the ownership of the asset being transferred, interest is paid to a lender by a borrower who gains access to the money for a time before paying it back. By letting the borrower have access to the money, the lender has sacrificed the exchange value of this money, and is compensated for it in the form of interest. The initial amount of the borrowed funds is less than the total amount of money paid to the lender.

Exam Probability: **Medium**

43. *Answer choices:*

(see index for correct answer)

- a. Econophysics
- b. Adjusted present value
- c. Simple Dietz method
- d. Present value

Guidance: level 1

:: Statistical terminology ::

_____ es can be learned implicitly within cultural contexts. People may develop _____ es toward or against an individual, an ethnic group, a sexual or gender identity, a nation, a religion, a social class, a political party, theoretical paradigms and ideologies within academic domains, or a species. _____ ed means one-sided, lacking a neutral viewpoint, or not having an open mind. _____ can come in many forms and is related to prejudice and intuition.

Exam Probability: **Low**

44. *Answer choices:*
(see index for correct answer)

- a. Bias
- b. Probable error
- c. Burstiness
- d. Scale parameter

Guidance: level 1

:: Generally Accepted Accounting Principles ::

Expenditure is an outflow of money to another person or group to pay for an item or service, or for a category of costs. For a tenant, rent is an _____. For students or parents, tuition is an _____. Buying food, clothing, furniture or an automobile is often referred to as an _____. An _____ is a cost that is "paid" or "remitted", usually in exchange for something of value. Something that seems to cost a great deal is "expensive". Something that seems to cost little is "inexpensive". "_____ s of the table" are _____ s of dining, refreshments, a feast, etc.

Exam Probability: **Low**

45. *Answer choices:*

(see index for correct answer)

- a. Cost principle
- b. Operating income
- c. Expense
- d. Contributed capital

Guidance: level 1

:: Infographics ::

A _____ is a symbolic representation of information according to visualization technique. _____ s have been used since ancient times, but became more prevalent during the Enlightenment. Sometimes, the technique uses a three-dimensional visualization which is then projected onto a two-dimensional surface. The word graph is sometimes used as a synonym for _____ .

Exam Probability: **Medium**

46. *Answer choices:*

(see index for correct answer)

- a. Admiralty chart
- b. House sign
- c. Funnel chart
- d. Diagram

Guidance: level 1

:: Shareholders ::

A _____ is a payment made by a corporation to its shareholders, usually as a distribution of profits. When a corporation earns a profit or surplus, the corporation is able to re-invest the profit in the business and pay a proportion of the profit as a _____ to shareholders. Distribution to shareholders may be in cash or, if the corporation has a _____ reinvestment plan, the amount can be paid by the issue of further shares or share repurchase. When _____ s are paid, shareholders typically must pay income taxes, and the corporation does not receive a corporate income tax deduction for the _____ payments.

Exam Probability: **Medium**

47. *Answer choices:*

(see index for correct answer)

- a. Dividend
- b. Australian Shareholders Association
- c. Shareholder Executive
- d. Shareholder ownership value

Guidance: level 1

:: Strategic management ::

_____ is a strategic planning technique used to help a person or organization identify strengths, weaknesses, opportunities, and threats related to business competition or project planning. It is intended to specify the objectives of the business venture or project and identify the internal and external factors that are favorable and unfavorable to achieving those objectives. Users of a _____ often ask and answer questions to generate meaningful information for each category to make the tool useful and identify their competitive advantage. SWOT has been described as the tried-and-true tool of strategic analysis.

Exam Probability: **High**

48. *Answer choices:*

(see index for correct answer)

- a. SWOT analysis
- b. The New Age of Innovation
- c. IT strategy alignment
- d. Results-based management

Guidance: level 1

:: Financial accounting ::

_____ is a financial metric which represents operating liquidity available to a business, organisation or other entity, including governmental entities. Along with fixed assets such as plant and equipment, _____ is considered a part of operating capital. Gross _____ is equal to current assets. _____ is calculated as current assets minus current liabilities. If current assets are less than current liabilities, an entity has a _____ deficiency, also called a _____ deficit.

Exam Probability: **Low**

49. *Answer choices:*

(see index for correct answer)

- a. Working capital
- b. Deferred financing cost
- c. Hidden asset
- d. Authorised capital

Guidance: level 1

:: Majority–minority relations ::

_____ , also known as reservation in India and Nepal, positive discrimination / action in the United Kingdom, and employment equity in Canada and South Africa, is the policy of promoting the education and employment of members of groups that are known to have previously suffered from discrimination. Historically and internationally, support for _____ has sought to achieve goals such as bridging inequalities in employment and pay, increasing access to education, promoting diversity, and redressing apparent past wrongs, harms, or hindrances.

Exam Probability: **Low**

50. *Answer choices:*

(see index for correct answer)

- a. Affirmative action
- b. cultural Relativism
- c. cultural dissonance

Guidance: level 1

:: Real estate valuation ::

_____ or OMV is the price at which an asset would trade in a competitive auction setting. _____ is often used interchangeably with open _____ , fair value or fair _____ , although these terms have distinct definitions in different standards, and may or may not differ in some circumstances.

Exam Probability: **Medium**

51. *Answer choices:*

(see index for correct answer)

- a. Appraisal Standards Board
- b. Sales comparison approach
- c. Chartered Surveyor
- d. Lamudi

Guidance: level 1

:: Telecommunication theory ::

In reliability theory and reliability engineering, the term _____ has the following meanings.

Exam Probability: **Low**

52. *Answer choices:*

(see index for correct answer)

- a. Availability
- b. Balance return loss
- c. Coded set
- d. Release time

Guidance: level 1

:: Employment ::

The _____ is an individual's metaphorical "journey" through learning, work and other aspects of life. There are a number of ways to define _____ and the term is used in a variety of ways.

Exam Probability: **Medium**

53. *Answer choices:*

(see index for correct answer)

- a. Performance improvement
- b. Transformation in economics
- c. Paradox of toil
- d. Customized employment

Guidance: level 1

:: Problem solving ::

In other words, _____ is a situation where a group of people meet to generate new ideas and solutions around a specific domain of interest by removing inhibitions. People are able to think more freely and they suggest as many spontaneous new ideas as possible. All the ideas are noted down and those ideas are not criticized and after _____ session the ideas are evaluated. The term was popularized by Alex Faickney Osborn in the 1953 book Applied Imagination.

Exam Probability: **High**

54. *Answer choices:*

(see index for correct answer)

- a. Eight Disciplines Problem Solving
- b. Karl Duncker
- c. Brainstorming
- d. Divergent thinking

Guidance: level 1

:: Foreign direct investment ::

A _____ is an investment in the form of a controlling ownership in a business in one country by an entity based in another country. It is thus distinguished from a foreign portfolio investment by a notion of direct control.

Exam Probability: **Low**

55. Answer choices:

(see index for correct answer)

- a. Foreign direct investment
- b. International Centre for Settlement of Investment Disputes
- c. FDi magazine
- d. EB-5 visa

Guidance: level 1

:: Auditing ::

_____, as defined by accounting and auditing, is a process for assuring of an organization's objectives in operational effectiveness and efficiency, reliable financial reporting, and compliance with laws, regulations and policies. A broad concept, _____ involves everything that controls risks to an organization.

Exam Probability: **High**

56. Answer choices:

(see index for correct answer)

- a. Inherent risk
- b. Sales tax audit
- c. Internal control
- d. Performance audit

Guidance: level 1

:: ::

_____ or accountancy is the measurement, processing, and communication of financial information about economic entities such as businesses and corporations. The modern field was established by the Italian mathematician Luca Pacioli in 1494. _____ , which has been called the "language of business", measures the results of an organization's economic activities and conveys this information to a variety of users, including investors, creditors, management, and regulators. Practitioners of _____ are known as accountants. The terms "_____" and "financial reporting" are often used as synonyms.

Exam Probability: **High**

57. *Answer choices:*

(see index for correct answer)

- a. Character
- b. cultural
- c. personal values
- d. Accounting

Guidance: level 1

:: Training ::

_____ is teaching, or developing in oneself or others, any skills and knowledge that relate to specific useful competencies. _____ has specific goals of improving one's capability, capacity, productivity and performance. It forms the core of apprenticeships and provides the backbone of content at institutes of technology. In addition to the basic _____ required for a trade, occupation or profession, observers of the labor-market recognize as of 2008 the need to continue _____ beyond initial qualifications: to maintain, upgrade and update skills throughout working life. People within many professions and occupations may refer to this sort of _____ as professional development.

Exam Probability: **Medium**

58. *Answer choices:*

(see index for correct answer)

- a. Voluntary Protection Program
- b. Overlearning
- c. Strength and conditioning coach
- d. American Council on Exercise

Guidance: level 1

:: Semiconductor companies ::

_____ Corporation is a Japanese multinational conglomerate corporation headquartered in Konan, Minato, Tokyo. Its diversified business includes consumer and professional electronics, gaming, entertainment and financial services. The company owns the largest music entertainment business in the world, the largest video game console business and one of the largest video game publishing businesses, and is one of the leading manufacturers of electronic products for the consumer and professional markets, and a leading player in the film and television entertainment industry. _____ was ranked 97th on the 2018 Fortune Global 500 list.

Exam Probability: **Medium**

59. *Answer choices:*

(see index for correct answer)

- a. Hana Micron
- b. STMicroelectronics
- c. Zilog
- d. Sony

Guidance: level 1

Management

Management is the administration of an organization, whether it is a business, a not-for-profit organization, or government body. Management includes the activities of setting the strategy of an organization and coordinating the efforts of its employees (or of volunteers) to accomplish its objectives through the application of available resources, such as financial, natural, technological, and human resources.

An _____ is, most an organized examination or formal evaluation exercise. In engineering activities _____ involves the measurements, tests, and gauges applied to certain characteristics in regard to an object or activity. The results are usually compared to specified requirements and standards for determining whether the item or activity is in line with these targets, often with a Standard _____ Procedure in place to ensure consistent checking. _____ s are usually non-destructive.

Exam Probability: **High**

1. *Answer choices:*

(see index for correct answer)

- a. Inspection
- b. co-culture
- c. open system
- d. hierarchical

Guidance: level 1

:: ::

_____ refers to a business or organization attempting to acquire goods or services to accomplish its goals. Although there are several organizations that attempt to set standards in the _____ process, processes can vary greatly between organizations. Typically the word " _____ " is not used interchangeably with the word "procurement", since procurement typically includes expediting, supplier quality, and transportation and logistics in addition to _____ .

Exam Probability: **Medium**

2. *Answer choices:*

(see index for correct answer)

- a. Purchasing
- b. surface-level diversity
- c. corporate values
- d. cultural

Guidance: level 1

:: ::

_____ consists of using generic or ad hoc methods in an orderly manner to find solutions to problems. Some of the problem-solving techniques developed and used in philosophy, artificial intelligence, computer science, engineering, mathematics, or medicine are related to mental problem-solving techniques studied in psychology.

Exam Probability: **Low**

3. *Answer choices:*

(see index for correct answer)

- a. surface-level diversity
- b. hierarchical

- c. Problem solving
- d. imperative

Guidance: level 1

:: Project management ::

In economics, _____ is the assignment of available resources to various uses. In the context of an entire economy, resources can be allocated by various means, such as markets or central planning.

Exam Probability: **Medium**

4. *Answer choices:*

(see index for correct answer)

- a. Virtual design and construction
- b. Fast-track construction
- c. Resource allocation
- d. Scope

Guidance: level 1

:: Human resource management ::

_____ means increasing the scope of a job through extending the range of its job duties and responsibilities generally within the same level and periphery. _____ involves combining various activities at the same level in the organization and adding them to the existing job. It is also called the horizontal expansion of job activities. This contradicts the principles of specialisation and the division of labour whereby work is divided into small units, each of which is performed repetitively by an individual worker and the responsibilities are always clear. Some motivational theories suggest that the boredom and alienation caused by the division of labour can actually cause efficiency to fall. Thus, _____ seeks to motivate workers through reversing the process of specialisation. A typical approach might be to replace assembly lines with modular work; instead of an employee repeating the same step on each product, they perform several tasks on a single item. In order for employees to be provided with _____ they will need to be retrained in new fields to understand how each field works.

Exam Probability: **Medium**

5. *Answer choices:*

(see index for correct answer)

- a. Restructuring
- b. Occupational burnout
- c. Domestic inquiry
- d. Job enlargement

Guidance: level 1

:: Employee relations ::

_____ ownership, or employee share ownership, is an ownership interest in a company held by the company's workforce. The ownership interest may be facilitated by the company as part of employees' remuneration or incentive compensation for work performed, or the company itself may be employee owned.

Exam Probability: **Low**

6. *Answer choices:*

(see index for correct answer)

- a. Industry Federation of the State of Rio de Janeiro
- b. Employee handbook
- c. Employee stock
- d. Employee surveys

Guidance: level 1

:: Project management ::

_____ is the right to exercise power, which can be formalized by a state and exercised by way of judges, appointed executives of government, or the ecclesiastical or priestly appointed representatives of a God or other deities.

Exam Probability: **High**

7. *Answer choices:*

(see index for correct answer)

- a. The Transformation Project
- b. Extreme project management
- c. Task
- d. Problem domain analysis

Guidance: level 1

:: Management ::

In organizational studies, _____ is the efficient and effective development of an organization's resources when they are needed. Such resources may include financial resources, inventory, human skills, production resources, or information technology and natural resources.

Exam Probability: **Low**

8. *Answer choices:*

(see index for correct answer)

- a. Resource management
- b. Project stakeholder
- c. Managerial hubris
- d. Supply management

Guidance: level 1

:: Business models ::

A _____ is "an autonomous association of persons united voluntarily to meet their common economic, social, and cultural needs and aspirations through a jointly-owned and democratically-controlled enterprise". _____ s may include.

Exam Probability: **Medium**

9. *Answer choices:*
(see index for correct answer)

- a. Product-service system
- b. Parent company
- c. Cooperative
- d. Microfranchising

Guidance: level 1

:: Organizational behavior ::

_____ is the term now used more commonly in business management, particularly human resource management. _____ refers to the number of subordinates a supervisor has.

Exam Probability: **Low**

10. *Answer choices:*

(see index for correct answer)

- a. Span of control
- b. Counterproductive norms
- c. Organizational citizenship behavior
- d. Conformity

Guidance: level 1

:: Industrial Revolution ::

The _____, now also known as the First _____, was the transition to new manufacturing processes in Europe and the US, in the period from about 1760 to sometime between 1820 and 1840. This transition included going from hand production methods to machines, new chemical manufacturing and iron production processes, the increasing use of steam power and water power, the development of machine tools and the rise of the mechanized factory system. The _____ also led to an unprecedented rise in the rate of population growth.

Exam Probability: **Medium**

11. *Answer choices:*

(see index for correct answer)

- a. Lunar Society of Birmingham

- b. Sykes Bleaching Company
- c. Industrial Revolution
- d. Surplus women

Guidance: level 1

:: ::

_____ is the consumption and saving opportunity gained by an entity within a specified timeframe, which is generally expressed in monetary terms. For households and individuals, " _____ is the sum of all the wages, salaries, profits, interest payments, rents, and other forms of earnings received in a given period of time."

Exam Probability: **Low**

12. *Answer choices:*

(see index for correct answer)

- a. surface-level diversity
- b. functional perspective
- c. interpersonal communication
- d. empathy

Guidance: level 1

:: ::

____ involves the development of an action plan designed to motivate and guide a person or group toward a goal. ____ can be guided by goal-setting criteria such as SMART criteria. ____ is a major component of personal-development and management literature.

Exam Probability: **Medium**

13. *Answer choices:*

(see index for correct answer)

- a. deep-level diversity
- b. Goal setting
- c. interpersonal communication
- d. process perspective

Guidance: level 1

:: Evaluation ::

____ solving consists of using generic or ad hoc methods in an orderly manner to find solutions to ____ s. Some of the ____ -solving techniques developed and used in philosophy, artificial intelligence, computer science, engineering, mathematics, or medicine are related to mental ____ -solving techniques studied in psychology.

Exam Probability: **Low**

14. *Answer choices:*

(see index for correct answer)

- a. Formative assessment
- b. Problem
- c. American Evaluation Association
- d. Educational assessment

Guidance: level 1

:: Statistical terminology ::

_____ is the magnitude or dimensions of a thing. _____ can be measured as length, width, height, diameter, perimeter, area, volume, or mass.

Exam Probability: **Medium**

15. *Answer choices:*

(see index for correct answer)

- a. Data binning
- b. Size
- c. P-value
- d. Skewness risk

Guidance: level 1

:: Information science ::

_____ is the resolution of uncertainty; it is that which answers the question of "what an entity is" and thus defines both its essence and nature of its characteristics. _____ relates to both data and knowledge, as data is meaningful _____ representing values attributed to parameters, and knowledge signifies understanding of a concept. _____ is uncoupled from an observer, which is an entity that can access _____ and thus discern what it specifies; _____ exists beyond an event horizon for example. In the case of knowledge, the _____ itself requires a cognitive observer to be obtained.

Exam Probability: **Medium**

16. *Answer choices:*

(see index for correct answer)

- a. Information
- b. Scientific communication
- c. Upper ontology
- d. Controlled vocabulary

Guidance: level 1

:: Systems thinking ::

In business management, a _____ is a company that facilitates the learning of its members and continuously transforms itself. The concept was coined through the work and research of Peter Senge and his colleagues.

Exam Probability: **Low**

17. *Answer choices:*

(see index for correct answer)

- a. Business continuity planning
- b. The Letters of Utrecht
- c. Scenario analysis
- d. Learning organization

Guidance: level 1

:: Industry ::

_____ describes various measures of the efficiency of production. Often , a _____ measure is expressed as the ratio of an aggregate output to a single input or an aggregate input used in a production process, i.e. output per unit of input. Most common example is the labour _____ measure, e.g., such as GDP per worker. There are many different definitions of _____ and the choice among them depends on the purpose of the _____ measurement and/or data availability. The key source of difference between various _____ measures is also usually related to how the outputs and the inputs are aggregated into scalars to obtain such a ratio-type measure of _____ .

Exam Probability: **Medium**

18. *Answer choices:*

(see index for correct answer)

- a. PROFINET
- b. Precision mechanics
- c. Productivity
- d. Mass production

Guidance: level 1

:: Scientific method ::

In the social sciences and life sciences, a _____ is a research method involving an up-close, in-depth, and detailed examination of a subject of study, as well as its related contextual conditions.

Exam Probability: **Medium**

19. *Answer choices:*

(see index for correct answer)

- a. Preference test
- b. Causal research
- c. explanatory research
- d. pilot project

Guidance: level 1

:: Business ethics ::

_____ is a type of harassment technique that relates to a sexual nature and the unwelcome or inappropriate promise of rewards in exchange for sexual favors. _____ includes a range of actions from mild transgressions to sexual abuse or assault. Harassment can occur in many different social settings such as the workplace, the home, school, churches, etc. Harassers or victims may be of any gender.

Exam Probability: **Low**

20. *Answer choices:*

(see index for correct answer)

- a. Institute for Business and Professional Ethics
- b. Sexual harassment
- c. Hostile work environment
- d. Centre for Research on Multinational Corporations

Guidance: level 1

:: ::

_____ involves decision making. It can include judging the merits of multiple options and selecting one or more of them. One can make a _____ between imagined options or between real options followed by the corresponding action. For example, a traveler might choose a route for a journey based on the preference of arriving at a given destination as soon as possible. The preferred route can then follow from information such as the length of each of the possible routes, traffic conditions, etc. The arrival at a _____ can include more complex motivators such as cognition, instinct, and feeling.

Exam Probability: **Low**

21. *Answer choices:*

(see index for correct answer)

- a. Choice
- b. deep-level diversity
- c. co-culture
- d. cultural

Guidance: level 1

:: ::

Some scenarios associate "this kind of planning" with learning "life skills". Schedules are necessary, or at least useful, in situations where individuals need to know what time they must be at a specific location to receive a specific service, and where people need to accomplish a set of goals within a set time period.

Exam Probability: **Low**

22. *Answer choices:*

(see index for correct answer)

- a. deep-level diversity
- b. hierarchical perspective
- c. Character
- d. imperative

Guidance: level 1

:: E-commerce ::

_____ is the activity of buying or selling of products on online services or over the Internet. Electronic commerce draws on technologies such as mobile commerce, electronic funds transfer, supply chain management, Internet marketing, online transaction processing, electronic data interchange , inventory management systems, and automated data collection systems.

Exam Probability: **Medium**

23. *Answer choices:*

(see index for correct answer)

- a. Electronic commerce
- b. Government-to-business

- c. E-commerce
- d. Click Frenzy

Guidance: level 1

:: ::

_____ is the stock of habits, knowledge, social and personality attributes embodied in the ability to perform labor so as to produce economic value.

Exam Probability: **High**

24. *Answer choices:*
(see index for correct answer)

- a. corporate values
- b. cultural
- c. functional perspective
- d. process perspective

Guidance: level 1

:: ::

Business is the activity of making one's living or making money by producing or buying and selling products. Simply put, it is "any activity or enterprise entered into for profit. It does not mean it is a company, a corporation, partnership, or have any such formal organization, but it can range from a street peddler to General Motors."

Exam Probability: **Low**

25. *Answer choices:*

(see index for correct answer)

- a. Firm
- b. Character
- c. surface-level diversity
- d. levels of analysis

Guidance: level 1

:: Life skills ::

_____, emotional leadership, emotional quotient and _____ quotient, is the capability of individuals to recognize their own emotions and those of others, discern between different feelings and label them appropriately, use emotional information to guide thinking and behavior, and manage and/or adjust emotions to adapt to environments or achieve one's goal.

Exam Probability: **High**

26. *Answer choices:*

(see index for correct answer)

- a. Social intelligence
- b. Emotional intelligence
- c. emotion work
- d. multiple intelligence

Guidance: level 1

:: Power (social and political) ::

_____ is a form of reverence gained by a leader who has strong interpersonal relationship skills. _____ , as an aspect of personal power, becomes particularly important as organizational leadership becomes increasingly about collaboration and influence, rather than command and control.

Exam Probability: **Medium**

27. *Answer choices:*

(see index for correct answer)

- a. Hard power
- b. Referent power
- c. need for power

Guidance: level 1

:: Systems theory ::

A _____ is a set of policies, processes and procedures used by an organization to ensure that it can fulfill the tasks required to achieve its objectives. These objectives cover many aspects of the organization's operations. For instance, an environmental _____ enables organizations to improve their environmental performance and an occupational health and safety _____ enables an organization to control its occupational health and safety risks, etc.

Exam Probability: **Medium**

28. *Answer choices:*
(see index for correct answer)

- a. decentralized system
- b. Management system
- c. Viable System Model
- d. Black box

Guidance: level 1

:: Electronic feedback ::

_____ occurs when outputs of a system are routed back as inputs as part of a chain of cause-and-effect that forms a circuit or loop. The system can then be said to feed back into itself. The notion of cause-and-effect has to be handled carefully when applied to _____ systems.

Exam Probability: **Low**

29. *Answer choices:*

(see index for correct answer)

- a. Feedback
- b. feedback loop

Guidance: level 1

:: ::

_____ comprises all of the processes of governing – whether undertaken by the government of a state, by a market or by a network – over a social system and whether through the laws, norms, power or language of an organized society. It relates to "the processes of interaction and decision-making among the actors involved in a collective problem that lead to the creation, reinforcement, or reproduction of social norms and institutions". In lay terms, it could be described as the political processes that exist in and between formal institutions.

Exam Probability: **Low**

30. *Answer choices:*

(see index for correct answer)

- a. surface-level diversity
- b. imperative
- c. Governance
- d. corporate values

Guidance: level 1

:: Labour relations ::

_____ is a field of study that can have different meanings depending on the context in which it is used. In an international context, it is a subfield of labor history that studies the human relations with regard to work – in its broadest sense – and how this connects to questions of social inequality. It explicitly encompasses unregulated, historical, and non-Western forms of labor. Here, _____ define "for or with whom one works and under what rules. These rules determine the type of work, type and amount of remuneration, working hours, degrees of physical and psychological strain, as well as the degree of freedom and autonomy associated with the work."

Exam Probability: **Low**

31. *Answer choices:*

(see index for correct answer)

- a. Boulwarism
- b. European Trade Union Confederation

- c. Global Unions
- d. Labor relations

Guidance: level 1

:: Management ::

The _____ is a strategy performance management tool – a semi-standard structured report, that can be used by managers to keep track of the execution of activities by the staff within their control and to monitor the consequences arising from these actions.

Exam Probability: **Medium**

32. *Answer choices:*

(see index for correct answer)

- a. Crisis management
- b. Executive compensation
- c. Main Street Manager
- d. Control limits

Guidance: level 1

:: Production and manufacturing ::

_____ is a theory of management that analyzes and synthesizes workflows. Its main objective is improving economic efficiency, especially labor productivity. It was one of the earliest attempts to apply science to the engineering of processes and to management. _____ is sometimes known as Taylorism after its founder, Frederick Winslow Taylor.

Exam Probability: **Low**

33. *Answer choices:*

(see index for correct answer)

- a. Mockup
- b. Nuffield Tools and Gauges
- c. Scientific management
- d. First pass yield

Guidance: level 1

:: ::

The _____ officer or just _____, is the most senior corporate, executive, or administrative officer in charge of managing an organization especially an independent legal entity such as a company or nonprofit institution. CEOs lead a range of organizations, including public and private corporations, non-profit organizations and even some government organizations. The CEO of a corporation or company typically reports to the board of directors and is charged with maximizing the value of the entity, which may include maximizing the share price, market share, revenues or another element. In the non-profit and government sector, CEOs typically aim at achieving outcomes related to the organization's mission, such as reducing poverty, increasing literacy, etc.

Exam Probability: **Medium**

34. *Answer choices:*

(see index for correct answer)

- a. surface-level diversity
- b. open system
- c. Sarbanes-Oxley act of 2002
- d. information systems assessment

Guidance: level 1

:: Logistics ::

_____ is generally the detailed organization and implementation of a complex operation. In a general business sense, _____ is the management of the flow of things between the point of origin and the point of consumption in order to meet requirements of customers or corporations. The resources managed in _____ may include tangible goods such as materials, equipment, and supplies, as well as food and other consumable items. The _____ of physical items usually involves the integration of information flow, materials handling, production, packaging, inventory, transportation, warehousing, and often security.

Exam Probability: **High**

35. *Answer choices:*

(see index for correct answer)

- a. Terminal Operating System
- b. Medical logistics
- c. The Institute of Transport Management
- d. Logistics

Guidance: level 1

:: Supply chain management ::

_____ is the process of finding and agreeing to terms, and acquiring goods, services, or works from an external source, often via a tendering or competitive bidding process. _____ is used to ensure the buyer receives goods, services, or works at the best possible price when aspects such as quality, quantity, time, and location are compared. Corporations and public bodies often define processes intended to promote fair and open competition for their business while minimizing risks such as exposure to fraud and collusion.

Exam Probability: **High**

36. *Answer choices:*

(see index for correct answer)

- a. Procurement
- b. Delivery Performance
- c. Pharmacode
- d. Security risk

Guidance: level 1

:: Business ::

_____ is a trade policy that does not restrict imports or exports; it can also be understood as the free market idea applied to international trade. In government, _____ is predominantly advocated by political parties that hold liberal economic positions while economically left-wing and nationalist political parties generally support protectionism, the opposite of _____ .

Exam Probability: **Medium**

37. *Answer choices:*

(see index for correct answer)

- a. Free trade
- b. Post-transaction marketing
- c. Co-creation
- d. Employee experience management

Guidance: level 1

:: Management ::

_____ is a technique used by some employers to rotate their employees' assigned jobs throughout their employment. Employers practice this technique for a number of reasons. It was designed to promote flexibility of employees and to keep employees interested into staying with the company/organization which employs them. There is also research that shows how _____ s help relieve the stress of employees who work in a job that requires manual labor.

Exam Probability: **Low**

38. *Answer choices:*

(see index for correct answer)

- a. Managing stage boundaries
- b. Intopia

- c. Director
- d. Continuous-flow manufacturing

Guidance: level 1

:: Income ::

In business and accounting, net income is an entity's income minus cost of goods sold, expenses and taxes for an accounting period. It is computed as the residual of all revenues and gains over all expenses and losses for the period, and has also been defined as the net increase in shareholders' equity that results from a company's operations. In the context of the presentation of financial statements, the IFRS Foundation defines net income as synonymous with profit and loss. The difference between revenue and the cost of making a product or providing a service, before deducting overheads, payroll, taxation, and interest payments. This is different from operating income.

Exam Probability: **High**

39. *Answer choices:*

(see index for correct answer)

- a. Return on investment
- b. Bottom line
- c. Windfall gain
- d. Aggregate expenditure

Guidance: level 1

:: Mereology ::

_____ , in the abstract, is what belongs to or with something, whether as an attribute or as a component of said thing. In the context of this article, it is one or more components , whether physical or incorporeal, of a person's estate; or so belonging to, as in being owned by, a person or jointly a group of people or a legal entity like a corporation or even a society. Depending on the nature of the _____ , an owner of _____ has the right to consume, alter, share, redefine, rent, mortgage, pawn, sell, exchange, transfer, give away or destroy it, or to exclude others from doing these things, as well as to perhaps abandon it; whereas regardless of the nature of the _____ , the owner thereof has the right to properly use it , or at the very least exclusively keep it.

Exam Probability: **Low**

40. *Answer choices:*
(see index for correct answer)

- a. Mereotopology
- b. Mereology
- c. Mereological essentialism
- d. Property

Guidance: level 1

:: Human resource management ::

_____ , also known as management by results, was first popularized by Peter Drucker in his 1954 book The Practice of Management. _____ is the process of defining specific objectives within an organization that management can convey to organization members, then deciding on how to achieve each objective in sequence. This process allows managers to take work that needs to be done one step at a time to allow for a calm, yet productive work environment. This process also helps organization members to see their accomplishments as they achieve each objective, which reinforces a positive work environment and a sense of achievement. An important part of MBO is the measurement and comparison of an employee's actual performance with the standards set. Ideally, when employees themselves have been involved with the goal-setting and choosing the course of action to be followed by them, they are more likely to fulfill their responsibilities. According to George S. Odiorne, the system of _____ can be described as a process whereby the superior and subordinate jointly identify common goals, define each individual's major areas of responsibility in terms of the results expected of him or her, and use these measures as guides for operating the unit and assessing the contribution of each of its members.

Exam Probability: **Medium**

41. *Answer choices:*

(see index for correct answer)

- a. Competency-based management
- b. Management by objectives
- c. Recruitment process outsourcing
- d. Lego Serious Play

Guidance: level 1

:: Data collection ::

A _____ is an utterance which typically functions as a request for information. _____ s can thus be understood as a kind of illocutionary act in the field of pragmatics or as special kinds of propositions in frameworks of formal semantics such as alternative semantics or inquisitive semantics. The information requested is expected to be provided in the form of an answer. _____ s are often conflated with interrogatives, which are the grammatical forms typically used to achieve them. Rhetorical _____ s, for example, are interrogative in form but may not be considered true _____ s as they are not expected to be answered. Conversely, non-interrogative grammatical structures may be considered _____ s as in the case of the imperative sentence "tell me your name".

Exam Probability: **High**

42. *Answer choices:*

(see index for correct answer)

- a. IPUMS
- b. Question
- c. Interpellation
- d. Guardian

Guidance: level 1

:: Analysis ::

_____ is the process of breaking a complex topic or substance into smaller parts in order to gain a better understanding of it. The technique has been applied in the study of mathematics and logic since before Aristotle, though _____ as a formal concept is a relatively recent development.

Exam Probability: **Low**

43. *Answer choices:*

(see index for correct answer)

- a. Situational analysis
- b. Irreducibility
- c. Analysis
- d. Divergent question

Guidance: level 1

:: ::

_____ is the administration of an organization, whether it is a business, a not-for-profit organization, or government body. _____ includes the activities of setting the strategy of an organization and coordinating the efforts of its employees to accomplish its objectives through the application of available resources, such as financial, natural, technological, and human resources. The term "_____" may also refer to those people who manage an organization.

Exam Probability: **High**

44. Answer choices:

(see index for correct answer)

- a. Sarbanes-Oxley act of 2002
- b. information systems assessment
- c. cultural
- d. co-culture

Guidance: level 1

:: Marketing techniques ::

> In industry, product lifecycle management is the process of managing the entire lifecycle of a product from inception, through engineering design and manufacture, to service and disposal of manufactured products. PLM integrates people, data, processes and business systems and provides a product information backbone for companies and their extended enterprise.

Exam Probability: **High**

45. Answer choices:

(see index for correct answer)

- a. unique selling point
- b. Continuity marketing
- c. Product life cycle
- d. Appeal to fear

Guidance: level 1

:: Management ::

In business, a _____ is the attribute that allows an organization to outperform its competitors. A _____ may include access to natural resources, such as high-grade ores or a low-cost power source, highly skilled labor, geographic location, high entry barriers, and access to new technology.

Exam Probability: **Low**

46. *Answer choices:*

(see index for correct answer)

- a. Product breakdown structure
- b. Professional performances
- c. Competitive advantage
- d. Dominant design

Guidance: level 1

:: Management ::

A _____ is when two or more people come together to discuss one or more topics, often in a formal or business setting, but _____ s also occur in a variety of other environments. Many various types of _____ s exist.

Exam Probability: **Medium**

47. *Answer choices:*

(see index for correct answer)

- a. Task-oriented and relationship-oriented leadership
- b. Linear scheduling method
- c. Meeting
- d. Purchasing management

Guidance: level 1

:: ::

In sales, commerce and economics, a _____ is the recipient of a good, service, product or an idea - obtained from a seller, vendor, or supplier via a financial transaction or exchange for money or some other valuable consideration.

Exam Probability: **High**

48. *Answer choices:*

(see index for correct answer)

- a. levels of analysis
- b. surface-level diversity
- c. hierarchical perspective
- d. Customer

Guidance: level 1

:: ::

_____ is the process of making predictions of the future based on past and present data and most commonly by analysis of trends. A commonplace example might be estimation of some variable of interest at some specified future date. Prediction is a similar, but more general term. Both might refer to formal statistical methods employing time series, cross-sectional or longitudinal data, or alternatively to less formal judgmental methods. Usage can differ between areas of application: for example, in hydrology the terms "forecast" and "_____" are sometimes reserved for estimates of values at certain specific future times, while the term "prediction" is used for more general estimates, such as the number of times floods will occur over a long period.

Exam Probability: **Medium**

49. *Answer choices:*

(see index for correct answer)

- a. corporate values
- b. hierarchical perspective
- c. Forecasting

- d. interpersonal communication

Guidance: level 1

:: Quality management ::

A _____ or quality control circle is a group of workers who do the same or similar work, who meet regularly to identify, analyze and solve work-related problems. Normally small in size, the group is usually led by a supervisor or manager and presents its solutions to management; where possible, workers implement the solutions themselves in order to improve the performance of the organization and motivate employees. _____ s were at their most popular during the 1980s, but continue to exist in the form of Kaizen groups and similar worker participation schemes.

Exam Probability: **High**

50. *Answer choices:*

(see index for correct answer)

- a. Test bay
- b. Allied Quality Assurance Publications
- c. Good Clinical Laboratory Practice
- d. Quality circle

Guidance: level 1

:: Human resource management ::

An organizational chart is a diagram that shows the structure of an organization and the relationships and relative ranks of its parts and positions/jobs. The term is also used for similar diagrams, for example ones showing the different elements of a field of knowledge or a group of languages.

Exam Probability: **Low**

51. *Answer choices:*

(see index for correct answer)

- a. Work activity management
- b. Co-determination
- c. Employee exit management
- d. Organization chart

Guidance: level 1

:: Business models ::

A _____, _____ company or daughter company is a company that is owned or controlled by another company, which is called the parent company, parent, or holding company. The _____ can be a company, corporation, or limited liability company. In some cases it is a government or state-owned enterprise. In some cases, particularly in the music and book publishing industries, subsidiaries are referred to as imprints.

Exam Probability: **High**

52. *Answer choices:*

(see index for correct answer)

- a. Sustainable business
- b. Volatility, uncertainty, complexity and ambiguity
- c. Professional open source
- d. Subsidiary

Guidance: level 1

:: Management ::

> A _____ describes the rationale of how an organization creates, delivers, and captures value, in economic, social, cultural or other contexts. The process of _____ construction and modification is also called _____ innovation and forms a part of business strategy.

Exam Probability: **Low**

53. *Answer choices:*

(see index for correct answer)

- a. Meeting system
- b. Industrial forensics
- c. Business model

- d. Project stakeholder

Guidance: level 1

:: Statistical terminology ::

_____ es can be learned implicitly within cultural contexts. People may develop _____ es toward or against an individual, an ethnic group, a sexual or gender identity, a nation, a religion, a social class, a political party, theoretical paradigms and ideologies within academic domains, or a species. _____ ed means one-sided, lacking a neutral viewpoint, or not having an open mind. _____ can come in many forms and is related to prejudice and intuition.

Exam Probability: **Medium**

54. *Answer choices:*

(see index for correct answer)

- a. Shape parameter
- b. Fair coin
- c. Skewness risk
- d. Statistical error

Guidance: level 1

:: Evaluation ::

_____ is a way of preventing mistakes and defects in manufactured products and avoiding problems when delivering products or services to customers; which ISO 9000 defines as "part of quality management focused on providing confidence that quality requirements will be fulfilled". This defect prevention in _____ differs subtly from defect detection and rejection in quality control and has been referred to as a shift left since it focuses on quality earlier in the process.

Exam Probability: **Medium**

55. *Answer choices:*
(see index for correct answer)

- a. Formative assessment
- b. Expression
- c. Teaching and Learning International Survey
- d. Quality assurance

Guidance: level 1

:: Telecommuting ::

_____, also called telework, teleworking, working from home, mobile work, remote work, and flexible workplace, is a work arrangement in which employees do not commute or travel to a central place of work, such as an office building, warehouse, or store. Teleworkers in the 21st century often use mobile telecommunications technology such as Wi-Fi-equipped laptop or tablet computers and smartphones to work from coffee shops; others may use a desktop computer and a landline phone at their home. According to a Reuters poll, approximately "one in five workers around the globe, particularly employees in the Middle East, Latin America and Asia, telecommute frequently and nearly 10 percent work from home every day." In the 2000s, annual leave or vacation in some organizations was seen as absence from the workplace rather than ceasing work, and some office employees used telework to continue to check work e-mails while on vacation.

Exam Probability: **Low**

56. *Answer choices:*

(see index for correct answer)

- a. Yuuguu
- b. Telecommuting
- c. Home Work Convention, 1996
- d. IvanAnywhere

Guidance: level 1

:: Critical thinking ::

An _____ is a set of statements usually constructed to describe a set of facts which clarifies the causes, context, and consequences of those facts. This description of the facts et cetera may establish rules or laws, and may clarify the existing rules or laws in relation to any objects, or phenomena examined. The components of an _____ can be implicit, and interwoven with one another.

Exam Probability: **Medium**

57. *Answer choices:*
(see index for correct answer)

- a. Critical-Creative Thinking and Behavioral Research Laboratory
- b. Explanation
- c. Inquiry: Critical Thinking Across the Disciplines
- d. Adviser

Guidance: level 1

:: Management ::

A _____ is an idea of the future or desired result that a person or a group of people envisions, plans and commits to achieve. People endeavor to reach _____ s within a finite time by setting deadlines.

Exam Probability: **High**

58. *Answer choices:*

(see index for correct answer)

- a. Line management
- b. Technology scouting
- c. Quality control
- d. Industrial forensics

Guidance: level 1

:: ::

A _____ is a type of job aid used to reduce failure by compensating for potential limits of human memory and attention. It helps to ensure consistency and completeness in carrying out a task. A basic example is the "to do list". A more advanced _____ would be a schedule, which lays out tasks to be done according to time of day or other factors. A primary task in _____ is documentation of the task and auditing against the documentation.

Exam Probability: **Medium**

59. *Answer choices:*

(see index for correct answer)

- a. deep-level diversity
- b. cultural
- c. Checklist
- d. interpersonal communication

Guidance: level 1

Business law

Corporate law (also known as business law) is the body of law governing the rights, relations, and conduct of persons, companies, organizations and businesses. It refers to the legal practice relating to, or the theory of corporations. Corporate law often describes the law relating to matters which derive directly from the life-cycle of a corporation. It thus encompasses the formation, funding, governance, and death of a corporation.

:: Product liability ::

_____ is the area of law in which manufacturers, distributors, suppliers, retailers, and others who make products available to the public are held responsible for the injuries those products cause. Although the word "product" has broad connotations, _____ as an area of law is traditionally limited to products in the form of tangible personal property.

Exam Probability: **Low**

1. *Answer choices:*

(see index for correct answer)

- a. Consumer Protection Act 1987
- b. Product Liability Directive
- c. Product liability
- d. Dalkon Shield

Guidance: level 1

:: Criminal law ::

_____ is the body of law that relates to crime. It proscribes conduct perceived as threatening, harmful, or otherwise endangering to the property, health, safety, and moral welfare of people inclusive of one's self. Most _____ is established by statute, which is to say that the laws are enacted by a legislature. _____ includes the punishment and rehabilitation of people who violate such laws. _____ varies according to jurisdiction, and differs from civil law, where emphasis is more on dispute resolution and victim compensation, rather than on punishment or rehabilitation. Criminal procedure is a formalized official activity that authenticates the fact of commission of a crime and authorizes punitive or rehabilitative treatment of the offender.

Exam Probability: **Medium**

2. *Answer choices:*

(see index for correct answer)

- a. complicit
- b. Criminal law

- c. Mala in se
- d. Mala prohibita

Guidance: level 1

:: Treaties ::

A _____ is an agreement under international law entered into by actors in international law, namely sovereign states and international organizations. A _____ may also be known as an agreement, protocol, covenant, convention, pact, or exchange of letters, among other terms. Regardless of terminology, all of these forms of agreements are, under international law, equally considered treaties and the rules are the same.

Exam Probability: **Medium**

3. *Answer choices:*

(see index for correct answer)

- a. Clausula rebus sic stantibus
- b. Bilateral treaty
- c. Full Powers
- d. Treaty

Guidance: level 1

:: ::

_____ is the study and management of exchange relationships. _____ is the business process of creating relationships with and satisfying customers. With its focus on the customer, _____ is one of the premier components of business management.

Exam Probability: **High**

4. *Answer choices:*

(see index for correct answer)

- a. corporate values
- b. open system
- c. hierarchical
- d. Sarbanes-Oxley act of 2002

Guidance: level 1

:: ::

The U.S. _____ is an independent agency of the United States federal government. The SEC holds primary responsibility for enforcing the federal securities laws, proposing securities rules, and regulating the securities industry, the nation's stock and options exchanges, and other activities and organizations, including the electronic securities markets in the United States.

Exam Probability: **High**

5. *Answer choices:*

(see index for correct answer)

- a. Sarbanes-Oxley act of 2002
- b. interpersonal communication
- c. Securities and Exchange Commission
- d. Character

Guidance: level 1

:: Commercial item transport and distribution ::

A _____ in common law countries is a person or company that transports goods or people for any person or company and that is responsible for any possible loss of the goods during transport. A _____ offers its services to the general public under license or authority provided by a regulatory body. The regulatory body has usually been granted "ministerial authority" by the legislation that created it. The regulatory body may create, interpret, and enforce its regulations upon the _____ with independence and finality, as long as it acts within the bounds of the enabling legislation.

Exam Probability: **Low**

6. *Answer choices:*

(see index for correct answer)

- a. E2open
- b. Private carrier

- c. Export Yellow Pages
- d. Fuel cell forklift

Guidance: level 1

:: Business law ::

A _____ is a form of security interest granted over an item of property to secure the payment of a debt or performance of some other obligation. The owner of the property, who grants the _____ , is referred to as the _____ ee and the person who has the benefit of the _____ is referred to as the _____ or or _____ holder.

Exam Probability: **Medium**

7. *Answer choices:*
(see index for correct answer)

- a. Extraordinary resolution
- b. Recharacterisation
- c. Inslaw
- d. WIPO Copyright Treaty

Guidance: level 1

:: Insolvency ::

_____ is a legal process through which people or other entities who cannot repay debts to creditors may seek relief from some or all of their debts. In most jurisdictions, _____ is imposed by a court order, often initiated by the debtor.

Exam Probability: **Medium**

8. *Answer choices:*

(see index for correct answer)

- a. Liquidator
- b. Financial distress
- c. Insolvency
- d. Liquidation

Guidance: level 1

:: Commercial crimes ::

_____ is the process of concealing the origins of money obtained illegally by passing it through a complex sequence of banking transfers or commercial transactions. The overall scheme of this process returns the money to the launderer in an obscure and indirect way.

Exam Probability: **Medium**

9. *Answer choices:*

(see index for correct answer)

- a. Price fixing
- b. Legal abuse
- c. Trademark infringement
- d. Money laundering

Guidance: level 1

:: ::

> An _____ is an area of the production, distribution, or trade, and consumption of goods and services by different agents. Understood in its broadest sense, 'The _____ is defined as a social domain that emphasize the practices, discourses, and material expressions associated with the production, use, and management of resources'. Economic agents can be individuals, businesses, organizations, or governments. Economic transactions occur when two parties agree to the value or price of the transacted good or service, commonly expressed in a certain currency. However, monetary transactions only account for a small part of the economic domain.

Exam Probability: **Low**

10. *Answer choices:*

(see index for correct answer)

- a. personal values
- b. cultural
- c. Economy

- d. levels of analysis

Guidance: level 1

:: ::

The _____ is an intergovernmental organization that is concerned with the regulation of international trade between nations. The WTO officially commenced on 1 January 1995 under the Marrakesh Agreement, signed by 124 nations on 15 April 1994, replacing the General Agreement on Tariffs and Trade , which commenced in 1948. It is the largest international economic organization in the world.

Exam Probability: **High**

11. *Answer choices:*

(see index for correct answer)

- a. World Trade Organization
- b. information systems assessment
- c. hierarchical perspective
- d. Character

Guidance: level 1

:: ::

Competition arises whenever at least two parties strive for a goal which cannot be shared: where one's gain is the other's loss.

Exam Probability: **Medium**

12. *Answer choices:*

(see index for correct answer)

- a. Competitor
- b. co-culture
- c. imperative
- d. Character

Guidance: level 1

:: Legal doctrines and principles ::

_____ , land acquisition , compulsory purchase , resumption , resumption/compulsory acquisition , or expropriation is the power of a state, provincial, or national government to take private property for public use. However, this power can be legislatively delegated by the state to municipalities, government subdivisions, or even to private persons or corporations, when they are authorized by the legislature to exercise the functions of public character.

Exam Probability: **Low**

13. Answer choices:

(see index for correct answer)

- a. Acquiescence
- b. Eminent domain
- c. Res ipsa loquitur
- d. Contributory negligence

Guidance: level 1

:: ::

In law, an _____ is the process in which cases are reviewed, where parties request a formal change to an official decision. _____ s function both as a process for error correction as well as a process of clarifying and interpreting law. Although appellate courts have existed for thousands of years, common law countries did not incorporate an affirmative right to _____ into their jurisprudence until the 19th century.

Exam Probability: **Low**

14. Answer choices:

(see index for correct answer)

- a. deep-level diversity
- b. Appeal
- c. Sarbanes-Oxley act of 2002
- d. interpersonal communication

Guidance: level 1

:: ::

> _____ is widespread, interconnected digital technology. The term entered the popular culture from science fiction and the arts but is now used by technology strategists, security professionals, government, military and industry leaders and entrepreneurs to describe the domain of the global technology environment. Others consider _____ to be just a notional environment in which communication over computer networks occurs. The word became popular in the 1990s when the uses of the Internet, networking, and digital communication were all growing dramatically and the term "_____" was able to represent the many new ideas and phenomena that were emerging. It has been called the largest unregulated and uncontrolled domain in the history of mankind, and is also unique because it is a domain created by people vice the traditional physical domains.

Exam Probability: **Medium**

15. *Answer choices:*
(see index for correct answer)

- a. Cyberspace
- b. similarity-attraction theory
- c. hierarchical
- d. personal values

Guidance: level 1

:: Shareholders ::

A _____ is a payment made by a corporation to its shareholders, usually as a distribution of profits. When a corporation earns a profit or surplus, the corporation is able to re-invest the profit in the business and pay a proportion of the profit as a _____ to shareholders. Distribution to shareholders may be in cash or, if the corporation has a _____ reinvestment plan, the amount can be paid by the issue of further shares or share repurchase. When _____ s are paid, shareholders typically must pay income taxes, and the corporation does not receive a corporate income tax deduction for the _____ payments.

Exam Probability: **Medium**

16. *Answer choices:*

(see index for correct answer)

- a. Say on pay
- b. UK Individual Shareholders Society
- c. Shareholder Protection Act
- d. Proxy statement

Guidance: level 1

:: Contract law ::

In contract law, a _____ is a promise which is not a condition of the contract or an innominate term: it is a term "not going to the root of the contract", and which only entitles the innocent party to damages if it is breached: i.e. the _____ is not true or the defaulting party does not perform the contract in accordance with the terms of the _____. A _____ is not guarantee. It is a mere promise. It may be enforced if it is breached by an award for the legal remedy of damages.

Exam Probability: **Low**

17. *Answer choices:*

(see index for correct answer)

- a. Cover
- b. Warranty
- c. first refusal
- d. Secured transaction

Guidance: level 1

An _____ is a written sworn statement of fact voluntarily made by an affiant or deponent under an oath or affirmation administered by a person authorized to do so by law. Such statement is witnessed as to the authenticity of the affiant's signature by a taker of oaths, such as a notary public or commissioner of oaths. An _____ is a type of verified statement or showing, or in other words, it contains a verification, meaning it is under oath or penalty of perjury, and this serves as evidence to its veracity and is required for court proceedings.

Exam Probability: **Medium**

18. *Answer choices:*

(see index for correct answer)

- a. Affidavit
- b. surface-level diversity
- c. similarity-attraction theory
- d. Sarbanes-Oxley act of 2002

Guidance: level 1

:: ::

A _____ is a person or firm who arranges transactions between a buyer and a seller for a commission when the deal is executed. A _____ who also acts as a seller or as a buyer becomes a principal party to the deal. Neither role should be confused with that of an agent—one who acts on behalf of a principal party in a deal.

Exam Probability: **Medium**

19. *Answer choices:*

(see index for correct answer)

- a. surface-level diversity
- b. Broker
- c. functional perspective
- d. process perspective

Guidance: level 1

:: Meetings ::

A _____ is a body of one or more persons that is subordinate to a deliberative assembly. Usually, the assembly sends matters into a _____ as a way to explore them more fully than would be possible if the assembly itself were considering them. _____ s may have different functions and their type of work differ depending on the type of the organization and its needs.

Exam Probability: **Medium**

20. *Answer choices:*

(see index for correct answer)

- a. Tertulia
- b. Popular assembly

- c. Brown bag seminar
- d. Speed thinking

Guidance: level 1

:: ::

A _____ is a formal presentation of a matter such as a complaint, indictment or bill of exchange. In early-medieval England, juries of _____ would hear inquests in order to establish whether someone should be presented for a crime.

Exam Probability: **High**

21. *Answer choices:*

(see index for correct answer)

- a. surface-level diversity
- b. interpersonal communication
- c. empathy
- d. personal values

Guidance: level 1

:: Marketing ::

_____ comes from the Latin neg and otsia referring to businessmen who, unlike the patricians, had no leisure time in their industriousness; it held the meaning of business until the 17th century when it took on the diplomatic connotation as a dialogue between two or more people or parties intended to reach a beneficial outcome over one or more issues where a conflict exists with respect to at least one of these issues. Thus, _____ is a process of combining divergent positions into a joint agreement under a decision rule of unanimity.

Exam Probability: **Low**

22. *Answer choices:*

(see index for correct answer)

- a. Packshot
- b. Mass-market theory
- c. Interruption marketing
- d. Promise marketing

Guidance: level 1

:: Intention ::

_____ is the mental element of a person's intention to commit a crime; or knowledge that one's action or lack of action would cause a crime to be committed. It is a necessary element of many crimes.

Exam Probability: **Medium**

23. Answer choices:

(see index for correct answer)

- a. Letter of Intent
- b. Mens rea

Guidance: level 1

:: Labour relations ::

_____ is a field of study that can have different meanings depending on the context in which it is used. In an international context, it is a subfield of labor history that studies the human relations with regard to work – in its broadest sense – and how this connects to questions of social inequality. It explicitly encompasses unregulated, historical, and non-Western forms of labor. Here, _____ define "for or with whom one works and under what rules. These rules determine the type of work, type and amount of remuneration, working hours, degrees of physical and psychological strain, as well as the degree of freedom and autonomy associated with the work."

Exam Probability: **High**

24. Answer choices:

(see index for correct answer)

- a. Scranton Declaration
- b. Minnesota Nurses Association
- c. Labor relations
- d. Boulwarism

Guidance: level 1

:: Consumer theory ::

> A _____ is a technical term in psychology, economics and philosophy usually used in relation to choosing between alternatives. For example, someone prefers A over B if they would rather choose A than B.

Exam Probability: **High**

25. *Answer choices:*

(see index for correct answer)

- a. Quality bias
- b. End-of-life
- c. Rational addiction
- d. Preference

Guidance: level 1

:: ::

An _____ is a formal or official change made to a law, contract, constitution, or other legal document. It is based on the verb to amend, which means to change for better. _____ s can add, remove, or update parts of these agreements. They are often used when it is better to change the document than to write a new one.

Exam Probability: **High**

26. *Answer choices:*

(see index for correct answer)

- a. similarity-attraction theory
- b. surface-level diversity
- c. empathy
- d. personal values

Guidance: level 1

:: ::

_____ is the act or practice of forbidding something by law; more particularly the term refers to the banning of the manufacture, storage, transportation, sale, possession, and consumption of alcoholic beverages. The word is also used to refer to a period of time during which such bans are enforced.

Exam Probability: **Medium**

27. Answer choices:

(see index for correct answer)

- a. functional perspective
- b. cultural
- c. deep-level diversity
- d. Prohibition

Guidance: level 1

:: White-collar criminals ::

_____ refers to financially motivated, nonviolent crime committed by businesses and government professionals. It was first defined by the sociologist Edwin Sutherland in 1939 as "a crime committed by a person of respectability and high social status in the course of their occupation". Typical _____ s could include wage theft, fraud, bribery, Ponzi schemes, insider trading, labor racketeering, embezzlement, cybercrime, copyright infringement, money laundering, identity theft, and forgery. Lawyers can specialize in _____ .

Exam Probability: **High**

28. Answer choices:

(see index for correct answer)

- a. White-collar crime
- b. Du Jun

Guidance: level 1

:: Legal terms ::

_____s may be governments, corporations or investment trusts. _____s are legally responsible for the obligations of the issue and for reporting financial conditions, material developments and any other operational activities as required by the regulations of their jurisdictions.

Exam Probability: **Low**

29. *Answer choices:*

(see index for correct answer)

- a. Issuer
- b. Bifurcation
- c. Gag order
- d. Curator bonis

Guidance: level 1

:: Business law ::

An _____ is an agreement in which a producer agrees to sell his or her entire production to the buyer, who in turn agrees to purchase the entire output. Example: an almond grower enters into an _____ with an almond packer: thus the producer has a "home" for output of nuts, and the packer of nuts is happy to try the particular product. The converse of this situation is a requirements contract, under which a seller agrees to supply the buyer with as much of a good or service as the buyer wants, in exchange for the buyer's agreement not to buy that good or service elsewhere.

Exam Probability: **Low**

30. *Answer choices:*

(see index for correct answer)

- a. Double ticketing
- b. Ladenschlussgesetz
- c. Unfair business practices
- d. Business method patent

Guidance: level 1

:: Business law ::

An _____ is a natural person, business, or corporation that provides goods or services to another entity under terms specified in a contract or within a verbal agreement. Unlike an employee, an _____ does not work regularly for an employer but works as and when required, during which time they may be subject to law of agency. _____ s are usually paid on a freelance basis. Contractors often work through a limited company or franchise, which they themselves own, or may work through an umbrella company.

Exam Probability: **Medium**

31. *Answer choices:*

(see index for correct answer)

- a. Joint venture
- b. General assignment
- c. Court auction
- d. Independent contractor

Guidance: level 1

:: Personal property law ::

Bailment describes a legal relationship in common law where physical possession of personal property, or a chattel, is transferred from one person to another person who subsequently has possession of the property. It arises when a person gives property to someone else for safekeeping, and is a cause of action independent of contract or tort.

Exam Probability: **High**

32. *Answer choices:*

(see index for correct answer)

- a. bailment
- b. bailor

Guidance: level 1

:: Contract law ::

> A _____ is a contract in which one party agrees to supply as much of a good or service as is required by the other party, and in exchange the other party expressly or implicitly promises that it will obtain its goods or services exclusively from the first party. For example, a grocery store might enter into a contract with the farmer who grows oranges under which the farmer would supply the grocery store with as many oranges as the store could sell. The farmer could sue for breach of contract if the store were thereafter to purchase oranges for this purpose from any other party. The converse of this situation is an output contract, in which one buyer agrees to purchase however much of a good or service the seller is able to produce.

Exam Probability: **High**

33. *Answer choices:*

(see index for correct answer)

- a. Illegal agreement

- b. Escalator clause
- c. Doctrine of concurrent delay
- d. The Rise and Fall of Freedom of Contract

Guidance: level 1

:: ::

Business is the activity of making one's living or making money by producing or buying and selling products. Simply put, it is "any activity or enterprise entered into for profit. It does not mean it is a company, a corporation, partnership, or have any such formal organization, but it can range from a street peddler to General Motors."

Exam Probability: **High**

34. *Answer choices:*

(see index for correct answer)

- a. cultural
- b. Firm
- c. surface-level diversity
- d. similarity-attraction theory

Guidance: level 1

:: Business law ::

> A _____, also known as the sole trader, individual entrepreneurship or proprietorship, is a type of enterprise that is owned and run by one person and in which there is no legal distinction between the owner and the business entity. A sole trader does not necessarily work `alone`—it is possible for the sole trader to employ other people.

Exam Probability: **High**

35. *Answer choices:*

(see index for correct answer)

- a. Trading while insolvent
- b. Equity of redemption
- c. Sole proprietorship
- d. Independent contractor

Guidance: level 1

:: ::

Advertising is a marketing communication that employs an openly sponsored, non-personal message to promote or sell a product, service or idea. Sponsors of advertising are typically businesses wishing to promote their products or services. Advertising is differentiated from public relations in that an advertiser pays for and has control over the message. It differs from personal selling in that the message is non-personal, i.e., not directed to a particular individual.Advertising is communicated through various mass media, including traditional media such as newspapers, magazines, television, radio, outdoor advertising or direct mail; and new media such as search results, blogs, social media, websites or text messages. The actual presentation of the message in a medium is referred to as an _____ , or "ad" or advert for short.

Exam Probability: **Low**

36. *Answer choices:*

(see index for correct answer)

- a. deep-level diversity
- b. co-culture
- c. Advertisement
- d. imperative

Guidance: level 1

:: Contract law ::

A _____ is an event or state of affairs that is required before something else will occur. In contract law, a _____ is an event which must occur, unless its non-occurrence is excused, before performance under a contract becomes due, i.e., before any contractual duty exists.

Exam Probability: **Low**

37. *Answer choices:*

(see index for correct answer)

- a. first refusal
- b. Collateral warranty
- c. Accommodation
- d. Offer and acceptance

Guidance: level 1

:: ::

In contract law, rescission is an equitable remedy which allows a contractual party to cancel the contract. Parties may _____ if they are the victims of a vitiating factor, such as misrepresentation, mistake, duress, or undue influence. Rescission is the unwinding of a transaction. This is done to bring the parties, as far as possible, back to the position in which they were before they entered into a contract.

Exam Probability: **Low**

38. Answer choices:

(see index for correct answer)

- a. empathy
- b. process perspective
- c. co-culture
- d. levels of analysis

Guidance: level 1

:: ::

_____ is the collection of techniques, skills, methods, and processes used in the production of goods or services or in the accomplishment of objectives, such as scientific investigation. _____ can be the knowledge of techniques, processes, and the like, or it can be embedded in machines to allow for operation without detailed knowledge of their workings. Systems applying _____ by taking an input, changing it according to the system's use, and then producing an outcome are referred to as _____ systems or technological systems.

Exam Probability: **Low**

39. Answer choices:

(see index for correct answer)

- a. Technology
- b. functional perspective

- c. process perspective
- d. hierarchical

Guidance: level 1

:: Mereology ::

_____ , in the abstract, is what belongs to or with something, whether as an attribute or as a component of said thing. In the context of this article, it is one or more components, whether physical or incorporeal, of a person's estate; or so belonging to, as in being owned by, a person or jointly a group of people or a legal entity like a corporation or even a society. Depending on the nature of the _____ , an owner of _____ has the right to consume, alter, share, redefine, rent, mortgage, pawn, sell, exchange, transfer, give away or destroy it, or to exclude others from doing these things, as well as to perhaps abandon it; whereas regardless of the nature of the _____ , the owner thereof has the right to properly use it , or at the very least exclusively keep it.

Exam Probability: **High**

40. *Answer choices:*

(see index for correct answer)

- a. Property
- b. Mereological essentialism
- c. Simple
- d. Non-wellfounded mereology

Guidance: level 1

:: ::

_____ is the practical authority granted to a legal body to administer justice within a defined field of responsibility, e.g., Michigan tax law. In federations like the United States, areas of _____ apply to local, state, and federal levels; e.g. the court has _____ to apply federal law.

Exam Probability: **Medium**

41. *Answer choices:*

(see index for correct answer)

- a. Jurisdiction
- b. co-culture
- c. imperative
- d. hierarchical perspective

Guidance: level 1

:: Real property law ::

_____ is an area of criminal law or tort law broadly divided into three groups: _____ to the person, _____ to chattels and _____ to land.

Exam Probability: **High**

42. *Answer choices:*

(see index for correct answer)

- a. Avulsion
- b. Commissioner of deeds
- c. Project 70 Land Acquisition and Borrowing Act
- d. Frank-marriage

Guidance: level 1

:: United States securities law ::

_____ is a legal term for intent or knowledge of wrongdoing. An offending party then has knowledge of the "wrongness" of an act or event prior to committing it.

Exam Probability: **Low**

43. *Answer choices:*

(see index for correct answer)

- a. Scienter
- b. Registered representative
- c. General Securities Principal Exam
- d. Investment Banking Exam

Guidance: level 1

:: ::

_____ is the administration of an organization, whether it is a business, a not-for-profit organization, or government body. _____ includes the activities of setting the strategy of an organization and coordinating the efforts of its employees to accomplish its objectives through the application of available resources, such as financial, natural, technological, and human resources. The term "_____" may also refer to those people who manage an organization.

Exam Probability: **Low**

44. *Answer choices:*
(see index for correct answer)

- a. co-culture
- b. functional perspective
- c. open system
- d. hierarchical perspective

Guidance: level 1

:: Information technology audit ::

_____ is the act of using a computer to take or alter electronic data, or to gain unlawful use of a computer or system. In the United States, _____ is specifically proscribed by the _____ and Abuse Act, which criminalizes computer-related acts under federal jurisdiction. Types of _____ include.

Exam Probability: **Low**

45. *Answer choices:*

(see index for correct answer)

- a. David Coderre
- b. Information security audit
- c. Mobile device forensics
- d. Computer fraud

Guidance: level 1

:: Employment discrimination ::

_____ is a form of discrimination based on race, gender, religion, national origin, physical or mental disability, age, sexual orientation, and gender identity by employers. Earnings differentials or occupational differentiation—where differences in pay come from differences in qualifications or responsibilities—should not be confused with _____. Discrimination can be intended and involve disparate treatment of a group or be unintended, yet create disparate impact for a group.

Exam Probability: **Low**

46. *Answer choices:*

(see index for correct answer)

- a. New South Wales selection bias
- b. Glass ceiling
- c. Employment discrimination
- d. United Kingdom employment equality law

Guidance: level 1

:: ::

A _____ is a person who trades in commodities produced by other people. Historically, a _____ is anyone who is involved in business or trade. _____ s have operated for as long as industry, commerce, and trade have existed. During the 16th-century, in Europe, two different terms for _____ s emerged: One term, meerseniers, described local traders such as bakers, grocers, etc.; while a new term, koopman (Dutch: koopman, described _____ s who operated on a global stage, importing and exporting goods over vast distances, and offering added-value services such as credit and finance.

Exam Probability: **High**

47. *Answer choices:*

(see index for correct answer)

- a. Merchant
- b. imperative
- c. Character
- d. personal values

Guidance: level 1

:: Marketing ::

A _____ is an overall experience of a customer that distinguishes an organization or product from its rivals in the eyes of the customer. _____ s are used in business, marketing, and advertising. Name _____ s are sometimes distinguished from generic or store _____ s.

48. *Answer choices:*

(see index for correct answer)

- a. Disruptive innovation
- b. Pitching engine
- c. Brandweek
- d. Brand

Guidance: level 1

:: ::

The _____ is the central philosophical concept in the deontological moral philosophy of Immanuel Kant. Introduced in Kant's 1785 Groundwork of the Metaphysics of Morals, it may be defined as a way of evaluating motivations for action.

Exam Probability: **High**

49. *Answer choices:*

(see index for correct answer)

- a. information systems assessment
- b. personal values
- c. Categorical imperative

- d. levels of analysis

Guidance: level 1

:: Manufactured goods ::

A _____ or final good is any commodity that is produced or consumed by the consumer to satisfy current wants or needs. _____ s are ultimately consumed, rather than used in the production of another good. For example, a microwave oven or a bicycle that is sold to a consumer is a final good or _____, but the components that are sold to be used in those goods are intermediate goods. For example, textiles or transistors can be used to make some further goods.

Exam Probability: **High**

50. *Answer choices:*

(see index for correct answer)

- a. Bespoke
- b. Product ecosystem theory
- c. Tarpaulin
- d. Final good

Guidance: level 1

:: ::

_____ is the assignment of any responsibility or authority to another person to carry out specific activities. It is one of the core concepts of management leadership. However, the person who delegated the work remains accountable for the outcome of the delegated work. _____ empowers a subordinate to make decisions, i.e. it is a shifting of decision-making authority from one organizational level to a lower one. _____, if properly done, is not fabrication. The opposite of effective _____ is micromanagement, where a manager provides too much input, direction, and review of delegated work. In general, _____ is good and can save money and time, help in building skills, and motivate people. On the other hand, poor _____ might cause frustration and confusion to all the involved parties. Some agents, however, do not favour a _____ and consider the power of making a decision rather burdensome.

Exam Probability: **High**

51. *Answer choices:*

(see index for correct answer)

- a. imperative
- b. Delegation
- c. personal values
- d. hierarchical

Guidance: level 1

:: Contract law ::

In common law jurisdictions, an _____ is a contract law term for certain assurances that are presumed to be made in the sale of products or real property, due to the circumstances of the sale. These assurances are characterized as warranties irrespective of whether the seller has expressly promised them orally or in writing. They include an _____ of fitness for a particular purpose, an _____ of merchantability for products, _____ of workmanlike quality for services, and an _____ of habitability for a home.

Exam Probability: **High**

52. *Answer choices:*

(see index for correct answer)

- a. Mistake
- b. Implied warranty
- c. Peppercorn
- d. Forum selection clause

Guidance: level 1

:: ::

_____ is the principled guide to action taken by the administrative executive branches of the state with regard to a class of issues, in a manner consistent with law and institutional customs.

Exam Probability: **Low**

53. *Answer choices:*

(see index for correct answer)

- a. empathy
- b. hierarchical
- c. functional perspective
- d. Public policy

Guidance: level 1

:: ::

_____ is a type of government support for the citizens of that society. _____ may be provided to people of any income level, as with social security, but it is usually intended to ensure that the poor can meet their basic human needs such as food and shelter. _____ attempts to provide poor people with a minimal level of well-being, usually either a free- or a subsidized-supply of certain goods and social services, such as healthcare, education, and vocational training.

Exam Probability: **Medium**

54. *Answer choices:*

(see index for correct answer)

- a. similarity-attraction theory
- b. hierarchical perspective
- c. co-culture

- d. surface-level diversity

Guidance: level 1

:: Insurance terms ::

_____ is the assumption by a third party of another party's legal right to collect a debt or damages. It is a legal doctrine whereby one person is entitled to enforce the subsisting or revived rights of another for one's own benefit. A right of _____ typically arises by operation of law, but can also arise by statute or by agreement. _____ is an equitable remedy, having first developed in the English Court of Chancery. It is a familiar feature of common law systems. Analogous doctrines exist in civil law jurisdictions.

Exam Probability: **High**

55. *Answer choices:*

(see index for correct answer)

- a. Insurance broker
- b. Additional insured
- c. Subrogation
- d. Contingent coverage

Guidance: level 1

:: ::

_____ refers to a business or organization attempting to acquire goods or services to accomplish its goals. Although there are several organizations that attempt to set standards in the _____ process, processes can vary greatly between organizations. Typically the word " _____ " is not used interchangeably with the word "procurement", since procurement typically includes expediting, supplier quality, and transportation and logistics in addition to _____ .

Exam Probability: **Medium**

56. *Answer choices:*

(see index for correct answer)

- a. personal values
- b. Sarbanes-Oxley act of 2002
- c. Purchasing
- d. corporate values

Guidance: level 1

:: Project management ::

A _____ is a source or supply from which a benefit is produced and it has some utility. _____ s can broadly be classified upon their availability—they are classified into renewable and non-renewable _____ s. Examples of non renewable _____ s are coal, crude oil natural gas nuclear energy etc. Examples of renewable _____ s are air, water, wind, solar energy etc. They can also be classified as actual and potential on the basis of level of development and use, on the basis of origin they can be classified as biotic and abiotic, and on the basis of their distribution, as ubiquitous and localized. An item becomes a _____ with time and developing technology. Typically, _____ s are materials, energy, services, staff, knowledge, or other assets that are transformed to produce benefit and in the process may be consumed or made unavailable. Benefits of _____ utilization may include increased wealth, proper functioning of a system, or enhanced well-being. From a human perspective a natural _____ is anything obtained from the environment to satisfy human needs and wants. From a broader biological or ecological perspective a _____ satisfies the needs of a living organism.

Exam Probability: **Low**

57. *Answer choices:*

(see index for correct answer)

- a. Resource
- b. Logical framework approach
- c. Extreme project management
- d. Project Management Institute

Guidance: level 1

:: Fraud ::

In law, _____ is intentional deception to secure unfair or unlawful gain, or to deprive a victim of a legal right. _____ can violate civil law, a criminal law, or it may cause no loss of money, property or legal right but still be an element of another civil or criminal wrong. The purpose of _____ may be monetary gain or other benefits, for example by obtaining a passport, travel document, or driver's license, or mortgage _____, where the perpetrator may attempt to qualify for a mortgage by way of false statements.

Exam Probability: **High**

58. *Answer choices:*

(see index for correct answer)

- a. Wine fraud
- b. Insurance fraud
- c. Fraud
- d. Address fraud

Guidance: level 1

:: Commerce ::

_____ relates to "the exchange of goods and services, especially on a large scale". It includes legal, economic, political, social, cultural and technological systems that operate in a country or in international trade.

Exam Probability: **Low**

59. *Answer choices:*

(see index for correct answer)

- a. Sales quote
- b. Group buying
- c. Commerce
- d. Gumball machine

Guidance: level 1

Finance

Finance is a field that is concerned with the allocation (investment) of assets and liabilities over space and time, often under conditions of risk or uncertainty. Finance can also be defined as the science of money management. Participants in the market aim to price assets based on their risk level, fundamental value, and their expected rate of return. Finance can be split into three sub-categories: public finance, corporate finance and personal finance.

:: Business economics ::

_____ is one of the constituents of a leasing calculus or operation. It describes the future value of a good in terms of absolute value in monetary terms and it is sometimes abbreviated into a percentage of the initial price when the item was new.

Exam Probability: **Low**

1. *Answer choices:*

(see index for correct answer)

- a. Residual value
- b. Risk-seeking
- c. Round-tripping
- d. Model audit

Guidance: level 1

:: Debt ::

_____, in finance and economics, is payment from a borrower or deposit-taking financial institution to a lender or depositor of an amount above repayment of the principal sum , at a particular rate. It is distinct from a fee which the borrower may pay the lender or some third party. It is also distinct from dividend which is paid by a company to its shareholders from its profit or reserve, but not at a particular rate decided beforehand, rather on a pro rata basis as a share in the reward gained by risk taking entrepreneurs when the revenue earned exceeds the total costs.

Exam Probability: **High**

2. *Answer choices:*

(see index for correct answer)

- a. Debit commission
- b. Credit crunch
- c. Interest
- d. Borrowing base

Guidance: level 1

:: ::

An _____ is a contingent motivator. Traditional _____ s are extrinsic motivators which reward actions to yield a desired outcome. The effectiveness of traditional _____ s has changed as the needs of Western society have evolved. While the traditional _____ model is effective when there is a defined procedure and goal for a task, Western society started to require a higher volume of critical thinkers, so the traditional model became less effective. Institutions are now following a trend in implementing strategies that rely on intrinsic motivations rather than the extrinsic motivations that the traditional _____ s foster.

Exam Probability: **Medium**

3. *Answer choices:*

(see index for correct answer)

- a. Sarbanes-Oxley act of 2002
- b. Incentive
- c. interpersonal communication
- d. similarity-attraction theory

Guidance: level 1

:: ::

_____ is an eight-block-long street running roughly northwest to southeast from Broadway to South Street, at the East River, in the Financial District of Lower Manhattan in New York City. Over time, the term has become a metonym for the financial markets of the United States as a whole, the American financial services industry, or New York–based financial interests.

Exam Probability: **Medium**

4. *Answer choices:*
(see index for correct answer)

- a. imperative
- b. functional perspective
- c. Wall Street
- d. open system

Guidance: level 1

:: Financial accounting ::

_____ is the value of all the non-financial and financial assets owned by an institutional unit or sector minus the value of all its outstanding liabilities. Since financial assets minus outstanding liabilities equal net financial assets, _____ can also be conveniently expressed as non-financial assets plus net financial assets. _____ can apply to companies, individuals, governments or economic sectors such as the sector of financial corporations or to entire countries.

Exam Probability: **Low**

5. *Answer choices:*

(see index for correct answer)

- a. Accelerated depreciation
- b. Asset recovery
- c. Net worth
- d. Tax amortization benefit

Guidance: level 1

:: Subprime mortgage crisis ::

The _____ Group, Inc., is an American multinational investment bank and financial services company headquartered in New York City. It offers services in investment management, securities, asset management, prime brokerage, and securities underwriting.

Exam Probability: **Low**

6. Answer choices:

(see index for correct answer)

- a. National City acquisition by PNC
- b. Money market fund
- c. Housing and Economic Recovery Act of 2008
- d. Goldman Sachs

Guidance: level 1

:: Contract law ::

A _____ is a legally-binding agreement which recognises and governs the rights and duties of the parties to the agreement. A _____ is legally enforceable because it meets the requirements and approval of the law. An agreement typically involves the exchange of goods, services, money, or promises of any of those. In the event of breach of _____, the law awards the injured party access to legal remedies such as damages and cancellation.

Exam Probability: **Low**

7. Answer choices:

(see index for correct answer)

- a. Offeror
- b. Escalator clause
- c. Convention on the Law Applicable to Contractual Obligations 1980
- d. Warranty

Guidance: level 1

:: ::

In financial markets, a share is a unit used as mutual funds, limited partnerships, and real estate investment trusts. The owner of _____ in the corporation/company is a shareholder of the corporation. A share is an indivisible unit of capital, expressing the ownership relationship between the company and the shareholder. The denominated value of a share is its face value, and the total of the face value of issued _____ represent the capital of a company, which may not reflect the market value of those _____.

Exam Probability: **High**

8. *Answer choices:*

(see index for correct answer)

- a. co-culture
- b. imperative
- c. corporate values
- d. empathy

Guidance: level 1

:: Financial markets ::

The _____ , also called the aftermarket and follow on public offering is the financial market in which previously issued financial instruments such as stock, bonds, options, and futures are bought and sold. Another frequent usage of " _____ " is to refer to loans which are sold by a mortgage bank to investors such as Fannie Mae and Freddie Mac.

Exam Probability: **Low**

9. *Answer choices:*

(see index for correct answer)

- a. dark pool
- b. Private equity fund
- c. Marketcetera
- d. Money market in India

Guidance: level 1

:: Costs ::

The _____ is computed by dividing the total cost of goods available for sale by the total units available for sale. This gives a weighted-average unit cost that is applied to the units in the ending inventory.

Exam Probability: **Medium**

10. *Answer choices:*

(see index for correct answer)

- a. Quality costs
- b. Explicit cost
- c. Average Cost
- d. Cost per paper

Guidance: level 1

:: Financial accounting ::

In accounting, _____ is the value of an asset according to its balance sheet account balance. For assets, the value is based on the original cost of the asset less any depreciation, amortization or impairment costs made against the asset. Traditionally, a company's _____ is its total assets minus intangible assets and liabilities. However, in practice, depending on the source of the calculation, _____ may variably include goodwill, intangible assets, or both. The value inherent in its workforce, part of the intellectual capital of a company, is always ignored. When intangible assets and goodwill are explicitly excluded, the metric is often specified to be "tangible _____ ".

Exam Probability: **Low**

11. *Answer choices:*
(see index for correct answer)

- a. Deferred Acquisition Costs
- b. Advance payment

- c. Accelerated depreciation
- d. Commuted cash value

Guidance: level 1

:: Generally Accepted Accounting Principles ::

Expenditure is an outflow of money to another person or group to pay for an item or service, or for a category of costs. For a tenant, rent is an _____ . For students or parents, tuition is an _____ . Buying food, clothing, furniture or an automobile is often referred to as an _____ . An _____ is a cost that is "paid" or "remitted", usually in exchange for something of value. Something that seems to cost a great deal is "expensive". Something that seems to cost little is "inexpensive". " _____ s of the table" are _____ s of dining, refreshments, a feast, etc.

Exam Probability: **High**

12. *Answer choices:*
(see index for correct answer)

- a. Liability
- b. Access to finance
- c. Matching principle
- d. Expense

Guidance: level 1

:: ::

_____ is the collection of mechanisms, processes and relations by which corporations are controlled and operated. Governance structures and principles identify the distribution of rights and responsibilities among different participants in the corporation and include the rules and procedures for making decisions in corporate affairs. _____ is necessary because of the possibility of conflicts of interests between stakeholders, primarily between shareholders and upper management or among shareholders.

Exam Probability: **Low**

13. *Answer choices:*

(see index for correct answer)

- a. cultural
- b. process perspective
- c. open system
- d. levels of analysis

Guidance: level 1

:: Stock market ::

A _____, securities exchange or bourse, is a facility where stock brokers and traders can buy and sell securities, such as shares of stock and bonds and other financial instruments. _____ s may also provide for facilities the issue and redemption of such securities and instruments and capital events including the payment of income and dividends. Securities traded on a _____ include stock issued by listed companies, unit trusts, derivatives, pooled investment products and bonds. _____ s often function as "continuous auction" markets with buyers and sellers consummating transactions via open outcry at a central location such as the floor of the exchange or by using an electronic trading platform.

Exam Probability: **Medium**

14. *Answer choices:*

(see index for correct answer)

- a. Beneficial ownership
- b. American Depositary Share
- c. Stock split
- d. Leading stock

Guidance: level 1

:: Financial risk ::

The _____ on a financial investment is the expected value of its return. It is a measure of the center of the distribution of the random variable that is the return.

Exam Probability: **High**

15. *Answer choices:*

(see index for correct answer)

- a. Age at risk
- b. Bielard, Biehl and Kaiser five-way model
- c. Expected return
- d. Interest rate risk

Guidance: level 1

:: Materials ::

A _____, also known as a feedstock, unprocessed material, or primary commodity, is a basic material that is used to produce goods, finished products, energy, or intermediate materials which are feedstock for future finished products. As feedstock, the term connotes these materials are bottleneck assets and are highly important with regard to producing other products. An example of this is crude oil, which is a _____ and a feedstock used in the production of industrial chemicals, fuels, plastics, and pharmaceutical goods; lumber is a _____ used to produce a variety of products including all types of furniture. The term "_____" denotes materials in minimally processed or unprocessed in states; e.g., raw latex, crude oil, cotton, coal, raw biomass, iron ore, air, logs, or water i.e. "...any product of agriculture, forestry, fishing and any other mineral that is in its natural form or which has undergone the transformation required to prepare it for internationally marketing in substantial volumes."

Exam Probability: **Low**

16. *Answer choices:*

(see index for correct answer)

- a. Tensometer
- b. Wattle
- c. Tego film
- d. Raw material

Guidance: level 1

:: Bonds (finance) ::

A _____ is a fund established by an economic entity by setting aside revenue over a period of time to fund a future capital expense, or repayment of a long-term debt.

Exam Probability: **Medium**

17. *Answer choices:*

(see index for correct answer)

- a. Social impact bond
- b. Mezzanine capital
- c. Puttable bond
- d. Regional Bond Dealers Association

Guidance: level 1

:: Business law ::

The expression " _____ " is somewhat confusing as it has a different meaning based on the context that is under consideration. From a product characteristic stand point, this type of a lease, as distinguished from a finance lease, is one where the lessor takes residual risk. As such, the lease is non full payout. From an accounting stand point, this type of lease results in off balance sheet financing.

Exam Probability: **Medium**

18. *Answer choices:*

(see index for correct answer)

- a. Fraudulent trading
- b. Operating lease
- c. Power harassment
- d. Lex mercatoria

Guidance: level 1

:: Mereology ::

_____, in the abstract, is what belongs to or with something, whether as an attribute or as a component of said thing. In the context of this article, it is one or more components, whether physical or incorporeal, of a person's estate; or so belonging to, as in being owned by, a person or jointly a group of people or a legal entity like a corporation or even a society. Depending on the nature of the _____, an owner of _____ has the right to consume, alter, share, redefine, rent, mortgage, pawn, sell, exchange, transfer, give away or destroy it, or to exclude others from doing these things, as well as to perhaps abandon it; whereas regardless of the nature of the _____, the owner thereof has the right to properly use it, or at the very least exclusively keep it.

Exam Probability: **High**

19. *Answer choices:*

(see index for correct answer)

- a. Mereological nihilism
- b. Mereotopology
- c. Gunk
- d. Mereological essentialism

Guidance: level 1

:: Stock market ::

_____ or stock market launch is a type of public offering in which shares of a company are sold to institutional investors and usually also retail investors; an IPO is underwritten by one or more investment banks, who also arrange for the shares to be listed on one or more stock exchanges. Through this process, colloquially known as floating, or going public, a privately held company is transformed into a public company. _____ s can be used: to raise new equity capital for the company concerned; to monetize the investments of private shareholders such as company founders or private equity investors; and to enable easy trading of existing holdings or future capital raising by becoming publicly traded enterprises.

Exam Probability: **Low**

20. *Answer choices:*

(see index for correct answer)

- a. Initial public offering
- b. BATS Chi-X Europe
- c. Tech Buzz
- d. Xetra

Guidance: level 1

:: Financial ratios ::

The _____ is a financial ratio indicating the relative proportion of shareholders' equity and debt used to finance a company's assets. Closely related to leveraging, the ratio is also known as risk, gearing or leverage. The two components are often taken from the firm's balance sheet or statement of financial position, but the ratio may also be calculated using market values for both, if the company's debt and equity are publicly traded, or using a combination of book value for debt and market value for equity financially.

Exam Probability: **Medium**

21. *Answer choices:*

(see index for correct answer)

- a. Yield gap
- b. Debt-to-equity ratio
- c. Greeks
- d. Fixed-asset turnover

Guidance: level 1

:: Stock market ::

The _____ of a corporation is all of the shares into which ownership of the corporation is divided. In American English, the shares are commonly known as "_____s". A single share of the _____ represents fractional ownership of the corporation in proportion to the total number of shares. This typically entitles the _____ holder to that fraction of the company's earnings, proceeds from liquidation of assets , or voting power, often dividing these up in proportion to the amount of money each _____ holder has invested. Not all _____ is necessarily equal, as certain classes of _____ may be issued for example without voting rights, with enhanced voting rights, or with a certain priority to receive profits or liquidation proceeds before or after other classes of shareholders.

Exam Probability: **Low**

22. *Answer choices:*

(see index for correct answer)

- a. Purple chip
- b. Stock
- c. Red chip
- d. Barbell strategy

Guidance: level 1

:: Finance ::

_____ is a field that is concerned with the allocation of assets and liabilities over space and time, often under conditions of risk or uncertainty. _____ can also be defined as the art of money management. Participants in the market aim to price assets based on their risk level, fundamental value, and their expected rate of return. _____ can be split into three sub-categories: public _____, corporate _____ and personal _____.

Exam Probability: **Medium**

23. *Answer choices:*

(see index for correct answer)

- a. Investment Policy Statement
- b. Finance
- c. Qualifying floating charge
- d. Weighted-average loan age

Guidance: level 1

:: Accounting terminology ::

In accounting/accountancy, _____ are journal entries usually made at the end of an accounting period to allocate income and expenditure to the period in which they actually occurred. The revenue recognition principle is the basis of making _____ that pertain to unearned and accrued revenues under accrual-basis accounting. They are sometimes called Balance Day adjustments because they are made on balance day.

Exam Probability: **Medium**

24. *Answer choices:*

(see index for correct answer)

- a. Adjusting entries
- b. Enterprise liquidity
- c. Absorption costing
- d. outstanding balance

Guidance: level 1

:: Occupations ::

An _____ is a practitioner of accounting or accountancy, which is the measurement, disclosure or provision of assurance about financial information that helps managers, investors, tax authorities and others make decisions about allocating resource.

Exam Probability: **Low**

25. *Answer choices:*

(see index for correct answer)

- a. Accountant
- b. Cigarette girl
- c. International Standard Classification of Occupations

- d. Shopkeeper

Guidance: level 1

:: Stock market ::

A share price is the price of a single share of a number of saleable stocks of a company, derivative or other financial asset. In layman's terms, the _____ is the highest amount someone is willing to pay for the stock, or the lowest amount that it can be bought for.

Exam Probability: **Low**

26. *Answer choices:*

(see index for correct answer)

- a. High-frequency trading
- b. Slippage
- c. Big boy letter
- d. Stock price

Guidance: level 1

:: ::

_____ or accountancy is the measurement, processing, and communication of financial information about economic entities such as businesses and corporations. The modern field was established by the Italian mathematician Luca Pacioli in 1494. _____ , which has been called the "language of business", measures the results of an organization's economic activities and conveys this information to a variety of users, including investors, creditors, management, and regulators. Practitioners of _____ are known as accountants. The terms "_____" and "financial reporting" are often used as synonyms.

Exam Probability: **Low**

27. *Answer choices:*

(see index for correct answer)

- a. levels of analysis
- b. Accounting
- c. imperative
- d. surface-level diversity

Guidance: level 1

:: ::

The U.S. _____ is an independent agency of the United States federal government. The SEC holds primary responsibility for enforcing the federal securities laws, proposing securities rules, and regulating the securities industry, the nation's stock and options exchanges, and other activities and organizations, including the electronic securities markets in the United States.

Exam Probability: **Low**

28. *Answer choices:*

(see index for correct answer)

- a. hierarchical perspective
- b. corporate values
- c. Character
- d. Securities and Exchange Commission

Guidance: level 1

:: Accounting terminology ::

In management accounting or _____, managers use the provisions of accounting information in order to better inform themselves before they decide matters within their organizations, which aids their management and performance of control functions.

Exam Probability: **Low**

29. Answer choices:

(see index for correct answer)

- a. Managerial accounting
- b. Internal auditing
- c. Cash flow management
- d. General ledger

Guidance: level 1

:: Costs ::

In microeconomic theory, the _____, or alternative cost, of making a particular choice is the value of the most valuable choice out of those that were not taken. In other words, opportunity that will require sacrifices.

Exam Probability: **Medium**

30. Answer choices:

(see index for correct answer)

- a. Sliding scale fees
- b. Opportunity cost
- c. Incremental cost-effectiveness ratio
- d. Opportunity cost of capital

Guidance: level 1

:: Generally Accepted Accounting Principles ::

An _____ or profit and loss account is one of the financial statements of a company and shows the company's revenues and expenses during a particular period.

Exam Probability: **Low**

31. *Answer choices:*

(see index for correct answer)

- a. Income statement
- b. Expense
- c. Consolidation
- d. Gross income

Guidance: level 1

:: Competition (economics) ::

_____ arises whenever at least two parties strive for a goal which cannot be shared: where one's gain is the other's loss.

Exam Probability: **Low**

32. Answer choices:

(see index for correct answer)

- a. Category killer
- b. Regulatory competition
- c. National Competitiveness Report of Armenia
- d. Self-competition

Guidance: level 1

:: Basic financial concepts ::

_____ is a sustained increase in the general price level of goods and services in an economy over a period of time. When the general price level rises, each unit of currency buys fewer goods and services; consequently, _____ reflects a reduction in the purchasing power per unit of money a loss of real value in the medium of exchange and unit of account within the economy. The measure of _____ is the _____ rate, the annualized percentage change in a general price index, usually the consumer price index, over time. The opposite of _____ is deflation.

Exam Probability: **Medium**

33. Answer choices:

(see index for correct answer)

- a. Leverage cycle
- b. Inflation

- c. Financial transaction
- d. Eurodollar

Guidance: level 1

:: Inventory ::

> Costs are associated with particular goods using one of the several formulas, including specific identification, first-in first-out, or average cost. Costs include all costs of purchase, costs of conversion and other costs that are incurred in bringing the inventories to their present location and condition. Costs of goods made by the businesses include material, labor, and allocated overhead. The costs of those goods which are not yet sold are deferred as costs of inventory until the inventory is sold or written down in value.

Exam Probability: **Medium**

34. *Answer choices:*

(see index for correct answer)

- a. Stock keeping unit
- b. GMROII
- c. Cost of goods sold
- d. Stock-taking

Guidance: level 1

:: Bonds (finance) ::

An _____ is a legal contract that reflects or covers a debt or purchase obligation. It specifically refers to two types of practices: in historical usage, an _____ d servant status, and in modern usage, it is an instrument used for commercial debt or real estate transaction.

Exam Probability: **Low**

35. *Answer choices:*

(see index for correct answer)

- a. Global bond
- b. Kimchi bond
- c. Indenture
- d. Variable rate debt obligation

Guidance: level 1

:: Data analysis ::

In statistics, the _____ is a measure that is used to quantify the amount of variation or dispersion of a set of data values. A low _____ indicates that the data points tend to be close to the mean of the set, while a high _____ indicates that the data points are spread out over a wider range of values.

Exam Probability: **Medium**

36. *Answer choices:*

(see index for correct answer)

- a. Neighbourhood components analysis
- b. Topological data analysis
- c. Imputation
- d. Inverse-variance weighting

Guidance: level 1

:: ::

A shareholder is an individual or institution that legally owns one or more shares of stock in a public or private corporation. Shareholders may be referred to as members of a corporation. Legally, a person is not a shareholder in a corporation until their name and other details are entered in the corporation's register of shareholders or members.

Exam Probability: **High**

37. *Answer choices:*

(see index for correct answer)

- a. hierarchical perspective
- b. personal values

- c. Stockholder
- d. information systems assessment

Guidance: level 1

:: ::

In accounting, the _____ is a measure of the number of times inventory is sold or used in a time period such as a year. It is calculated to see if a business has an excessive inventory in comparison to its sales level. The equation for _____ equals the cost of goods sold divided by the average inventory. _____ is also known as inventory turns, merchandise turnover, stockturn, stock turns, turns, and stock turnover.

Exam Probability: **High**

38. *Answer choices:*

(see index for correct answer)

- a. Inventory turnover
- b. deep-level diversity
- c. process perspective
- d. open system

Guidance: level 1

:: Asset ::

In accounting, a _____ is any asset which can reasonably be expected to be sold, consumed, or exhausted through the normal operations of a business within the current fiscal year or operating cycle. Typical _____ s include cash, cash equivalents, short-term investments, accounts receivable, stock inventory, supplies, and the portion of prepaid liabilities which will be paid within a year. In simple words, assets which are held for a short period are known as _____ s. Such assets are expected to be realised in cash or consumed during the normal operating cycle of the business.

Exam Probability: **High**

39. *Answer choices:*

(see index for correct answer)

- a. Fixed asset
- b. Current asset

Guidance: level 1

:: Actuarial science ::

The _____ is the greater benefit of receiving money now rather than an identical sum later. It is founded on time preference.

Exam Probability: **Medium**

40. *Answer choices:*

(see index for correct answer)

- a. Life expectancy
- b. Time value of money
- c. Medical underwriting
- d. Confidence weighting

Guidance: level 1

:: Options (finance) ::

A _____, often simply labeled a "call", is a financial contract between two parties, the buyer and the seller of this type of option. The buyer of the _____ has the right, but not the obligation, to buy an agreed quantity of a particular commodity or financial instrument from the seller of the option at a certain time for a certain price. The seller is obligated to sell the commodity or financial instrument to the buyer if the buyer so decides. The buyer pays a fee for this right. The term "call" comes from the fact that the owner has the right to "call the stock away" from the seller.

Exam Probability: **Low**

41. *Answer choices:*

(see index for correct answer)

- a. callable
- b. Rainbow option
- c. Call option

- d. Credit default option

Guidance: level 1

:: ::

In the field of analysis of algorithms in computer science, the _____ is a method of amortized analysis based on accounting. The _____ often gives a more intuitive account of the amortized cost of an operation than either aggregate analysis or the potential method. Note, however, that this does not guarantee such analysis will be immediately obvious; often, choosing the correct parameters for the _____ requires as much knowledge of the problem and the complexity bounds one is attempting to prove as the other two methods.

Exam Probability: **Medium**

42. *Answer choices:*

(see index for correct answer)

- a. Accounting method
- b. interpersonal communication
- c. empathy
- d. deep-level diversity

Guidance: level 1

:: Stock market ::

_____ is a form of stock which may have any combination of features not possessed by common stock including properties of both an equity and a debt instrument, and is generally considered a hybrid instrument. _____ s are senior to common stock, but subordinate to bonds in terms of claim and may have priority over common stock in the payment of dividends and upon liquidation. Terms of the _____ are described in the issuing company's articles of association or articles of incorporation.

Exam Probability: **Low**

43. *Answer choices:*

(see index for correct answer)

- a. Block premium
- b. Preferred stock
- c. Indirect finance
- d. Red chip

Guidance: level 1

:: Options (finance) ::

In finance, a put or _____ is a stock market device which gives the owner the right, but not the obligation, to sell an asset, at a specified price, by a predetermined date to a given party. The purchase of a _____ is interpreted as a negative sentiment about the future value of theunderlying stock. The term "put" comes from the fact that the owner has the right to "put up for sale" the stock or index.

Exam Probability: **High**

44. *Answer choices:*

(see index for correct answer)

- a. LEAPS
- b. Warrant
- c. Barrier option
- d. Margrabe's formula

Guidance: level 1

:: Financial ratios ::

The _____ shows the percentage of how profitable a company's assets are in generating revenue.

Exam Probability: **Medium**

45. *Answer choices:*

(see index for correct answer)

- a. Statutory liquidity ratio
- b. Quick ratio
- c. Return on assets
- d. Average propensity to save

Guidance: level 1

:: Generally Accepted Accounting Principles ::

In accrual accounting, the revenue recognition principle states that expenses should be recorded during the period in which they are incurred, regardless of when the transfer of cash occurs. Conversely, cash basis accounting calls for the recognition of an expense when the cash is paid, regardless of when the expense was actually incurred.

Exam Probability: **Medium**

46. *Answer choices:*

(see index for correct answer)

- a. Liability
- b. Matching principle
- c. Historical cost
- d. Petty cash

Guidance: level 1

:: Financial ratios ::

> _____ is a financial ratio that indicates the percentage of a company's assets that are provided via debt. It is the ratio of total debt and total assets.

Exam Probability: **High**

47. *Answer choices:*
(see index for correct answer)

- a. Debt ratio
- b. Equity ratio
- c. DuPont analysis
- d. Market-to-book

Guidance: level 1

:: Debt ::

_____ is the trust which allows one party to provide money or resources to another party wherein the second party does not reimburse the first party immediately, but promises either to repay or return those resources at a later date. In other words, _____ is a method of making reciprocity formal, legally enforceable, and extensible to a large group of unrelated people.

Exam Probability: **Low**

48. *Answer choices:*

(see index for correct answer)

- a. Exchangeable bond
- b. Credit
- c. Rule of 72
- d. Arrears

Guidance: level 1

:: Accounting terminology ::

A _____ contains all the accounts for recording transactions relating to a company's assets, liabilities, owners' equity, revenue, and expenses. In modern accounting software or ERP, the _____ works as a central repository for accounting data transferred from all subledgers or modules like accounts payable, accounts receivable, cash management, fixed assets, purchasing and projects. The _____ is the backbone of any accounting system which holds financial and non-financial data for an organization. The collection of all accounts is known as the _____ . Each account is known as a ledger account. In a manual or non-computerized system this may be a large book. The statement of financial position and the statement of income and comprehensive income are both derived from the _____ . Each account in the _____ consists of one or more pages. The _____ is where posting to the accounts occurs. Posting is the process of recording amounts as credits , and amounts as debits , in the pages of the _____ . Additional columns to the right hold a running activity total .

Exam Probability: **High**

49. *Answer choices:*

(see index for correct answer)

- a. Accounting equation
- b. Adjusting entries
- c. Chart of accounts
- d. General ledger

Guidance: level 1

:: Corporate governance ::

The _____ is the officer of a company that has primary responsibility for managing the company's finances, including financial planning, management of financial risks, record-keeping, and financial reporting. In some sectors, the CFO is also responsible for analysis of data. Some CFOs have the title CFOO for chief financial and operating officer. In the United Kingdom, the typical term for a CFO is finance director. The CFO typically reports to the chief executive officer and the board of directors and may additionally have a seat on the board. The CFO supervises the finance unit and is the chief financial spokesperson for the organization. The CFO directly assists the chief operating officer on all strategic and tactical matters relating to budget management, cost–benefit analysis, forecasting needs, and securing of new funding.

Exam Probability: **Low**

50. *Answer choices:*

(see index for correct answer)

- a. Chief operating officer
- b. Chartered Secretaries New Zealand
- c. Chief content officer
- d. Chief financial officer

Guidance: level 1

:: Financial markets ::

For an individual, a _____ is the minimum amount of money by which the expected return on a risky asset must exceed the known return on a risk-free asset in order to induce an individual to hold the risky asset rather than the risk-free asset. It is positive if the person is risk averse. Thus it is the minimum willingness to accept compensation for the risk.

Exam Probability: **Low**

51. *Answer choices:*

(see index for correct answer)

- a. Internal financing
- b. Faroese Securities Market
- c. Spread trade
- d. Block trade

Guidance: level 1

:: Fundamental analysis ::

_____ is the monetary value of earnings per outstanding share of common stock for a company.

Exam Probability: **Low**

52. *Answer choices:*

(see index for correct answer)

- a. Goldman Sachs asset management factor model
- b. Growth stock
- c. Earnings per share
- d. Fundamental analysis

Guidance: level 1

:: Accounting ::

_____ is a process of providing relief to shared service organization's cost centers that provide a product or service. In turn, the associated expense is assigned to internal clients' cost centers that consume the products and services. For example, the CIO may provide all IT services within the company and assign the costs back to the business units that consume each offering.

Exam Probability: **High**

53. *Answer choices:*

(see index for correct answer)

- a. CPA Site Solutions
- b. FreeAgent
- c. Cash sweep
- d. Cost allocation

Guidance: level 1

:: Hazard analysis ::

Broadly speaking, a _____ is the combined effort of 1. identifying and analyzing potential events that may negatively impact individuals, assets, and/or the environment ; and 2. making judgments "on the tolerability of the risk on the basis of a risk analysis" while considering influencing factors . Put in simpler terms, a _____ analyzes what can go wrong, how likely it is to happen, what the potential consequences are, and how tolerable the identified risk is. As part of this process, the resulting determination of risk may be expressed in a quantitative or qualitative fashion. The _____ is an inherent part of an overall risk management strategy, which attempts to, after a _____ , "introduce control measures to eliminate or reduce" any potential risk-related consequences.

Exam Probability: **Medium**

54. *Answer choices:*

(see index for correct answer)

- a. Hazard
- b. Swiss cheese model
- c. Hazardous Materials Identification System
- d. Risk assessment

Guidance: level 1

:: Accounting systems ::

In bookkeeping, a _____ statement is a process that explains the difference on a specified date between the bank balance shown in an organization's bank statement, as supplied by the bank and the corresponding amount shown in the organization's own accounting records.

Exam Probability: **High**

55. *Answer choices:*

(see index for correct answer)

- a. Unified ledger accounting
- b. Invoice processing
- c. Substance over form
- d. control account

Guidance: level 1

:: Income ::

_____ is a ratio between the net profit and cost of investment resulting from an investment of some resources. A high ROI means the investment's gains favorably to its cost. As a performance measure, ROI is used to evaluate the efficiency of an investment or to compare the efficiencies of several different investments. In purely economic terms, it is one way of relating profits to capital invested. _____ is a performance measure used by businesses to identify the efficiency of an investment or number of different investments.

Exam Probability: **High**

56. *Answer choices:*

(see index for correct answer)

- a. Return on investment
- b. Real estate investing
- c. Creative real estate investing
- d. Salary inversion

Guidance: level 1

:: Accounting terminology ::

Total _____ is a method of Accounting cost which entails the full cost of manufacturing or providing a service. TAC includes not just the costs of materials and labour, but also of all manufacturing overheads. The cost of each cost center can be direct or indirect. The direct cost can be easily identified with individual cost centers. Whereas indirect cost cannot be easily identified with the cost center. The distribution of overhead among the departments is called apportionment.

Exam Probability: **Medium**

57. *Answer choices:*

(see index for correct answer)

- a. Accounting equation

- b. Chart of accounts
- c. Cash flow management
- d. Capital surplus

Guidance: level 1

:: ::

In production, research, retail, and accounting, a _____ is the value of money that has been used up to produce something or deliver a service, and hence is not available for use anymore. In business, the _____ may be one of acquisition, in which case the amount of money expended to acquire it is counted as _____. In this case, money is the input that is gone in order to acquire the thing. This acquisition _____ may be the sum of the _____ of production as incurred by the original producer, and further _____s of transaction as incurred by the acquirer over and above the price paid to the producer. Usually, the price also includes a mark-up for profit over the _____ of production.

Exam Probability: **Low**

58. *Answer choices:*

(see index for correct answer)

- a. interpersonal communication
- b. Cost
- c. corporate values
- d. co-culture

Guidance: level 1

:: Generally Accepted Accounting Principles ::

> A _____ is a reduction of the recognized value of something. In accounting, this is a recognition of the reduced or zero value of an asset. In income tax statements, this is a reduction of taxable income, as a recognition of certain expenses required to produce the income.

Exam Probability: **High**

59. *Answer choices:*

(see index for correct answer)

- a. Net realizable value
- b. Fin 48
- c. French generally accepted accounting principles
- d. Write-off

Guidance: level 1

Human resource management

Human resource (HR) management is the strategic approach to the effective management of organization workers so that they help the business gain a competitive advantage. It is designed to maximize employee performance in service of an employer's strategic objectives. HR is primarily concerned with the management of people within organizations, focusing on policies and on systems. HR departments are responsible for overseeing employee-benefits design, employee recruitment, training and development, performance appraisal, and rewarding (e.g., managing pay and benefit systems). HR also concerns itself with organizational change and industrial relations, that is, the balancing of organizational practices with requirements arising from collective bargaining and from governmental laws.

:: Offshoring ::

A _____ is the temporary suspension or permanent termination of employment of an employee or, more commonly, a group of employees for business reasons, such as personnel management or downsizing an organization. Originally, _____ referred exclusively to a temporary interruption in work, or employment but this has evolved to a permanent elimination of a position in both British and US English, requiring the addition of "temporary" to specify the original meaning of the word. A _____ is not to be confused with wrongful termination. Laid off workers or displaced workers are workers who have lost or left their jobs because their employer has closed or moved, there was insufficient work for them to do, or their position or shift was abolished. Downsizing in a company is defined to involve the reduction of employees in a workforce. Downsizing in companies became a popular practice in the 1980s and early 1990s as it was seen as a way to deliver better shareholder value as it helps to reduce the costs of employers. Indeed, recent research on downsizing in the U.S., UK, and Japan suggests that downsizing is being regarded by management as one of the preferred routes to help declining organizations, cutting unnecessary costs, and improve organizational performance. Usually a _____ occurs as a cost cutting measure.

Exam Probability: **Low**

1. *Answer choices:*

(see index for correct answer)

- a. Layoff
- b. Offshore company
- c. Offshore outsourcing
- d. Global labor arbitrage

Guidance: level 1

:: Fundamental analysis ::

_____, also known as letter stock or restricted securities, is stock of a company that is not fully transferable until certain conditions have been met. Upon satisfaction of those conditions, the stock is no longer restricted, and becomes transferable to the person holding the award. _____ is often used as a form of employee compensation, in which case it typically becomes transferrable upon the satisfaction of certain conditions, such as continued employment for a period of time or the achievement of particular product-development milestones, earnings per share goals or other financial targets. _____ is a popular alternative to stock options, particularly for executives, due to favorable accounting rules and income tax treatment.

Exam Probability: **Low**

2. *Answer choices:*

(see index for correct answer)

- a. Earnings per share
- b. Trading Advantage
- c. Restricted stock
- d. Equity value

Guidance: level 1

:: Power (social and political) ::

In a notable study of power conducted by social psychologists John R. P. French and Bertram Raven in 1959, power is divided into five separate and distinct forms. In 1965 Raven revised this model to include a sixth form by separating the informational power base as distinct from the _____ base.

Exam Probability: **Medium**

3. *Answer choices:*

(see index for correct answer)

- a. need for power
- b. Referent power
- c. Hard power

Guidance: level 1

:: Nepotism ::

_____ is the granting of favour to relatives in various fields, including business, politics, entertainment, sports, religion and other activities. The term originated with the assignment of nephews to important positions by Catholic popes and bishops. Trading parliamentary employment for favors is a modern-day example of _____ . Criticism of _____ , however, can be found in ancient Indian texts such as the Kural literature.

Exam Probability: **High**

4. Answer choices:

(see index for correct answer)

- a. Monklandsgate
- b. Crachach
- c. Nepotism
- d. Ethnic nepotism

Guidance: level 1

:: ::

According to Torrington, a _____ is usually developed by conducting a job analysis, which includes examining the tasks and sequences of tasks necessary to perform the job. The analysis considers the areas of knowledge and skills needed for the job. A job usually includes several roles. According to Hall, the _____ might be broadened to form a person specification or may be known as "terms of reference". The person/job specification can be presented as a stand-alone document, but in practice it is usually included within the _____ . A _____ is often used by employers in the recruitment process.

Exam Probability: **Low**

5. Answer choices:

(see index for correct answer)

- a. surface-level diversity
- b. similarity-attraction theory

- c. Job description
- d. functional perspective

Guidance: level 1

:: Employment ::

> A _____, a concept developed in contemporary research by organizational scholar Denise Rousseau, represents the mutual beliefs, perceptions and informal obligations between an employer and an employee. It sets the dynamics for the relationship and defines the detailed practicality of the work to be done. It is distinguishable from the formal written contract of employment which, for the most part, only identifies mutual duties and responsibilities in a generalized form.

Exam Probability: **High**

6. *Answer choices:*

(see index for correct answer)

- a. Work sharing
- b. The Kingdom of Could Be You
- c. PATCOB
- d. Psychological contract

Guidance: level 1

:: Systems thinking ::

Systems theory is the interdisciplinary study of systems. A system is a cohesive conglomeration of interrelated and interdependent parts that is either natural or man-made. Every system is delineated by its spatial and temporal boundaries, surrounded and influenced by its environment, described by its structure and purpose or nature and expressed in its functioning. In terms of its effects, a system can be more than the sum of its parts if it expresses synergy or emergent behavior. Changing one part of the system usually affects other parts and the whole system, with predictable patterns of behavior. For systems that are self-learning and self-adapting, the positive growth and adaptation depend upon how well the system is adjusted with its environment. Some systems function mainly to support other systems by aiding in the maintenance of the other system to prevent failure. The goal of systems theory is systematically discovering a system's dynamics, constraints, conditions and elucidating principles that can be discerned and applied to systems at every level of nesting, and in every field for achieving optimized equifinality.

Exam Probability: **Medium**

7. *Answer choices:*

(see index for correct answer)

- a. Thought leader
- b. Business continuity planning
- c. Delphi method
- d. Interdependence

Guidance: level 1

:: Recruitment ::

A _____ is a quantitative research method commonly employed in survey research. The aim of this approach is to ensure that each interview is presented with exactly the same questions in the same order. This ensures that answers can be reliably aggregated and that comparisons can be made with confidence between sample subgroups or between different survey periods.

Exam Probability: **High**

8. *Answer choices:*
(see index for correct answer)

- a. ProClinical
- b. Global Career Development Facilitator
- c. Institute of Recruiters
- d. Structured interview

Guidance: level 1

:: Employment compensation ::

A _____ is an agreement between a company and an employee specifying that the employee will receive certain significant benefits if employment is terminated. Most definitions specify the employment termination is as a result of a merger or takeover, also known as "Change-in-control benefits", but more recently the term has been used to describe perceived excessive CEO severance packages unrelated to change in ownership. The benefits may include severance pay, cash bonuses, stock options, or other benefits.

Exam Probability: **High**

9. *Answer choices:*

(see index for correct answer)

- a. ADP, LLC
- b. Health Reimbursement Account
- c. Golden parachute
- d. salary sacrifice

Guidance: level 1

_____ is the moral stance, political philosophy, ideology, or social outlook that emphasizes the moral worth of the individual. Individualists promote the exercise of one's goals and desires and so value independence and self-reliance and advocate that interests of the individual should achieve precedence over the state or a social group, while opposing external interference upon one's own interests by society or institutions such as the government. _____ is often defined in contrast to totalitarianism, collectivism, and more corporate social forms.

Exam Probability: **Medium**

10. *Answer choices:*

(see index for correct answer)

- a. information systems assessment
- b. Individualism
- c. interpersonal communication
- d. similarity-attraction theory

Guidance: level 1

:: Training ::

_____ is a phase of training needs analysis directed at identifying which individuals within an organization should receive training.

Exam Probability: **High**

11. *Answer choices:*

(see index for correct answer)

- a. Person Analysis
- b. Teletraining
- c. Arts-based training
- d. Boardcast

Guidance: level 1

:: Stress ::

_____ means beneficial stress—either psychological, physical, or biochemical/radiological.

Exam Probability: **High**

12. *Answer choices:*

(see index for correct answer)

- a. Critical incident stress management
- b. Perceived Stress Scale
- c. Emotional exhaustion
- d. Freezing behavior

Guidance: level 1

:: Business law ::

_____ or employment relations is the multidisciplinary academic field that studies the employment relationship; that is, the complex interrelations between employers and employees, labor/trade unions, employer organizations and the state.

Exam Probability: **High**

13. *Answer choices:*

(see index for correct answer)

- a. Process agent
- b. Industrial relations
- c. Lien
- d. Novation

Guidance: level 1

:: Human resource management ::

_____ refers to the anticipation of required human capital for an organization and the planning to meet those needs. The field increased in popularity after McKinsey's 1997 research and the 2001 book on The War for Talent. _____ in this context does not refer to the management of entertainers.

Exam Probability: **High**

14. *Answer choices:*

(see index for correct answer)

- a. Work activity management
- b. Talent management
- c. Cross-training
- d. Sham peer review

Guidance: level 1

:: Unemployment ::

_____ is the support service provided by responsible organizations, keen to support individuals who are exiting the business – to help former employees transition to new jobs and help them re-orient themselves in the job market. A consultancy firm usually provides the _____ services which are paid for by the former employer and are achieved usually through practical advice, training materials and workshops. Some companies may offer psychological support.

Exam Probability: **High**

15. *Answer choices:*

(see index for correct answer)

- a. Outplacement

- b. Male unemployment
- c. Structural unemployment
- d. Recession

Guidance: level 1

:: Business law ::

An _____ is a natural person, business, or corporation that provides goods or services to another entity under terms specified in a contract or within a verbal agreement. Unlike an employee, an _____ does not work regularly for an employer but works as and when required, during which time they may be subject to law of agency. _____ s are usually paid on a freelance basis. Contractors often work through a limited company or franchise, which they themselves own, or may work through an umbrella company.

Exam Probability: **Low**

16. *Answer choices:*
(see index for correct answer)

- a. Negative option billing
- b. Independent contractor
- c. Operating lease
- d. Personal Property Security Act

Guidance: level 1

:: Personal finance ::

_____ is an arrangement in which a portion of an employee's income is paid out at a later date after which the income was earned. Examples of _____ include pensions, retirement plans, and employee stock options. The primary benefit of most _____ is the deferral of tax to the date at which the employee receives the income.

Exam Probability: **Low**

17. *Answer choices:*

(see index for correct answer)

- a. Deferred compensation
- b. Home equity
- c. HiddenLevers
- d. Sharesave

Guidance: level 1

:: Meetings ::

A _____ is a formal meeting of the representatives of different countries, constituent states, organizations, trade unions, political parties or other groups. The term, originally denoting a parley during battle in the Late Middle Ages, is derived from the Latin _____ us.

Exam Probability: **Medium**

18. *Answer choices:*

(see index for correct answer)

- a. Annual general meeting
- b. Congress
- c. CodeCamp
- d. Parley

Guidance: level 1

:: Occupational safety and health law ::

The _____ of 1970 is a US labor law governing the federal law of occupational health and safety in the private sector and federal government in the United States. It was enacted by Congress in 1970 and was signed by President Richard Nixon on December 29, 1970. Its main goal is to ensure that employers provide employees with an environment free from recognized hazards, such as exposure to toxic chemicals, excessive noise levels, mechanical dangers, heat or cold stress, or unsanitary conditions. The Act created the Occupational Safety and Health Administration and the National Institute for Occupational Safety and Health .

Exam Probability: **Low**

19. *Answer choices:*

(see index for correct answer)

- a. Factories Act 1961
- b. Factory and Workshop Act 1895
- c. Offices, Shops and Railway Premises Act 1963
- d. Health and Morals of Apprentices Act 1802

Guidance: level 1

:: Labor terms ::

_____ , often called DI or disability income insurance, or income protection, is a form of insurance that insures the beneficiary's earned income against the risk that a disability creates a barrier for a worker to complete the core functions of their work. For example, the worker may suffer from an inability to maintain composure in the case of psychological disorders or an injury, illness or condition that causes physical impairment or incapacity to work. It encompasses paid sick leave, short-term disability benefits , and long-term disability benefits . Statistics show that in the US a disabling accident occurs, on average, once every second. In fact, nearly 18.5% of Americans are currently living with a disability, and 1 out of every 4 persons in the US workforce will suffer a disabling injury before retirement.

Exam Probability: **Medium**

20. *Answer choices:*

(see index for correct answer)

- a. Capital services
- b. Disability insurance
- c. Absence rate

- d. Displaced workers

Guidance: level 1

:: ::

On December 31, 2016, Xerox separated its business process service operations into a new publicly traded company, Conduent. Xerox focuses on its document technology and document outsourcing business, and continues to trade on the NYSE. On January 31, 2018, Xerox announced that it would sell a controlling stake to Fujifilm, which has maintained a joint venture in the Asia-Pacific region known as Fuji Xerox.

Exam Probability: **Medium**

21. *Answer choices:*

(see index for correct answer)

- a. hierarchical
- b. Xerox Corporation
- c. Character
- d. imperative

Guidance: level 1

:: Workplace ::

A _____, also referred to as a performance review, performance evaluation, development discussion, or employee appraisal is a method by which the job performance of an employee is documented and evaluated. _____s are a part of career development and consist of regular reviews of employee performance within organizations.

Exam Probability: **High**

22. *Answer choices:*

(see index for correct answer)

- a. Workplace strategy
- b. Performance appraisal
- c. Hostile environment sexual harassment
- d. Workplace harassment

Guidance: level 1

:: Labor relations in the United States ::

In the context of U.S. labor politics, "_____s" refers to state laws that prohibit union security agreements between companies and labor unions. Under these laws, employees in unionized workplaces are banned from negotiating contracts which require all members who benefit from the union contract to contribute to the costs of union representation.

Exam Probability: **Medium**

23. *Answer choices:*

(see index for correct answer)

- a. Strong Economy for All Coalition
- b. Right-to-work law
- c. Plan B free agency
- d. Terror of the Tug

Guidance: level 1

:: Foreign workers ::

> A _____ or guest worker is a human who works in a country other than the one of which he or she is a citizen. Some _____ s are using a guest worker program in a country with more preferred job prospects than their home country. Guest workers are often either sent or invited to work outside their home country, or have acquired a job before they left their home country, whereas migrant workers often leave their home country without having a specific job at hand.

Exam Probability: **Low**

24. *Answer choices:*

(see index for correct answer)

- a. Migrant domestic workers
- b. Host family
- c. Foreign worker

- d. Foreign workers in Saudi Arabia

Guidance: level 1

:: Training ::

_____ refers to practicing newly acquired skills beyond the point of initial mastery. The term is also often used to refer to the pedagogical theory that this form of practice leads to automaticity or other beneficial consequences.

Exam Probability: **Low**

25. *Answer choices:*
(see index for correct answer)

- a. Compliance training
- b. Arts-based training
- c. Hypoventilation training
- d. National Occupational Standards

Guidance: level 1

:: Employment compensation ::

A _____ is pay and benefits employees receive when they leave employment at a company unwillfully. In addition to their remaining regular pay, it may include some of the following.

Exam Probability: **Low**

26. *Answer choices:*

(see index for correct answer)

- a. Severance package
- b. Family wage
- c. Compa-ratio
- d. Employee assistance program

Guidance: level 1

:: ::

A _____ is a technical analysis of a biological specimen, for example urine, hair, blood, breath, sweat, and/or oral fluid/saliva—to determine the presence or absence of specified parent drugs or their metabolites. Major applications of _____ ing include detection of the presence of performance enhancing steroids in sport, employers and parole/probation officers screening for drugs prohibited by law and police officers testing for the presence and concentration of alcohol in the blood commonly referred to as BAC . BAC tests are typically administered via a breathalyzer while urinalysis is used for the vast majority of _____ ing in sports and the workplace. Numerous other methods with varying degrees of accuracy, sensitivity , and detection periods exist.

Exam Probability: **Low**

27. *Answer choices:*

(see index for correct answer)

- a. imperative
- b. levels of analysis
- c. Drug test
- d. Character

Guidance: level 1

:: United States employment discrimination case law ::

_____, 490 U.S. 228, was an important decision by the United States Supreme Court on the issues of prescriptive sex discrimination and employer liability for sex discrimination. The employee, Ann Hopkins, sued her former employer, the accounting firm Price Waterhouse. She argued that the firm denied her partnership because she didn't fit the partners' idea of what a female employee should look like and act like. The employer failed to prove that it would have denied her partnership anyway, and the Court held that constituted sex discrimination under Title VII of the Civil Rights Act of 1964. The significance of the Supreme Court's ruling was twofold. First, it established that gender stereotyping is actionable as sex discrimination. Second, it established the mixed-motive framework that enables employees to prove discrimination when other, lawful reasons for the adverse employment action exist alongside discriminatory motivations or reasons.

Exam Probability: **Medium**

28. Answer choices:

(see index for correct answer)

- a. Reeves v. Sanderson Plumbing Products, Inc.
- b. Executive Order 11375
- c. Vance v. Ball State University
- d. Price Waterhouse v. Hopkins

Guidance: level 1

:: ::

_____ is an enduring pattern of romantic or sexual attraction to persons of the opposite sex or gender, the same sex or gender, or to both sexes or more than one gender. These attractions are generally subsumed under heterosexuality, homosexuality, and bisexuality, while asexuality is sometimes identified as the fourth category.

Exam Probability: **Low**

29. Answer choices:

(see index for correct answer)

- a. Sexual orientation
- b. cultural
- c. Sarbanes-Oxley act of 2002
- d. deep-level diversity

Guidance: level 1

:: Labour law ::

A _____ is a "shop-floor" organization representing workers that functions as a local/firm-level complement to trade unions but is independent of these at least in some countries. _____ s exist with different names in a variety of related forms in a number of European countries, including Britain ; Germany and Austria ; Luxembourg ; the Netherlands and Flanders in Belgium ; Italy ; France ; Wallonia in Belgium and Spain .

Exam Probability: **Low**

30. *Answer choices:*

(see index for correct answer)

- a. Works council
- b. Danish Vacation Law
- c. Vesting
- d. Michele Tiraboschi

Guidance: level 1

:: ::

The U.S. _____ is a federal agency that administers and enforces civil rights laws against workplace discrimination. The EEOC investigates discrimination complaints based on an individual's race, children, national origin, religion, sex, age, disability, sexual orientation, gender identity, genetic information, and retaliation for reporting, participating in, and/or opposing a discriminatory practice.

Exam Probability: **Medium**

31. *Answer choices:*

(see index for correct answer)

- a. cultural
- b. deep-level diversity
- c. Equal Employment Opportunity Commission
- d. Sarbanes-Oxley act of 2002

Guidance: level 1

:: ::

_____ is the withdrawal from one's position or occupation or from one's active working life. A person may also semi-retire by reducing work hours.

Exam Probability: **Medium**

32. *Answer choices:*

(see index for correct answer)

- a. Character
- b. Retirement
- c. cultural
- d. co-culture

Guidance: level 1

:: Employment compensation ::

_____ refers to various incentive plans introduced by businesses that provide direct or indirect payments to employees that depend on company's profitability in addition to employees' regular salary and bonuses. In publicly traded companies these plans typically amount to allocation of shares to employees. One of the earliest pioneers of _____ was Englishman Theodore Cooke Taylor, who is known to have introduced the practice in his woollen mills during the late 1800s.

Exam Probability: **Low**

33. *Answer choices:*

(see index for correct answer)

- a. Seasonal bonuses
- b. Golden handshake
- c. General Schedule
- d. Real wage

Guidance: level 1

:: Labor ::

The workforce or labour force is the labour pool in employment. It is generally used to describe those working for a single company or industry, but can also apply to a geographic region like a city, state, or country. Within a company, its value can be labelled as its "Workforce in Place". The workforce of a country includes both the employed and the unemployed. The labour force participation rate, LFPR, is the ratio between the labour force and the overall size of their cohort. The term generally excludes the employers or management, and can imply those involved in manual labour. It may also mean all those who are available for work.

Exam Probability: **Low**

34. *Answer choices:*

(see index for correct answer)

- a. Labor force
- b. Quality of working life
- c. Labour economics
- d. Surplus labour

Guidance: level 1

:: Management ::

A _____ is a method or technique that has been generally accepted as superior to any alternatives because it produces results that are superior to those achieved by other means or because it has become a standard way of doing things, e.g., a standard way of complying with legal or ethical requirements.

Exam Probability: **Low**

35. *Answer choices:*

(see index for correct answer)

- a. Court of Assistants
- b. Concept of operations
- c. Best practice
- d. Marketing plan

Guidance: level 1

:: Employment compensation ::

A _____ is the minimum income necessary for a worker to meet their basic needs. Needs are defined to include food, housing, and other essential needs such as clothing. The goal of a _____ is to allow a worker to afford a basic but decent standard of living. Due to the flexible nature of the term "needs", there is not one universally accepted measure of what a _____ is and as such it varies by location and household type.

Exam Probability: **High**

36. Answer choices:

(see index for correct answer)

- a. Annual leave
- b. Living wage
- c. Seasonal bonuses
- d. Workers Compensation Act 1987

Guidance: level 1

:: ::

> _____ are interactive computer-mediated technologies that facilitate the creation and sharing of information, ideas, career interests and other forms of expression via virtual communities and networks. The variety of stand-alone and built-in _____ services currently available introduces challenges of definition; however, there are some common features.

Exam Probability: **High**

37. Answer choices:

(see index for correct answer)

- a. Social media
- b. Sarbanes-Oxley act of 2002
- c. personal values
- d. surface-level diversity

Guidance: level 1

:: Learning methods ::

_____ is an approach to problem solving. It involves taking action and reflecting upon the results. This helps improve the problem-solving process as well as simplify the solutions developed by the team.

Exam Probability: **High**

38. *Answer choices:*

(see index for correct answer)

- a. Double-loop learning
- b. Action learning
- c. double loop learning
- d. Audience response system

Guidance: level 1

:: Trade union legislation ::

The _____ is the name for several legislative bills on US labor law which have been proposed and sometimes introduced into one or both chambers of the U.S. Congress.

Exam Probability: **High**

39. *Answer choices:*

(see index for correct answer)

- a. Employment Act 1982
- b. Employee Free Choice Act
- c. Trade Union Reform and Employment Rights Act 1993
- d. Trade Disputes and Trade Unions Act 1946

Guidance: level 1

:: Occupational safety and health ::

> Note: Parts of this article are written from the perspective of aircraft safety analysis techniques and definitions; these may not represent current best practice and the article needs to be updated to represent a more generic description of _____ and discussion of more modern standards and techniques.

Exam Probability: **Medium**

40. *Answer choices:*

(see index for correct answer)

- a. Hazards
- b. Hazard analysis

- c. Comcare
- d. Health hazards in semiconductor manufacturing occupations

Guidance: level 1

:: Television terminology ::

Distance education or long- _____ is the education of students who may not always be physically present at a school. Traditionally, this usually involved correspondence courses wherein the student corresponded with the school via post. Today it involves online education. Courses that are conducted are either hybrid, blended or 100% _____ . Massive open online courses, offering large-scale interactive participation and open access through the World Wide Web or other network technologies, are recent developments in distance education. A number of other terms are used roughly synonymously with distance education.

Exam Probability: **High**

41. *Answer choices:*

(see index for correct answer)

- a. Distance learning
- b. Satellite television
- c. multiplexing
- d. nonprofit

Guidance: level 1

:: Human resource management ::

This term is often used in an employment or human resources context where rather than terminating employees for first or minor infractions, there is a system of escalating responses intended to correct the negative behavior rather than to punish the employee.

Exam Probability: **High**

42. *Answer choices:*

(see index for correct answer)

- a. Resource-based view
- b. Job enrichment
- c. Selection ratio
- d. Progressive discipline

Guidance: level 1

:: Human resource management ::

_____ assesses whether a person performs a job well. _____, studied academically as part of industrial and organizational psychology, also forms a part of human resources management. Performance is an important criterion for organizational outcomes and success. John P. Campbell describes _____ as an individual-level variable, or something a single person does. This differentiates it from more encompassing constructs such as organizational performance or national performance, which are higher-level variables.

Exam Probability: **Medium**

43. *Answer choices:*

(see index for correct answer)

- a. Person specification
- b. Employment testing
- c. Job performance
- d. Succession planning

Guidance: level 1

:: Human resource management ::

_____, also known as organizational socialization, is management jargon first created in 1988 that refers to the mechanism through which new employees acquire the necessary knowledge, skills, and behaviors in order to become effective organizational members and insiders.

Exam Probability: **High**

44. *Answer choices:*

(see index for correct answer)

- a. E-HRM
- b. Inclusion
- c. Incentive program
- d. Aspiring Minds

Guidance: level 1

:: Income ::

In business and accounting, net income is an entity's income minus cost of goods sold, expenses and taxes for an accounting period. It is computed as the residual of all revenues and gains over all expenses and losses for the period, and has also been defined as the net increase in shareholders' equity that results from a company's operations. In the context of the presentation of financial statements, the IFRS Foundation defines net income as synonymous with profit and loss. The difference between revenue and the cost of making a product or providing a service, before deducting overheads, payroll, taxation, and interest payments. This is different from operating income.

Exam Probability: **Medium**

45. *Answer choices:*

(see index for correct answer)

- a. Imputed income
- b. Creative real estate investing

- c. Bottom line
- d. Passive income

Guidance: level 1

:: United States federal labor legislation ::

The _____ of 1988 is a United States federal law that generally prevents employers from using polygraph tests, either for pre-employment screening or during the course of employment, with certain exemptions.

Exam Probability: **Medium**

46. *Answer choices:*

(see index for correct answer)

- a. Water Resources Development Act of 2007
- b. Employee Polygraph Protection Act
- c. Civil Rights Act of 1964
- d. Federal Employers Liability Act

Guidance: level 1

:: Bankruptcy ::

_____ is the concept of a person or group of people taking precedence over another person or group because the former is either older than the latter or has occupied a particular position longer than the latter. _____ is present between parents and children and may be present in other common relationships, such as among siblings of different ages or between workers and their managers.

Exam Probability: **High**

47. *Answer choices:*

(see index for correct answer)

- a. Bankruptcy remote
- b. Asset-protection trust
- c. Pre-packaged insolvency
- d. Strategic bankruptcy

Guidance: level 1

:: Problem solving ::

In other words, _____ is a situation where a group of people meet to generate new ideas and solutions around a specific domain of interest by removing inhibitions. People are able to think more freely and they suggest as many spontaneous new ideas as possible. All the ideas are noted down and those ideas are not criticized and after _____ session the ideas are evaluated. The term was popularized by Alex Faickney Osborn in the 1953 book Applied Imagination.

Exam Probability: **High**

48. *Answer choices:*

(see index for correct answer)

- a. Brainstorming
- b. Convergent and divergent production
- c. Trizics
- d. Divergent thinking

Guidance: level 1

:: ::

Domestic violence is violence or other abuse by one person against another in a domestic setting, such as in marriage or cohabitation. It may be termed intimate partner violence when committed by a spouse or partner in an intimate relationship against the other spouse or partner, and can take place in heterosexual or same-sex relationships, or between former spouses or partners. Domestic violence can also involve violence against children, parents, or the elderly. It takes a number of forms, including physical, verbal, emotional, economic, religious, reproductive, and sexual abuse, which can range from subtle, coercive forms to marital rape and to violent physical abuse such as choking, beating, female genital mutilation, and acid throwing that results in disfigurement or death. Domestic murders include stoning, bride burning, honor killings, and dowry deaths.

Exam Probability: **High**

49. *Answer choices:*

(see index for correct answer)

- a. corporate values
- b. interpersonal communication
- c. functional perspective
- d. imperative

Guidance: level 1

:: Validity (statistics) ::

In psychometrics, _____ is the extent to which a score on a scale or test predicts scores on some criterion measure.

Exam Probability: **Low**

50. *Answer choices:*

(see index for correct answer)

- a. Statistical conclusion
- b. Predictive validity
- c. Discriminant validity
- d. Construct validity

Guidance: level 1

:: ::

_____ is the extraction of valuable minerals or other geological materials from the earth, usually from an ore body, lode, vein, seam, reef or placer deposit. These deposits form a mineralized package that is of economic interest to the miner.

Exam Probability: **High**

51. *Answer choices:*

(see index for correct answer)

- a. corporate values
- b. open system
- c. similarity-attraction theory
- d. hierarchical

Guidance: level 1

:: Management education ::

_____ is the implementation of government policy and also an academic discipline that studies this implementation and prepares civil servants for working in the public service. As a "field of inquiry with a diverse scope" whose fundamental goal is to "advance management and policies so that government can function". Some of the various definitions which have been offered for the term are: "the management of public programs"; the "translation of politics into the reality that citizens see every day"; and "the study of government decision making, the analysis of the policies themselves, the various inputs that have produced them, and the inputs necessary to produce alternative policies."

Exam Probability: **Low**

52. *Answer choices:*

(see index for correct answer)

- a. Executive DBA Council
- b. Training simulation
- c. System Design and Management
- d. Public administration

Guidance: level 1

:: Human resource management ::

_____ or work sharing is an employment arrangement where typically two people are retained on a part-time or reduced-time basis to perform a job normally fulfilled by one person working full-time. Since all positions are shared thus leads to a net reduction in per-employee income. The people sharing the job work as a team to complete the job task and are equally responsible for the job workload. Compensation is apportioned between the workers. Working hours, pay and holidays are divided equally. The pay as you go system helps make deductions for national insurance and superannuations are made as a straightforward percentage.

Exam Probability: **High**

53. *Answer choices:*

(see index for correct answer)

- a. Job sharing
- b. Work activity management
- c. Expense management
- d. Employee relationship management

Guidance: level 1

:: Human resource management ::

_____ is a sub-discipline of human resources, focused on employee _____ policy-making. While _____ are tangible, there are intangible rewards such as recognition, work-life and development. Combined, these are referred to as total rewards . The term "_____" refers to the discipline as well as the rewards themselves.

Exam Probability: **High**

54. *Answer choices:*

(see index for correct answer)

- a. Organization chart
- b. Compensation and benefits
- c. Mergers and acquisitions
- d. Workforce planning

Guidance: level 1

:: ::

_____ is the process of collecting, analyzing and/or reporting information regarding the performance of an individual, group, organization, system or component. _____ is not a new concept, some of the earliest records of human activity relate to the counting or recording of activities.

Exam Probability: **High**

55. *Answer choices:*

(see index for correct answer)

- a. personal values
- b. open system
- c. Performance measurement

- d. functional perspective

Guidance: level 1

:: ::

_____, also known as drug abuse, is a patterned use of a drug in which the user consumes the substance in amounts or with methods which are harmful to themselves or others, and is a form of substance-related disorder. Widely differing definitions of drug abuse are used in public health, medical and criminal justice contexts. In some cases criminal or anti-social behaviour occurs when the person is under the influence of a drug, and long term personality changes in individuals may occur as well. In addition to possible physical, social, and psychological harm, use of some drugs may also lead to criminal penalties, although these vary widely depending on the local jurisdiction.

Exam Probability: **Medium**

56. *Answer choices:*

(see index for correct answer)

- a. hierarchical
- b. open system
- c. Substance abuse
- d. similarity-attraction theory

Guidance: level 1

:: Employment compensation ::

_____, merit increase or pay for performance, is performance-related pay, most frequently in the context of educational reform or government civil service reform. It provides bonuses for workers who perform their jobs effectively, according to easily measurable criteria. In the United States, policy makers are divided on whether _____ should be offered to public school teachers, and other public employees, as is commonly the case in the United Kingdom.

Exam Probability: **Medium**

57. *Answer choices:*

(see index for correct answer)

- a. Seasonal bonuses
- b. Merit pay
- c. ADP, LLC
- d. Real wage

Guidance: level 1

:: Systems thinking ::

In business management, a _____ is a company that facilitates the learning of its members and continuously transforms itself. The concept was coined through the work and research of Peter Senge and his colleagues.

Exam Probability: **High**

58. *Answer choices:*

(see index for correct answer)

- a. World Future Society
- b. Thought leader
- c. World Futures Studies Federation
- d. Business continuity planning

Guidance: level 1

:: Human resource management ::

An _____ is a software application that enables the electronic handling of recruitment needs. An ATS can be implemented or accessed online on an enterprise or small business level, depending on the needs of the company and there is also free and open source ATS software available. An ATS is very similar to customer relationship management systems, but are designed for recruitment tracking purposes. In many cases they filter applications automatically based on given criteria such as keywords, skills, former employers, years of experience and schools attended. This has caused many to adapt resume optimization techniques similar to those used in search engine optimization when creating and formatting their résumé.

Exam Probability: **Low**

59. *Answer choices:*

(see index for correct answer)

- a. Voluntary redundancy
- b. Employee retention
- c. Applicant tracking system
- d. Selection ratio

Guidance: level 1

Information systems

Information systems (IS) are formal, sociotechnical, organizational systems designed to collect, process, store, and distribute information. In a sociotechnical perspective Information Systems are composed by four components: technology, process, people and organizational structure.

:: Industrial design ::

Across the many fields concerned with _____, including information science, computer science, human-computer interaction, communication, and industrial design, there is little agreement over the meaning of the term "_____", although all are related to interaction with computers and other machines with a user interface.

Exam Probability: **Medium**

1. *Answer choices:*

(see index for correct answer)

- a. Interactivity
- b. AxSTREAM
- c. Industrial Designers Society of America
- d. WikID

Guidance: level 1

:: World Wide Web ::

> A _____ is a document that is suitable to act as a web resource on the World Wide Web. In order to graphically display a _____, a web browser is needed. This is a type of software that can retrieve _____ s from the Internet. When accessed by a web browser it may be displayed as a _____ on a monitor or mobile device. Typical _____ s are hypertext documents which contain hyperlinks, often referred to as links, for browsing to other _____ s.

Exam Probability: **Medium**

2. *Answer choices:*

(see index for correct answer)

- a. Website visitor tracking

- b. Mail.Ru Group
- c. Web documentary
- d. Web page

Guidance: level 1

:: Virtual reality ::

A _____ is a computer-based simulated environment which may be populated by many users who can create a personal avatar, and simultaneously and independently explore the _____ , participate in its activities and communicate with others. These avatars can be textual, two or three-dimensional graphical representations, or live video avatars with auditory and touch sensations. In general, _____ s allow for multiple users but single player computer games, such as Skyrim, can also be considered a type of _____ .

Exam Probability: **High**

3. *Answer choices:*

(see index for correct answer)

- a. Normal mapping
- b. Virtual world
- c. Immersive technology
- d. Mirror world

Guidance: level 1

:: Google services ::

_____ is a discontinued image organizer and image viewer for organizing and editing digital photos, plus an integrated photo-sharing website, originally created by a company named Lifescape in 2002. In July 2004, Google acquired _____ from Lifescape and began offering it as freeware. "_____" is a blend of the name of Spanish painter Pablo Picasso, the phrase mi casa and "pic" for pictures.

Exam Probability: **Low**

4. *Answer choices:*

(see index for correct answer)

- a. Google Translator Toolkit
- b. Google Cloud Connect
- c. Google Grants
- d. Picasa

Guidance: level 1

:: Google services ::

_____ is a web mapping service developed by Google. It offers satellite imagery, aerial photography, street maps, 360° panoramic views of streets, real-time traffic conditions, and route planning for traveling by foot, car, bicycle and air, or public transportation.

Exam Probability: **Low**

5. *Answer choices:*

(see index for correct answer)

- a. Google Classroom
- b. Google Maps
- c. App Inventor for Android
- d. Blogger

Guidance: level 1

:: Data management ::

Given organizations' increasing dependency on information technology to run their operations, Business continuity planning covers the entire organization, and Disaster recovery focuses on IT.

Exam Probability: **High**

6. *Answer choices:*

(see index for correct answer)

- a. Database-centric architecture
- b. Virtual data room
- c. Ontology merging
- d. SQL injection

Guidance: level 1

:: Contract law ::

> _____ refers to a situation where a statement's author cannot successfully dispute its authorship or the validity of an associated contract. The term is often seen in a legal setting when the authenticity of a signature is being challenged. In such an instance, the authenticity is being "repudiated".

Exam Probability: **Medium**

7. *Answer choices:*

(see index for correct answer)

- a. Verbal contract
- b. Terms of service
- c. Non-repudiation
- d. Proprietary estoppel

Guidance: level 1

:: Information technology ::

_____ is the reorientation of product and service designs to focus on the end user as an individual consumer, in contrast with an earlier era of only organization-oriented offerings. Technologies whose first commercialization was at the inter-organization level thus have potential for later _____. The emergence of the individual consumer as the primary driver of product and service design is most commonly associated with the IT industry, as large business and government organizations dominated the early decades of computer usage and development. Thus the microcomputer revolution, in which electronic computing moved from exclusively enterprise and government use to include personal computing, is a cardinal example of _____. But many technology-based products, such as calculators and mobile phones, have also had their origins in business markets, and only over time did they become dominated by high-volume consumer usage, as these products commoditized and prices fell. An example of enterprise software that became consumer software is optical character recognition software, which originated with banks and postal systems but eventually became personal productivity software.

Exam Probability: **Medium**

8. *Answer choices:*

(see index for correct answer)

- a. Digital transformation
- b. E-Governance
- c. Consumerization
- d. Environmental informatics

Guidance: level 1

:: Consumer behaviour ::

_____ is the ratio of users who click on a specific link to the number of total users who view a page, email, or advertisement. It is commonly used to measure the success of an online advertising campaign for a particular website as well as the effectiveness of email campaigns.

Exam Probability: **Low**

9. *Answer choices:*
(see index for correct answer)

- a. Internality
- b. Homo consumericus
- c. Click-through rate
- d. Buying decision process

Guidance: level 1

:: Survey methodology ::

A _____ is the procedure of systematically acquiring and recording information about the members of a given population. The term is used mostly in connection with national population and housing _____ es; other common _____ es include agriculture, business, and traffic _____ es. The United Nations defines the essential features of population and housing _____ es as "individual enumeration, universality within a defined territory, simultaneity and defined periodicity", and recommends that population _____ es be taken at least every 10 years. United Nations recommendations also cover _____ topics to be collected, official definitions, classifications and other useful information to co-ordinate international practice.

Exam Probability: **Low**

10. *Answer choices:*

(see index for correct answer)

- a. Survey research
- b. Census
- c. Group concept mapping
- d. National Health Interview Survey

Guidance: level 1

:: Sensitivity analysis ::

_____ is the study of how the uncertainty in the output of a mathematical model or system can be divided and allocated to different sources of uncertainty in its inputs. A related practice is uncertainty analysis, which has a greater focus on uncertainty quantification and propagation of uncertainty; ideally, uncertainty and _____ should be run in tandem.

Exam Probability: **Low**

11. *Answer choices:*

(see index for correct answer)

- a. Elementary effects method
- b. Sensitivity analysis
- c. Fourier amplitude sensitivity testing
- d. Tornado diagram

Guidance: level 1

:: Computer security standards ::

The _____ for Information Technology Security Evaluation is an international standard for computer security certification. It is currently in version 3.1 revision 5.

Exam Probability: **High**

12. *Answer choices:*

(see index for correct answer)

- a. IEC 60870-6
- b. ITSEC
- c. CVSS
- d. Common Criteria

Guidance: level 1

:: Geographic information systems ::

_____ is the computational process of transforming a physical address description to a location on the Earth's surface. Reverse _____, on the other hand, converts geographic coordinates to a description of a location, usually the name of a place or an addressable location. _____ relies on a computer representation of address points, the street / road network, together with postal and administrative boundaries.

Exam Probability: **Low**

13. *Answer choices:*

(see index for correct answer)

- a. Digital geologic mapping
- b. GvSIG
- c. Geoprocessing
- d. Geocoding

Guidance: level 1

:: History of human–computer interaction ::

A _____ , plural mice, is a small rodent characteristically having a pointed snout, small rounded ears, a body-length scaly tail and a high breeding rate. The best known _____ species is the common house _____ . It is also a popular pet. In some places, certain kinds of field mice are locally common. They are known to invade homes for food and shelter.

Exam Probability: **Low**

14. *Answer choices:*

(see index for correct answer)

- a. Mouse
- b. SpaceOrb 360
- c. Wired glove
- d. IBM 2741

Guidance: level 1

:: Knowledge representation ::

_____ is the system in which users apply public tags to online items, typically to make those items easier for themselves or others to find later. Over time, this can give rise to a classification system based on those tags and how often they are applied or searched for, in contrast to a taxonomic classification designed by the owners of the content and specified when it is published. This practice is also known as collaborative tagging, social classification, social indexing, and social tagging. _____ was originally "the result of personal free tagging of information [...] for one's own retrieval", but online sharing and interaction expanded it into collaborative forms. Social tagging is the application of tags in an open online environment where the tags of other users are available to others. Collaborative tagging is tagging performed by a group of users. This type of _____ is commonly used in cooperative and collaborative projects such as research, content repositories, and social bookmarking.

Exam Probability: **Low**

15. *Answer choices:*

(see index for correct answer)

- a. Digital curation
- b. Folksonomy
- c. Pretext
- d. Linear belief function

Guidance: level 1

:: SQL ::

SQL is a domain-specific language used in programming and designed for managing data held in a relational database management system , or for stream processing in a relational data stream management system . It is particularly useful in handling structured data where there are relations between different entities/variables of the data. SQL offers two main advantages over older read/write APIs like ISAM or VSAM. First, it introduced the concept of accessing many records with one single command; and second, it eliminates the need to specify how to reach a record, e.g. with or without an index.

Exam Probability: **Low**

16. *Answer choices:*

(see index for correct answer)

- a. Structured query language
- b. SQL/JRT
- c. HSQLDB
- d. Meta-SQL

Guidance: level 1

:: ::

_____ Holdings, Inc. is an American company operating a worldwide online payments system that supports online money transfers and serves as an electronic alternative to traditional paper methods like checks and money orders. The company operates as a payment processor for online vendors, auction sites, and many other commercial users, for which it charges a fee in exchange for benefits such as one-click transactions and password memory. _____'s payment system, also called _____ , is considered a type of payment rail.

Exam Probability: **Medium**

17. *Answer choices:*

(see index for correct answer)

- a. PayPal
- b. Character
- c. Sarbanes-Oxley act of 2002
- d. cultural

Guidance: level 1

:: Data collection ::

_____ is information that either does not have a pre-defined data model or is not organized in a pre-defined manner. Unstructured information is typically text-heavy, but may contain data such as dates, numbers, and facts as well. This results in irregularities and ambiguities that make it difficult to understand using traditional programs as compared to data stored in fielded form in databases or annotated in documents.

Exam Probability: **Medium**

18. *Answer choices:*

(see index for correct answer)

- a. North Atlantic Population Project
- b. Unstructured data
- c. Concrete slump test
- d. General Social Survey

Guidance: level 1

:: Google services ::

A blog is a discussion or informational website published on the World Wide Web consisting of discrete, often informal diary-style text entries . Posts are typically displayed in reverse chronological order, so that the most recent post appears first, at the top of the web page. Until 2009, blogs were usually the work of a single individual, occasionally of a small group, and often covered a single subject or topic. In the 2010s, "multi-author blogs" emerged, featuring the writing of multiple authors and sometimes professionally edited. MABs from newspapers, other media outlets, universities, think tanks, advocacy groups, and similar institutions account for an increasing quantity of blog traffic. The rise of Twitter and other "microblogging" systems helps integrate MABs and single-author blogs into the news media. Blog can also be used as a verb, meaning to maintain or add content to a blog.

Exam Probability: **High**

19. *Answer choices:*

(see index for correct answer)

- a. WDYL
- b. Google News Archive
- c. Blogger
- d. Google Webmaster Tools

Guidance: level 1

:: Virtual reality ::

An _____, a concept in Hinduism that means "descent", refers to the material appearance or incarnation of a deity on earth. The relative verb to "alight, to make one's appearance" is sometimes used to refer to any guru or revered human being.

Exam Probability: **Medium**

20. *Answer choices:*

(see index for correct answer)

- a. Bump mapping
- b. Maurice Benayoun
- c. XVROS
- d. Avatar

Guidance: level 1

:: Commercial item transport and distribution ::

In commerce, supply-chain management, the management of the flow of goods and services, involves the movement and storage of raw materials, of work-in-process inventory, and of finished goods from point of origin to point of consumption. Interconnected or interlinked networks, channels and node businesses combine in the provision of products and services required by end customers in a supply chain. Supply-chain management has been defined as the "design, planning, execution, control, and monitoring of supply-chain activities with the objective of creating net value, building a competitive infrastructure, leveraging worldwide logistics, synchronizing supply with demand and measuring performance globally."SCM practice draws heavily from the areas of industrial engineering, systems engineering, operations management, logistics, procurement, information technology, and marketing and strives for an integrated approach. Marketing channels play an important role in supply-chain management. Current research in supply-chain management is concerned with topics related to sustainability and risk management, among others. Some suggest that the "people dimension" of SCM, ethical issues, internal integration, transparency/visibility, and human capital/talent management are topics that have, so far, been underrepresented on the research agenda.

Exam Probability: **High**

21. *Answer choices:*

(see index for correct answer)

- a. Human mail
- b. Containerization
- c. Supply chain management

- d. DCT Industrial Trust

Guidance: level 1

:: Ergonomics ::

_____ is the design of products, devices, services, or environments for people with disabilities. The concept of accessible design and practice of accessible development ensures both "direct access" and "indirect access" meaning compatibility with a person's assistive technology.

Exam Probability: **Medium**

22. *Answer choices:*
(see index for correct answer)

- a. Alain Wisner
- b. Soft ergonomics
- c. Accessibility
- d. Adapted automobile

Guidance: level 1

:: Infographics ::

A _____ is a symbolic representation of information according to visualization technique. _____ s have been used since ancient times, but became more prevalent during the Enlightenment. Sometimes, the technique uses a three-dimensional visualization which is then projected onto a two-dimensional surface. The word graph is sometimes used as a synonym for _____ .

Exam Probability: **Medium**

23. *Answer choices:*

(see index for correct answer)

- a. Sparkline
- b. Diagram
- c. Surya Majapahit
- d. Inspiration Software

Guidance: level 1

:: Information science ::

In discourse-based grammatical theory, _____ is any tracking of referential information by speakers. Information may be new, just introduced into the conversation; given, already active in the speakers' consciousness; or old, no longer active. The various types of activation, and how these are defined, are model-dependent.

Exam Probability: **High**

24. *Answer choices:*

(see index for correct answer)

- a. Programming the Universe
- b. Museum informatics
- c. Precision and recall
- d. Materiality

Guidance: level 1

:: Data management ::

_____ means protecting digital data, such as those in a database, from destructive forces and from the unwanted actions of unauthorized users, such as a cyberattack or a data breach.

Exam Probability: **Low**

25. *Answer choices:*

(see index for correct answer)

- a. Data security
- b. Data architect
- c. XML database
- d. Online analytical processing

Guidance: level 1

:: History of human–computer interaction ::

_____ is a line of motion sensing input devices produced by Microsoft. Initially, the _____ was developed as a gaming accessory for Xbox 360 and Xbox One video game consoles and Microsoft Windows PCs. Based around a webcam-style add-on peripheral, it enabled users to control and interact with their console/computer without the need for a game controller, through a natural user interface using gestures and spoken commands. While the gaming line did not gain much traction and eventually discontinued, third-party developers and researches found several after-market uses for _____'s advanced low-cost sensor features, leading Microsoft to drive the product line towards more application-neutral uses, including integrating the device with Microsoft's cloud computing platform Azure.

Exam Probability: **Medium**

26. *Answer choices:*

(see index for correct answer)

- a. Sketchpad
- b. File Retrieval and Editing System
- c. Kinect
- d. Mousepad

Guidance: level 1

:: Cryptography ::

In cryptography, _____ is the process of encoding a message or information in such a way that only authorized parties can access it and those who are not authorized cannot. _____ does not itself prevent interference, but denies the intelligible content to a would-be interceptor. In an _____ scheme, the intended information or message, referred to as plaintext, is encrypted using an _____ algorithm – a cipher – generating ciphertext that can be read only if decrypted. For technical reasons, an _____ scheme usually uses a pseudo-random _____ key generated by an algorithm. It is in principle possible to decrypt the message without possessing the key, but, for a well-designed _____ scheme, considerable computational resources and skills are required. An authorized recipient can easily decrypt the message with the key provided by the originator to recipients but not to unauthorized users.

Exam Probability: **Low**

27. *Answer choices:*

(see index for correct answer)

- a. Encryption
- b. cryptosystem
- c. Anonymous matching
- d. ciphertext

Guidance: level 1

:: ::

_____ is a kind of action that occur as two or more objects have an effect upon one another. The idea of a two-way effect is essential in the concept of _____ , as opposed to a one-way causal effect. A closely related term is interconnectivity, which deals with the _____ s of _____ s within systems: combinations of many simple _____ s can lead to surprising emergent phenomena. _____ has different tailored meanings in various sciences. Changes can also involve _____ .

Exam Probability: **Medium**

28. *Answer choices:*

(see index for correct answer)

- a. personal values
- b. empathy
- c. Sarbanes-Oxley act of 2002
- d. Interaction

Guidance: level 1

:: ::

_____ , Inc. is an American online social media and social networking service company based in Menlo Park, California. It was founded by Mark Zuckerberg, along with fellow Harvard College students and roommates Eduardo Saverin, Andrew McCollum, Dustin Moskovitz and Chris Hughes. It is considered one of the Big Four technology companies along with Amazon, Apple, and Google.

Exam Probability: **Low**

29. *Answer choices:*

(see index for correct answer)

- a. levels of analysis
- b. Facebook
- c. co-culture
- d. open system

Guidance: level 1

:: Information science ::

_____ has been defined as "the branch of ethics that focuses on the relationship between the creation, organization, dissemination, and use of information, and the ethical standards and moral codes governing human conduct in society". It examines the morality that comes from information as a resource, a product, or as a target. It provides a critical framework for considering moral issues concerning informational privacy, moral agency, new environmental issues, problems arising from the life-cycle of information. It is very vital to understand that librarians, archivists, information professionals among others, really understand the importance of knowing how to disseminate proper information as well as being responsible with their actions when addressing information.

Exam Probability: **Low**

30. *Answer choices:*

(see index for correct answer)

- a. Thesaurus
- b. EJB QL
- c. Information ethics
- d. Information Rules

Guidance: level 1

:: Behavioral and social facets of systemic risk ::

_____ is the difficulty in understanding an issue and effectively making decisions when one has too much information about that issue. Generally, the term is associated with the excessive quantity of daily information. _____ most likely originated from information theory, which are studies in the storage, preservation, communication, compression, and extraction of information. The term, _____, was first used in Bertram Gross' 1964 book, The Managing of Organizations, and it was further popularized by Alvin Toffler in his bestselling 1970 book Future Shock. Speier et al. stated.

Exam Probability: **High**

31. *Answer choices:*

(see index for correct answer)

- a. Herd behavior
- b. Attention management
- c. Crowd manipulation

- d. Connectionism

Guidance: level 1

:: Monopoly (economics) ::

A _____ exists when a specific person or enterprise is the only supplier of a particular commodity. This contrasts with a monopsony which relates to a single entity's control of a market to purchase a good or service, and with oligopoly which consists of a few sellers dominating a market. Monopolies are thus characterized by a lack of economic competition to produce the good or service, a lack of viable substitute goods, and the possibility of a high _____ price well above the seller's marginal cost that leads to a high _____ profit. The verb monopolise or monopolize refers to the process by which a company gains the ability to raise prices or exclude competitors. In economics, a _____ is a single seller. In law, a _____ is a business entity that has significant market power, that is, the power to charge overly high prices. Although monopolies may be big businesses, size is not a characteristic of a _____. A small business may still have the power to raise prices in a small industry.

Exam Probability: **Medium**

32. *Answer choices:*

(see index for correct answer)

- a. Monopoly
- b. Wartime Law on Industrial Property
- c. Cost per procedure
- d. Regulatory economics

Guidance: level 1

:: Data management ::

A _____ is a place where you can store data. Commonly used to refer to a column in a database or a field in a data entry form or web form.

Exam Probability: **High**

33. *Answer choices:*

(see index for correct answer)

- a. Match report
- b. DMAPI
- c. National Data Repository
- d. Data field

Guidance: level 1

:: Data quality ::

_____ or data cleaning is the process of detecting and correcting corrupt or inaccurate records from a record set, table, or database and refers to identifying incomplete, incorrect, inaccurate or irrelevant parts of the data and then replacing, modifying, or deleting the dirty or coarse data. _____ may be performed interactively with data wrangling tools, or as batch processing through scripting.

Exam Probability: **Low**

34. *Answer choices:*

(see index for correct answer)

- a. Data cleansing
- b. Dirty data
- c. Data Quality Campaign
- d. Data corruption

Guidance: level 1

:: Data management ::

_____ is a data management concept concerning the capability that enables an organization to ensure that high data quality exists throughout the complete lifecycle of the data. The key focus areas of _____ include availability, usability, consistency, data integrity and data security and includes establishing processes to ensure effective data management throughout the enterprise such as accountability for the adverse effects of poor data quality and ensuring that the data which an enterprise has can be used by the entire organization.

Exam Probability: **Medium**

35. *Answer choices:*

(see index for correct answer)

- a. Database server
- b. Signed overpunch
- c. Data governance
- d. Information governance

Guidance: level 1

:: Automatic identification and data capture ::

_____ uses electromagnetic fields to automatically identify and track tags attached to objects. The tags contain electronically stored information. Passive tags collect energy from a nearby RFID reader's interrogating radio waves. Active tags have a local power source and may operate hundreds of meters from the RFID reader. Unlike a barcode, the tag need not be within the line of sight of the reader, so it may be embedded in the tracked object. RFID is one method of automatic identification and data capture .

Exam Probability: **Medium**

36. *Answer choices:*

(see index for correct answer)

- a. Wireless identification and sensing platform

- b. Radio-frequency identification
- c. Forms processing
- d. Digital Automated Identification SYstem

Guidance: level 1

:: Information science ::

_____ is the resolution of uncertainty; it is that which answers the question of "what an entity is" and thus defines both its essence and nature of its characteristics. _____ relates to both data and knowledge, as data is meaningful _____ representing values attributed to parameters, and knowledge signifies understanding of a concept. _____ is uncoupled from an observer, which is an entity that can access _____ and thus discern what it specifies; _____ exists beyond an event horizon for example. In the case of knowledge, the _____ itself requires a cognitive observer to be obtained.

Exam Probability: **High**

37. *Answer choices:*

(see index for correct answer)

- a. Information
- b. Museum informatics
- c. Selective dissemination of information
- d. Datafication

Guidance: level 1

:: Critical thinking ::

In psychology, _____ is regarded as the cognitive process resulting in the selection of a belief or a course of action among several alternative possibilities. Every _____ process produces a final choice, which may or may not prompt action.

Exam Probability: **Medium**

38. *Answer choices:*

(see index for correct answer)

- a. Adviser
- b. Informal logic
- c. Project Reason
- d. Decision-making

Guidance: level 1

:: World Wide Web Consortium standards ::

_____ is a markup language that defines a set of rules for encoding documents in a format that is both human-readable and machine-readable. The W3C's XML 1.0 Specification and several other related specifications—all of them free open standards—define XML.

Exam Probability: **Medium**

39. *Answer choices:*

(see index for correct answer)

- a. Hypertext markup language
- b. Extensible Markup Language

Guidance: level 1

:: ::

A _____ is a published declaration of the intentions, motives, or views of the issuer, be it an individual, group, political party or government. A _____ usually accepts a previously published opinion or public consensus or promotes a new idea with prescriptive notions for carrying out changes the author believes should be made. It often is political or artistic in nature, but may present an individual's life stance. _____ s relating to religious belief are generally referred to as creeds.

Exam Probability: **Low**

40. *Answer choices:*

(see index for correct answer)

- a. process perspective
- b. co-culture
- c. Manifesto

- d. information systems assessment

Guidance: level 1

:: Management ::

The _____ is a strategy performance management tool – a semi-standard structured report, that can be used by managers to keep track of the execution of activities by the staff within their control and to monitor the consequences arising from these actions.

Exam Probability: **Low**

41. *Answer choices:*

(see index for correct answer)

- a. Completed Staff Work
- b. Planning
- c. Place management
- d. Energy management software

Guidance: level 1

:: ::

_____ is an American video-sharing website headquartered in San Bruno, California. Three former PayPal employees—Chad Hurley, Steve Chen, and Jawed Karim—created the service in February 2005. Google bought the site in November 2006 for US$1.65 billion; _____ now operates as one of Google's subsidiaries.

Exam Probability: **Low**

42. *Answer choices:*

(see index for correct answer)

- a. deep-level diversity
- b. interpersonal communication
- c. Character
- d. co-culture

Guidance: level 1

:: Customer relationship management software ::

_____ Software Corporation is a Global Business Software company based in Austin, TX and was founded in 1972. Its products are aimed at the manufacturing, distribution, retail and services industries.

Exam Probability: **Low**

43. *Answer choices:*

(see index for correct answer)

- a. Serial switcher
- b. Ebase
- c. OpenMFG
- d. Epicor

Guidance: level 1

:: Metadata ::

_____ s usage can be discovered by inspection of software applications or application data files through a process of manual or automated Application Discovery and Understanding. Once _____ s are discovered they can be registered in a metadata registry.

Exam Probability: **Medium**

44. *Answer choices:*

(see index for correct answer)

- a. MediaInfo
- b. MPEG-21
- c. Data element
- d. Filename extension

Guidance: level 1

:: Network architecture ::

An _____ is a controlled private network that allows access to partners, vendors and suppliers or an authorized set of customers – normally to a subset of the information accessible from an organization's intranet. An _____ is similar to a DMZ in that it provides access to needed services for authorized parties, without granting access to an organization's entire network. An _____ is a private network organization.

Exam Probability: **Medium**

45. *Answer choices:*

(see index for correct answer)

- a. Internetworking
- b. Extranet

Guidance: level 1

:: Computer data ::

In computer science, _____ is the ability to access an arbitrary element of a sequence in equal time or any datum from a population of addressable elements roughly as easily and efficiently as any other, no matter how many elements may be in the set. It is typically contrasted to sequential access.

Exam Probability: **High**

46. *Answer choices:*

(see index for correct answer)

- a. Continuous data protection
- b. Lilian date
- c. Data efficiency
- d. DataPortability

Guidance: level 1

:: Information systems ::

A _____ is an information system used for decision-making, and for the coordination, control, analysis, and visualization of information in an organization; especially in a company.

Exam Probability: **High**

47. *Answer choices:*

(see index for correct answer)

- a. Policy appliances
- b. Clinical decision support system
- c. Trust management
- d. Data system

Guidance: level 1

:: Data ::

_____ is a branch of mathematics working with data collection, organization, analysis, interpretation and presentation. In applying _____ to, for example, a scientific, industrial, or social problem, it is conventional to begin with a statistical population or a statistical model process to be studied. Populations can be diverse topics such as "all people living in a country" or "every atom composing a crystal". _____ deals with every aspect of data, including the planning of data collection in terms of the design of surveys and experiments. See glossary of probability and _____ .

Exam Probability: **Medium**

48. *Answer choices:*

(see index for correct answer)

- a. Data visualization
- b. Serial concatenated convolutional codes
- c. DataSplice
- d. Statistics

Guidance: level 1

:: ::

_____ consists of tailoring a service or a product to accommodate specific individuals, sometimes tied to groups or segments of individuals. A wide variety of organizations use _____ to improve customer satisfaction, digital sales conversion, marketing results, branding, and improved website metrics as well as for advertising. _____ is a key element in social media and recommender systems.

Exam Probability: **Medium**

49. *Answer choices:*

(see index for correct answer)

- a. co-culture
- b. imperative
- c. Personalization
- d. Sarbanes-Oxley act of 2002

Guidance: level 1

:: Global Positioning System ::

A _____ is a mechanism for determining the location of an object in space. Technologies for this task exist ranging from worldwide coverage with meter accuracy to workspace coverage with sub-millimetre accuracy.

Exam Probability: **High**

50. *Answer choices:*

(see index for correct answer)

- a. Defense Advanced GPS Receiver
- b. EUREF Permanent Network
- c. MoNav
- d. GPS Block IIIA

Guidance: level 1

:: Internet marketing ::

_____ is the process of increasing the quality and quantity of website traffic, increasing visibility of a website or a web page to users of a web search engine. SEO refers to the improvement of unpaid results, and excludes the purchase of paid placement.

Exam Probability: **High**

51. *Answer choices:*

(see index for correct answer)

- a. RedPoint Global
- b. Ad text optimization
- c. Microsoft pubCenter
- d. Search engine optimization

Guidance: level 1

:: Information technology management ::

_____ is the use of software to control machine tools and related ones in the manufacturing of workpieces. This is not the only definition for CAM, but it is the most common; CAM may also refer to the use of a computer to assist in all operations of a manufacturing plant, including planning, management, transportation and storage. Its primary purpose is to create a faster production process and components and tooling with more precise dimensions and material consistency, which in some cases, uses only the required amount of raw material , while simultaneously reducing energy consumption.CAM is now a system used in schools and lower educational purposes.CAM is a subsequent computer-aided process after computer-aided design and sometimes computer-aided engineering , as the model generated in CAD and verified in CAE can be input into CAM software, which then controls the machine tool. CAM is used in many schools alongside Computer-Aided Design to create objects.

Exam Probability: **Medium**

52. *Answer choices:*

(see index for correct answer)

- a. Cherwell Software
- b. Campustours
- c. Computer-aided manufacturing
- d. League Lab

Guidance: level 1

:: Web security exploits ::

A _____ is a baked or cooked food that is small, flat and sweet. It usually contains flour, sugar and some type of oil or fat. It may include other ingredients such as raisins, oats, chocolate chips, nuts, etc.

Exam Probability: **Low**

53. *Answer choices:*

(see index for correct answer)

- a. Browser exploit
- b. Session hijacking
- c. Session fixation
- d. Cookie

Guidance: level 1

:: Database theory ::

A _____ is a digital database based on the relational model of data, as proposed by E. F. Codd in 1970. A software system used to maintain _____ s is a _____ management system. Virtually all _____ systems use SQL for querying and maintaining the database.

Exam Probability: **Medium**

54. *Answer choices:*

(see index for correct answer)

- a. Database design
- b. Conjunctive query
- c. Nested set model
- d. Relational database

Guidance: level 1

:: Fraud ::

_____ is the deliberate use of someone else's identity, usually as a method to gain a financial advantage or obtain credit and other benefits in the other person's name, and perhaps to the other person's disadvantage or loss. The person whose identity has been assumed may suffer adverse consequences, especially if they are held responsible for the perpetrator's actions.
_____ occurs when someone uses another's personally identifying information, like their name, identifying number, or credit card number, without their permission, to commit fraud or other crimes. The term _____ was coined in 1964. Since that time, the definition of _____ has been statutorily prescribed throughout both the U.K. and the United States as the theft of personally identifying information, generally including a person's name, date of birth, social security number, driver's license number, bank account or credit card numbers, PIN numbers, electronic signatures, fingerprints, passwords, or any other information that can be used to access a person's financial resources.

Exam Probability: **Low**

55. *Answer choices:*

(see index for correct answer)

- a. Identity theft
- b. Pharma fraud
- c. Regummed stamp
- d. Card not present transaction

Guidance: level 1

:: Product testing ::

_____ is a characteristic of a product or system, whose interfaces are completely understood, to work with other products or systems, at present or in the future, in either implementation or access, without any restrictions.

Exam Probability: **Low**

56. *Answer choices:*

(see index for correct answer)

- a. Defect tracking
- b. Consumer organization
- c. Sensory analysis
- d. IBM Product Test

Guidance: level 1

:: Payment systems ::

An _____ is an electronic telecommunications device that enables customers of financial institutions to perform financial transactions, such as cash withdrawals, deposits, transfer funds, or obtaining account information, at any time and without the need for direct interaction with bank staff.

Exam Probability: **Low**

57. *Answer choices:*

(see index for correct answer)

- a. Automated teller machine
- b. Electronic Recording Machine, Accounting
- c. FreshBooks
- d. Adyen

Guidance: level 1

:: Help desk ::

Data center management is the collection of tasks performed by those responsible for managing ongoing operation of a data center This includes Business service management and planning for the future.

Exam Probability: **Medium**

58. *Answer choices:*

(see index for correct answer)

- a. OTRS
- b. EHelp Corporation
- c. Help desk
- d. HEAT

Guidance: level 1

:: ::

_____ is the fundamental facilities and systems serving a country, city, or other area, including the services and facilities necessary for its economy to function. _____ is composed of public and private physical improvements such as roads, bridges, tunnels, water supply, sewers, electrical grids, and telecommunications . In general, it has also been defined as "the physical components of interrelated systems providing commodities and services essential to enable, sustain, or enhance societal living conditions".

Exam Probability: **High**

59. *Answer choices:*
(see index for correct answer)

- a. Infrastructure
- b. empathy
- c. imperative
- d. Character

Guidance: level 1

Marketing

Marketing is the study and management of exchange relationships. Marketing is the business process of creating relationships with and satisfying customers. With its focus on the customer, marketing is one of the premier components of business management.

Marketing is defined by the American Marketing Association as "the activity, set of institutions, and processes for creating, communicating, delivering, and exchanging offerings that have value for customers, clients, partners, and society at large."

:: Summary statistics ::

_____ is the number of occurrences of a repeating event per unit of time. It is also referred to as temporal _____, which emphasizes the contrast to spatial _____ and angular _____. The period is the duration of time of one cycle in a repeating event, so the period is the reciprocal of the _____. For example: if a newborn baby's heart beats at a _____ of 120 times a minute, its period—the time interval between beats—is half a second. _____ is an important parameter used in science and engineering to specify the rate of oscillatory and vibratory phenomena, such as mechanical vibrations, audio signals, radio waves, and light.

Exam Probability: **Low**

1. *Answer choices:*

(see index for correct answer)

- a. Frequency
- b. Higher-order statistics
- c. Quantile
- d. Percentile

Guidance: level 1

:: ::

A _____ is a professional who provides expert advice in a particular area such as security, management, education, accountancy, law, human resources, marketing, finance, engineering, science or any of many other specialized fields.

Exam Probability: **Medium**

2. *Answer choices:*

(see index for correct answer)

- a. hierarchical perspective
- b. Sarbanes-Oxley act of 2002
- c. Consultant
- d. co-culture

Guidance: level 1

:: Marketing ::

_____, in marketing, manufacturing, call centres and management, is the use of flexible computer-aided manufacturing systems to produce custom output. Such systems combine the low unit costs of mass production processes with the flexibility of individual customization.

Exam Probability: **Medium**

3. *Answer choices:*

(see index for correct answer)

- a. Call centre
- b. Keyword research
- c. Packshot

- d. Mass customization

Guidance: level 1

:: Retailing ::

A _____ is a retail establishment offering a wide range of consumer goods in different product categories known as "departments". In modern major cities, the _____ made a dramatic appearance in the middle of the 19th century, and permanently reshaped shopping habits, and the definition of service and luxury. Similar developments were under way in London , in Paris and in New York .

Exam Probability: **Medium**

4. *Answer choices:*

(see index for correct answer)

- a. Survival store
- b. St. Vincent de Paul Thrift Store
- c. Planogram
- d. Department store

Guidance: level 1

:: International trade ::

_____ or globalisation is the process of interaction and integration among people, companies, and governments worldwide. As a complex and multifaceted phenomenon, _____ is considered by some as a form of capitalist expansion which entails the integration of local and national economies into a global, unregulated market economy. _____ has grown due to advances in transportation and communication technology. With the increased global interactions comes the growth of international trade, ideas, and culture. _____ is primarily an economic process of interaction and integration that's associated with social and cultural aspects. However, conflicts and diplomacy are also large parts of the history of _____, and modern _____.

Exam Probability: **Medium**

5. *Answer choices:*

(see index for correct answer)

- a. Trade creation
- b. Agreement on Agriculture
- c. Silver standard
- d. Globalization

Guidance: level 1

:: Data interchange standards ::

_____ is the concept of businesses electronically communicating information that was traditionally communicated on paper, such as purchase orders and invoices. Technical standards for EDI exist to facilitate parties transacting such instruments without having to make special arrangements.

Exam Probability: **High**

6. *Answer choices:*

(see index for correct answer)

- a. Common Alerting Protocol
- b. Electronic data interchange
- c. Interaction protocol
- d. Uniform Communication Standard

Guidance: level 1

:: Management ::

_____ is the process of thinking about the activities required to achieve a desired goal. It is the first and foremost activity to achieve desired results. It involves the creation and maintenance of a plan, such as psychological aspects that require conceptual skills. There are even a couple of tests to measure someone's capability of _____ well. As such, _____ is a fundamental property of intelligent behavior. An important further meaning, often just called "_____" is the legal context of permitted building developments.

Exam Probability: **High**

7. *Answer choices:*

(see index for correct answer)

- a. Evidence-based management
- b. Quality, cost, delivery
- c. Wireless informatics
- d. Business process improvement

Guidance: level 1

:: Marketing ::

_____ is based on a marketing concept which can be adopted by an organization as a strategy for business expansion. Where implemented, a franchisor licenses its know-how, procedures, intellectual property, use of its business model, brand, and rights to sell its branded products and services to a franchisee. In return the franchisee pays certain fees and agrees to comply with certain obligations, typically set out in a Franchise Agreement.

Exam Probability: **Low**

8. *Answer choices:*

(see index for correct answer)

- a. Business marketing
- b. Marketing automation

- c. Franchising
- d. Marketing intelligence

Guidance: level 1

:: Credit cards ::

The _____ Company, also known as Amex, is an American multinational financial services corporation headquartered in Three World Financial Center in New York City. The company was founded in 1850 and is one of the 30 components of the Dow Jones Industrial Average. The company is best known for its charge card, credit card, and traveler's cheque businesses.

Exam Probability: **Medium**

9. *Answer choices:*

(see index for correct answer)

- a. Alpha Card Services
- b. BC Card
- c. Credit Saison
- d. MPP Global Solutions

Guidance: level 1

:: ::

_____, also referred to as orthostasis, is a human position in which the body is held in an upright position and supported only by the feet.

Exam Probability: **Low**

10. *Answer choices:*

(see index for correct answer)

- a. Standing
- b. hierarchical
- c. cultural
- d. open system

Guidance: level 1

:: Marketing ::

_____ is "commercial competition characterized by the repeated cutting of prices below those of competitors". One competitor will lower its price, then others will lower their prices to match. If one of them reduces their price again, a new round of reductions starts. In the short term, _____ s are good for buyers, who can take advantage of lower prices. Often they are not good for the companies involved because the lower prices reduce profit margins and can threaten their survival.

Exam Probability: **Medium**

11. *Answer choices:*

(see index for correct answer)

- a. Interactive marketing
- b. Observatory of prices
- c. Digital billboard
- d. Price war

Guidance: level 1

:: Marketing ::

The _____ is a foundation model for businesses. The _____ has been defined as the "set of marketing tools that the firm uses to pursue its marketing objectives in the target market". Thus the _____ refers to four broad levels of marketing decision, namely: product, price, place, and promotion. Marketing practice has been occurring for millennia, but marketing theory emerged in the early twentieth century. The contemporary _____ , or the 4 Ps, which has become the dominant framework for marketing management decisions, was first published in 1960. In services marketing, an extended _____ is used, typically comprising 7 Ps, made up of the original 4 Ps extended by process, people, and physical evidence. Occasionally service marketers will refer to 8 Ps, comprising these 7 Ps plus performance.

Exam Probability: **Low**

12. *Answer choices:*

(see index for correct answer)

- a. Adobe Analytics
- b. Marketing mix
- c. Content creation
- d. Licensing International Expo

Guidance: level 1

:: ::

> In marketing jargon, product lining is offering several related products for sale individually. Unlike product bundling, where several products are combined into one group, which is then offered for sale as a units, product lining involves offering the products for sale separately. A line can comprise related products of various sizes, types, colors, qualities, or prices. Line depth refers to the number of subcategories a category has. Line consistency refers to how closely related the products that make up the line are. Line vulnerability refers to the percentage of sales or profits that are derived from only a few products in the line.

Exam Probability: **Low**

13. *Answer choices:*

(see index for correct answer)

- a. corporate values
- b. Product line
- c. personal values
- d. surface-level diversity

Guidance: level 1

:: ::

_____ LLC is an American multinational technology company that specializes in Internet-related services and products, which include online advertising technologies, search engine, cloud computing, software, and hardware. It is considered one of the Big Four technology companies, alongside Amazon, Apple and Facebook.

Exam Probability: **High**

14. *Answer choices:*

(see index for correct answer)

- a. information systems assessment
- b. Google
- c. open system
- d. corporate values

Guidance: level 1

:: ::

In law, an _____ is the process in which cases are reviewed, where parties request a formal change to an official decision. _____ s function both as a process for error correction as well as a process of clarifying and interpreting law. Although appellate courts have existed for thousands of years, common law countries did not incorporate an affirmative right to _____ into their jurisprudence until the 19th century.

Exam Probability: **Low**

15. *Answer choices:*

(see index for correct answer)

- a. similarity-attraction theory
- b. interpersonal communication
- c. Appeal
- d. levels of analysis

Guidance: level 1

:: E-commerce ::

_____ is the activity of buying or selling of products on online services or over the Internet. Electronic commerce draws on technologies such as mobile commerce, electronic funds transfer, supply chain management, Internet marketing, online transaction processing, electronic data interchange , inventory management systems, and automated data collection systems.

Exam Probability: **High**

16. Answer choices:

(see index for correct answer)

- a. E-commerce
- b. PaySafe
- c. Alternative currency
- d. UseMyServices

Guidance: level 1

:: ::

A _____ is a person who trades in commodities produced by other people. Historically, a _____ is anyone who is involved in business or trade. _____s have operated for as long as industry, commerce, and trade have existed. During the 16th-century, in Europe, two different terms for _____s emerged: One term, meerseniers, described local traders such as bakers, grocers, etc.; while a new term, koopman (Dutch: koopman, described _____s who operated on a global stage, importing and exporting goods over vast distances, and offering added-value services such as credit and finance.

Exam Probability: **High**

17. Answer choices:

(see index for correct answer)

- a. hierarchical perspective
- b. Merchant

- c. interpersonal communication
- d. deep-level diversity

Guidance: level 1

:: ::

In business and engineering, new _____ covers the complete process of bringing a new product to market. A central aspect of NPD is product design, along with various business considerations. New _____ is described broadly as the transformation of a market opportunity into a product available for sale. The product can be tangible or intangible, though sometimes services and other processes are distinguished from "products." NPD requires an understanding of customer needs and wants, the competitive environment, and the nature of the market. Cost, time and quality are the main variables that drive customer needs. Aiming at these three variables, innovative companies develop continuous practices and strategies to better satisfy customer requirements and to increase their own market share by a regular development of new products. There are many uncertainties and challenges which companies must face throughout the process. The use of best practices and the elimination of barriers to communication are the main concerns for the management of the NPD.

Exam Probability: **Medium**

18. *Answer choices:*

(see index for correct answer)

- a. surface-level diversity
- b. hierarchical
- c. Product development

- d. open system

Guidance: level 1

:: Competition (economics) ::

_____ arises whenever at least two parties strive for a goal which cannot be shared: where one's gain is the other's loss.

Exam Probability: **Medium**

19. *Answer choices:*
(see index for correct answer)

- a. Currency competition
- b. Competition
- c. Wantrapreneur
- d. Level playing field

Guidance: level 1

:: Promotion and marketing communications ::

Advertising mail, also known as _____ , junk mail, mailshot or admail, is the delivery of advertising material to recipients of postal mail. The delivery of advertising mail forms a large and growing service for many postal services, and direct-mail marketing forms a significant portion of the direct marketing industry. Some organizations attempt to help people opt out of receiving advertising mail, in many cases motivated by a concern over its negative environmental impact.

Exam Probability: **High**

20. *Answer choices:*

(see index for correct answer)

- a. Sleeper effect
- b. Trade Promotion Forecasting
- c. Next Jump
- d. Air Miles

Guidance: level 1

:: Budgets ::

A _____ is a financial plan for a defined period, often one year. It may also include planned sales volumes and revenues, resource quantities, costs and expenses, assets, liabilities and cash flows. Companies, governments, families and other organizations use it to express strategic plans of activities or events in measurable terms.

Exam Probability: **Medium**

21. *Answer choices:*

(see index for correct answer)

- a. Budget
- b. Public budgeting
- c. Programme budgeting
- d. Budgeted cost of work scheduled

Guidance: level 1

:: ::

_____ , known in Europe as research and technological development , refers to innovative activities undertaken by corporations or governments in developing new services or products, or improving existing services or products. _____ constitutes the first stage of development of a potential new service or the production process.

Exam Probability: **Medium**

22. *Answer choices:*

(see index for correct answer)

- a. Research and development
- b. Sarbanes-Oxley act of 2002

- c. functional perspective
- d. co-culture

Guidance: level 1

:: Marketing ::

_____ is multi-channel online marketing technique focused at reaching a specific audience on their smartphones, tablets, or any other related devices through websites, E-mail, SMS and MMS, social media, or mobile applications. _____ can provide customers with time and location sensitive, personalized information that promotes goods, services and ideas. In a more theoretical manner, academic Andreas Kaplan defines _____ as "any marketing activity conducted through a ubiquitous network to which consumers are constantly connected using a personal mobile device".

Exam Probability: **High**

23. *Answer choices:*

(see index for correct answer)

- a. Discoverability
- b. Call centre
- c. National brand
- d. Mobile marketing

Guidance: level 1

:: Product management ::

_____ or brand stretching is a marketing strategy in which a firm marketing a product with a well-developed image uses the same brand name in a different product category. The new product is called a spin-off. Organizations use this strategy to increase and leverage brand equity. An example of a _____ is Jello-gelatin creating Jello pudding pops. It increases awareness of the brand name and increases profitability from offerings in more than one product category.

Exam Probability: **Medium**

24. *Answer choices:*

(see index for correct answer)

- a. Product family engineering
- b. Obsolescence
- c. Dwinell-Wright Company
- d. Service life

Guidance: level 1

:: Data management ::

_____ is a form of intellectual property that grants the creator of an original creative work an exclusive legal right to determine whether and under what conditions this original work may be copied and used by others, usually for a limited term of years. The exclusive rights are not absolute but limited by limitations and exceptions to _____ law, including fair use. A major limitation on _____ on ideas is that _____ protects only the original expression of ideas, and not the underlying ideas themselves.

Exam Probability: **Low**

25. *Answer choices:*

(see index for correct answer)

- a. Distributed concurrency control
- b. ADO.NET
- c. Copyright
- d. Dynamic knowledge repository

Guidance: level 1

:: Direct marketing ::

_____ is a method of direct marketing in which a salesperson solicits prospective customers to buy products or services, either over the phone or through a subsequent face to face or Web conferencing appointment scheduled during the call. _____ can also include recorded sales pitches programmed to be played over the phone via automatic dialing.

Exam Probability: **High**

26. *Answer choices:*

(see index for correct answer)

- a. Robinson list
- b. Response Dynamics
- c. Multi-level marketing
- d. Telemarketing

Guidance: level 1

:: Contract law ::

A _____ is a legally-binding agreement which recognises and governs the rights and duties of the parties to the agreement. A _____ is legally enforceable because it meets the requirements and approval of the law. An agreement typically involves the exchange of goods, services, money, or promises of any of those. In the event of breach of _____ , the law awards the injured party access to legal remedies such as damages and cancellation.

Exam Probability: **Medium**

27. *Answer choices:*

(see index for correct answer)

- a. German contract law
- b. Retainer agreement

- c. Standard form contract
- d. Proprietary estoppel

Guidance: level 1

:: Public relations ::

_____ is the public visibility or awareness for any product, service or company. It may also refer to the movement of information from its source to the general public, often but not always via the media. The subjects of _____ include people, goods and services, organizations, and works of art or entertainment.

Exam Probability: **Medium**

28. *Answer choices:*

(see index for correct answer)

- a. Publicity
- b. Public affairs
- c. Litigation public relations
- d. Corporate Representatives for Ethical Wikipedia Engagement

Guidance: level 1

:: Communication design ::

An _____ is a series of advertisement messages that share a single idea and theme which make up an integrated marketing communication. An IMC is a platform in which a group of people can group their ideas, beliefs, and concepts into one large media base. _____ s utilize diverse media channels over a particular time frame and target identified audiences.

Exam Probability: **Low**

29. *Answer choices:*

(see index for correct answer)

- a. Copywriting agency
- b. MacDonald Gill
- c. Tango Desktop Project
- d. Ladislav Sutnar

Guidance: level 1

:: Industrial design ::

In physics and mathematics, the _____ of a mathematical space is informally defined as the minimum number of coordinates needed to specify any point within it. Thus a line has a _____ of one because only one coordinate is needed to specify a point on it for example, the point at 5 on a number line. A surface such as a plane or the surface of a cylinder or sphere has a _____ of two because two coordinates are needed to specify a point on it for example, both a latitude and longitude are required to locate a point on the surface of a sphere. The inside of a cube, a cylinder or a sphere is three-_____ al because three coordinates are needed to locate a point within these spaces.

Exam Probability: **Low**

30. *Answer choices:*

(see index for correct answer)

- a. Form factor
- b. Dimension
- c. Fab Lab Barcelona
- d. Geschmacksmuster

Guidance: level 1

:: ::

_____ is the study and management of exchange relationships. _____ is the business process of creating relationships with and satisfying customers. With its focus on the customer, _____ is one of the premier components of business management.

Exam Probability: **Medium**

31. *Answer choices:*

(see index for correct answer)

- a. process perspective
- b. empathy
- c. Marketing
- d. personal values

Guidance: level 1

:: ::

_____ is the means to see, hear, or become aware of something or someone through our fundamental senses. The term _____ derives from the Latin word perceptio, and is the organization, identification, and interpretation of sensory information in order to represent and understand the presented information, or the environment.

Exam Probability: **High**

32. *Answer choices:*

(see index for correct answer)

- a. interpersonal communication
- b. Perception

- c. functional perspective
- d. deep-level diversity

Guidance: level 1

:: Product development ::

In business and engineering, _____ covers the complete process of bringing a new product to market. A central aspect of NPD is product design, along with various business considerations. _____ is described broadly as the transformation of a market opportunity into a product available for sale. The product can be tangible or intangible , though sometimes services and other processes are distinguished from "products." NPD requires an understanding of customer needs and wants, the competitive environment, and the nature of the market.Cost, time and quality are the main variables that drive customer needs. Aiming at these three variables, innovative companies develop continuous practices and strategies to better satisfy customer requirements and to increase their own market share by a regular development of new products. There are many uncertainties and challenges which companies must face throughout the process. The use of best practices and the elimination of barriers to communication are the main concerns for the management of the NPD .

Exam Probability: **Medium**

33. *Answer choices:*

(see index for correct answer)

- a. WhiteBoard Product Solutions
- b. Design brief
- c. DFMA

- d. New product development

Guidance: level 1

:: International trade ::

> In finance, an _____ is the rate at which one currency will be exchanged for another. It is also regarded as the value of one country's currency in relation to another currency. For example, an interbank _____ of 114 Japanese yen to the United States dollar means that ¥114 will be exchanged for each US$1 or that US$1 will be exchanged for each ¥114. In this case it is said that the price of a dollar in relation to yen is ¥114, or equivalently that the price of a yen in relation to dollars is $1/114.

Exam Probability: **High**

34. *Answer choices:*

(see index for correct answer)

- a. Exchange rate
- b. Cairns Group
- c. Common external tariff
- d. Uranium market

Guidance: level 1

:: Marketing techniques ::

_____ is the activity of dividing a broad consumer or business market, normally consisting of existing and potential customers, into sub-groups of consumers based on some type of shared characteristics. In dividing or segmenting markets, researchers typically look for common characteristics such as shared needs, common interests, similar lifestyles or even similar demographic profiles. The overall aim of segmentation is to identify high yield segments – that is, those segments that are likely to be the most profitable or that have growth potential – so that these can be selected for special attention.

Exam Probability: **Low**

35. *Answer choices:*

(see index for correct answer)

- a. Prize
- b. Enterprise engagement
- c. Search engine submission
- d. Market segmentation

Guidance: level 1

:: Management ::

A _____ describes the rationale of how an organization creates, delivers, and captures value, in economic, social, cultural or other contexts. The process of _____ construction and modification is also called _____ innovation and forms a part of business strategy.

Exam Probability: **High**

36. *Answer choices:*

(see index for correct answer)

- a. Public sector consulting
- b. Business model
- c. Smiling curve
- d. Mission critical

Guidance: level 1

:: Monopoly (economics) ::

The _____ of 1890 was a United States antitrust law that regulates competition among enterprises, which was passed by Congress under the presidency of Benjamin Harrison.

Exam Probability: **High**

37. *Answer choices:*

(see index for correct answer)

- a. Government-granted monopoly
- b. Sherman Antitrust Act
- c. Special 301 Report
- d. Chamberlinian monopolistic competition

Guidance: level 1

Employment is a relationship between two parties, usually based on a contract where work is paid for, where one party, which may be a corporation, for profit, not-for-profit organization, co-operative or other entity is the employer and the other is the employee. Employees work in return for payment, which may be in the form of an hourly wage, by piecework or an annual salary, depending on the type of work an employee does or which sector she or he is working in. Employees in some fields or sectors may receive gratuities, bonus payment or stock options. In some types of employment, employees may receive benefits in addition to payment. Benefits can include health insurance, housing, disability insurance or use of a gym. Employment is typically governed by employment laws, regulations or legal contracts.

Exam Probability: **Low**

38. *Answer choices:*

(see index for correct answer)

- a. Personnel
- b. Sarbanes-Oxley act of 2002
- c. co-culture
- d. levels of analysis

Guidance: level 1

:: Contract law ::

In contract law, a _____ is a promise which is not a condition of the contract or an innominate term: it is a term "not going to the root of the contract", and which only entitles the innocent party to damages if it is breached: i.e. the _____ is not true or the defaulting party does not perform the contract in accordance with the terms of the _____. A _____ is not guarantee. It is a mere promise. It may be enforced if it is breached by an award for the legal remedy of damages.

Exam Probability: **Low**

39. *Answer choices:*
(see index for correct answer)

- a. Choice of law clause
- b. Condition subsequent
- c. Freedom of contract
- d. Warranty

Guidance: level 1

:: Marketing ::

_____ is a market strategy in which a firm decides to ignore market segment differences and appeal the whole market with one offer or one strategy, which supports the idea of broadcasting a message that will reach the largest number of people possible. Traditionally _____ has focused on radio, television and newspapers as the media used to reach this broad audience. By reaching the largest audience possible, exposure to the product is maximized, and in theory this would directly correlate with a larger number of sales or buys into the product.

Exam Probability: **Low**

40. *Answer choices:*

(see index for correct answer)

- a. Movie packaging
- b. Product proliferation
- c. Mass marketing
- d. Markup

Guidance: level 1

:: Library science ::

_____ refers to data which is collected by someone who is someone other than the user. Common sources of _____ for social science include censuses, information collected by government departments, organizational records and data that was originally collected for other research purposes. Primary data, by contrast, are collected by the investigator conducting the research.

Exam Probability: **Medium**

41. *Answer choices:*

(see index for correct answer)

- a. Scientific citation
- b. Secondary data
- c. Genreflecting
- d. Bibliometrics

Guidance: level 1

:: ::

In regulatory jurisdictions that provide for it, _____ is a group of laws and organizations designed to ensure the rights of consumers as well as fair trade, competition and accurate information in the marketplace. The laws are designed to prevent the businesses that engage in fraud or specified unfair practices from gaining an advantage over competitors. They may also provides additional protection for those most vulnerable in society. _____ laws are a form of government regulation that aim to protect the rights of consumers. For example, a government may require businesses to disclose detailed information about products—particularly in areas where safety or public health is an issue, such as food.

Exam Probability: **Low**

42. *Answer choices:*

(see index for correct answer)

- a. corporate values
- b. Character
- c. Consumer Protection
- d. hierarchical

Guidance: level 1

:: Monopoly (economics) ::

A _____ is a form of intellectual property that gives its owner the legal right to exclude others from making, using, selling, and importing an invention for a limited period of years, in exchange for publishing an enabling public disclosure of the invention. In most countries _____ rights fall under civil law and the _____ holder needs to sue someone infringing the _____ in order to enforce his or her rights. In some industries _____ s are an essential form of competitive advantage; in others they are irrelevant.

Exam Probability: **High**

43. *Answer choices:*

(see index for correct answer)

- a. Herfindahl index
- b. Ownership unbundling
- c. Intellectual property
- d. Legal monopoly

Guidance: level 1

:: Health promotion ::

_____ is a form of advertising, it has been a large industry for some time now. Originally with newspapers and billboards, but now we have advanced to huge LCD screens and online advertisement on social medias and websites. The most common use of _____ in today's society is through social media.. It has the primary goal of achieving "social good". Traditional commercial marketing aims are primarily financial, though they can have positive social affects as well. In the context of public health, _____ would promote general health, raise awareness and induce changes in behaviour. To see _____ as only the use of standard commercial marketing practices to achieve non-commercial goals is an oversimplified view.

Exam Probability: **High**

44. *Answer choices:*

(see index for correct answer)

- a. United States Army Public Health Command
- b. Social marketing
- c. Health risk assessment
- d. Health promotion in higher education

Guidance: level 1

:: ::

A _____ consists of one people who live in the same dwelling and share meals. It may also consist of a single family or another group of people. A dwelling is considered to contain multiple _____ s if meals or living spaces are not shared. The _____ is the basic unit of analysis in many social, microeconomic and government models, and is important to economics and inheritance.

Exam Probability: **High**

45. *Answer choices:*

(see index for correct answer)

- a. hierarchical
- b. corporate values
- c. Character
- d. Household

Guidance: level 1

_____ is the practice of deliberately managing the spread of information between an individual or an organization and the public. _____ may include an organization or individual gaining exposure to their audiences using topics of public interest and news items that do not require direct payment. This differentiates it from advertising as a form of marketing communications. _____ is the idea of creating coverage for clients for free, rather than marketing or advertising. But now, advertising is also a part of greater PR Activities. An example of good _____ would be generating an article featuring a client, rather than paying for the client to be advertised next to the article. The aim of _____ is to inform the public, prospective customers, investors, partners, employees, and other stakeholders and ultimately persuade them to maintain a positive or favorable view about the organization, its leadership, products, or political decisions. _____ professionals typically work for PR and marketing firms, businesses and companies, government, and public officials as PIOs and nongovernmental organizations, and nonprofit organizations. Jobs central to _____ include account coordinator, account executive, account supervisor, and media relations manager.

Exam Probability: **High**

46. *Answer choices:*

(see index for correct answer)

- a. interpersonal communication
- b. cultural
- c. surface-level diversity
- d. Public relations

Guidance: level 1

:: Marketing ::

_____ comes from the Latin neg and otsia referring to businessmen who, unlike the patricians, had no leisure time in their industriousness; it held the meaning of business until the 17th century when it took on the diplomatic connotation as a dialogue between two or more people or parties intended to reach a beneficial outcome over one or more issues where a conflict exists with respect to at least one of these issues. Thus, _____ is a process of combining divergent positions into a joint agreement under a decision rule of unanimity.

Exam Probability: **High**

47. *Answer choices:*

(see index for correct answer)

- a. Postmodern branding
- b. Food marketing
- c. Category management
- d. City marketing

Guidance: level 1

:: ::

In marketing, a _____ is a ticket or document that can be redeemed for a financial discount or rebate when purchasing a product.

Exam Probability: **Low**

48. *Answer choices:*

(see index for correct answer)

- a. surface-level diversity
- b. levels of analysis
- c. Coupon
- d. Character

Guidance: level 1

:: Business models ::

A _____ , _____ company or daughter company is a company that is owned or controlled by another company, which is called the parent company, parent, or holding company. The _____ can be a company, corporation, or limited liability company. In some cases it is a government or state-owned enterprise. In some cases, particularly in the music and book publishing industries, subsidiaries are referred to as imprints.

Exam Probability: **High**

49. *Answer choices:*

(see index for correct answer)

- a. Component business model
- b. Consumer cooperative

- c. Professional open source
- d. Subsidiary

Guidance: level 1

:: Monopoly (economics) ::

_____ is a category of property that includes intangible creations of the human intellect. _____ encompasses two types of rights: industrial property rights and copyright. It was not until the 19th century that the term " _____ " began to be used, and not until the late 20th century that it became commonplace in the majority of the world.

Exam Probability: **Low**

50. *Answer choices:*

(see index for correct answer)

- a. Regulatory economics
- b. Price-cap regulation
- c. Economies of scope
- d. Intellectual property

Guidance: level 1

:: Marketing ::

A _____ is an overall experience of a customer that distinguishes an organization or product from its rivals in the eyes of the customer. _____ s are used in business, marketing, and advertising. Name _____ s are sometimes distinguished from generic or store _____ s.

Exam Probability: **Low**

51. *Answer choices:*

(see index for correct answer)

- a. Business marketing
- b. Brand
- c. Customer reference program
- d. The Cellar

Guidance: level 1

:: ::

_____ is the process whereby a business sets the price at which it will sell its products and services, and may be part of the business's marketing plan. In setting prices, the business will take into account the price at which it could acquire the goods, the manufacturing cost, the market place, competition, market condition, brand, and quality of product.

Exam Probability: **Medium**

52. *Answer choices:*

(see index for correct answer)

- a. empathy
- b. levels of analysis
- c. functional perspective
- d. Pricing

Guidance: level 1

:: ::

In financial markets, a share is a unit used as mutual funds, limited partnerships, and real estate investment trusts. The owner of _____ in the corporation/company is a shareholder of the corporation. A share is an indivisible unit of capital, expressing the ownership relationship between the company and the shareholder. The denominated value of a share is its face value, and the total of the face value of issued _____ represent the capital of a company, which may not reflect the market value of those _____ .

Exam Probability: **High**

53. *Answer choices:*

(see index for correct answer)

- a. surface-level diversity
- b. Shares

- c. functional perspective
- d. imperative

Guidance: level 1

:: Market research ::

_____ , an acronym for Information through Disguised Experimentation is an annual market research fair conducted by the students of IIM-Lucknow. Students create games and use various other simulated environments to capture consumers' subconscious thoughts. This innovative method of market research removes the sensitization effect that might bias peoples answers to questions. This ensures that the most truthful answers are captured to research questions. The games are designed in such a way that the observers can elicit all the required information just by observing and noting down the behaviour and the responses of the participants.

Exam Probability: **High**

54. *Answer choices:*

(see index for correct answer)

- a. Product Intelligence
- b. Nielsen SoundScan
- c. High Mark Credit Information Services
- d. New economic order

Guidance: level 1

:: Promotion and marketing communications ::

_____ is one of the elements of the promotional mix. . _____ uses both media and non-media marketing communications for a pre-determined, limited time to increase consumer demand, stimulate market demand or improve product availability. Examples include contests, coupons, freebies, loss leaders, point of purchase displays, premiums, prizes, product samples, and rebates.

Exam Probability: **Low**

55. *Answer choices:*

(see index for correct answer)

- a. IB5k
- b. The Best Job In The World
- c. Sales promotion
- d. Reich Publishing and Marketing

Guidance: level 1

:: Marketing ::

_____ is a pricing strategy where the price of a product is initially set low to rapidly reach a wide fraction of the market and initiate word of mouth. The strategy works on the expectation that customers will switch to the new brand because of the lower price. _____ is most commonly associated with marketing objectives of enlarging market share and exploiting economies of scale or experience.

Exam Probability: **High**

56. *Answer choices:*
(see index for correct answer)

- a. Business stature
- b. Geographical pricing
- c. Marketspace
- d. Enterprise marketing management

Guidance: level 1

:: ::

In sales, commerce and economics, a _____ is the recipient of a good, service, product or an idea - obtained from a seller, vendor, or supplier via a financial transaction or exchange for money or some other valuable consideration.

Exam Probability: **Medium**

57. Answer choices:

(see index for correct answer)

- a. Customer
- b. levels of analysis
- c. imperative
- d. personal values

Guidance: level 1

:: Problem solving ::

In other words, _____ is a situation where a group of people meet to generate new ideas and solutions around a specific domain of interest by removing inhibitions. People are able to think more freely and they suggest as many spontaneous new ideas as possible. All the ideas are noted down and those ideas are not criticized and after _____ session the ideas are evaluated. The term was popularized by Alex Faickney Osborn in the 1953 book Applied Imagination.

Exam Probability: **High**

58. Answer choices:

(see index for correct answer)

- a. How to Solve it by Computer
- b. Calculation
- c. Disney method

- d. Brainstorming

Guidance: level 1

:: ::

_____ is the collection of techniques, skills, methods, and processes used in the production of goods or services or in the accomplishment of objectives, such as scientific investigation. _____ can be the knowledge of techniques, processes, and the like, or it can be embedded in machines to allow for operation without detailed knowledge of their workings. Systems applying _____ by taking an input, changing it according to the system's use, and then producing an outcome are referred to as _____ systems or technological systems.

Exam Probability: **Medium**

59. *Answer choices:*
(see index for correct answer)

- a. Character
- b. co-culture
- c. empathy
- d. Sarbanes-Oxley act of 2002

Guidance: level 1

Manufacturing

Manufacturing is the production of merchandise for use or sale using labor and machines, tools, chemical and biological processing, or formulation. The term may refer to a range of human activity, from handicraft to high tech, but is most commonly applied to industrial design, in which raw materials are transformed into finished goods on a large scale. Such finished goods may be sold to other manufacturers for the production of other, more complex products, such as aircraft, household appliances, furniture, sports equipment or automobiles, or sold to wholesalers, who in turn sell them to retailers, who then sell them to end users and consumers.

:: Mereology ::

_____ , in the abstract, is what belongs to or with something, whether as an attribute or as a component of said thing. In the context of this article, it is one or more components, whether physical or incorporeal, of a person's estate; or so belonging to, as in being owned by, a person or jointly a group of people or a legal entity like a corporation or even a society. Depending on the nature of the _____ , an owner of _____ has the right to consume, alter, share, redefine, rent, mortgage, pawn, sell, exchange, transfer, give away or destroy it, or to exclude others from doing these things, as well as to perhaps abandon it; whereas regardless of the nature of the _____ , the owner thereof has the right to properly use it, or at the very least exclusively keep it.

Exam Probability: **Low**

1. *Answer choices:*

(see index for correct answer)

- a. Non-wellfounded mereology
- b. Property
- c. Meronomy
- d. Mereotopology

Guidance: level 1

:: Production and manufacturing ::

_____ is a concept in purchasing and project management for securing the quality and timely delivery of goods and components.

Exam Probability: **Medium**

2. *Answer choices:*

(see index for correct answer)

- a. Expediting
- b. Production function
- c. ISO/TS 16949
- d. Screw conveyor

Guidance: level 1

:: Lean manufacturing ::

_____ is a Japanese term that means "mistake-proofing" or "inadvertent error prevention". A _____ is any mechanism in any process that helps an equipment operator avoid mistakes. Its purpose is to eliminate product defects by preventing, correcting, or drawing attention to human errors as they occur. The concept was formalised, and the term adopted, by Shigeo Shingo as part of the Toyota Production System. It was originally described as baka-yoke, but as this means "fool-proofing" the name was changed to the milder _____ .

Exam Probability: **High**

3. *Answer choices:*

(see index for correct answer)

- a. Poka-yoke
- b. Overall Labor Effectiveness
- c. Kanban board
- d. Frequent deliveries

Guidance: level 1

:: Costs ::

_____ is the process used by companies to reduce their costs and increase their profits. Depending on a company's services or product, the strategies can vary. Every decision in the product development process affects cost.

Exam Probability: **Low**

4. *Answer choices:*

(see index for correct answer)

- a. Cost reduction
- b. Road Logistics Costing in South Africa
- c. Economic cost
- d. Search cost

Guidance: level 1

:: Marketing ::

_____ or stock is the goods and materials that a business holds for the ultimate goal of resale.

Exam Probability: **Low**

5. *Answer choices:*
(see index for correct answer)

- a. Processing fluency
- b. Inventory
- c. Health marketing
- d. Analyst relations

Guidance: level 1

:: Chemical processes ::

_____ is the understanding and application of the fundamental principles and laws of nature that allow us to transform raw material and energy into products that are useful to society, at an industrial level. By taking advantage of the driving forces of nature such as pressure, temperature and concentration gradients, as well as the law of conservation of mass, process engineers can develop methods to synthesize and purify large quantities of desired chemical products. _____ focuses on the design, operation, control, optimization and intensification of chemical, physical, and biological processes. _____ encompasses a vast range of industries, such as agriculture, automotive, biotechnical, chemical, food, material development, mining, nuclear, petrochemical, pharmaceutical, and software development. The application of systematic computer-based methods to _____ is "process systems engineering".

Exam Probability: **High**

6. *Answer choices:*

(see index for correct answer)

- a. Chloralkali process
- b. Cracking
- c. Process engineering
- d. Downs cell

Guidance: level 1

:: Industrial design ::

In physics and mathematics, the _____ of a mathematical space is informally defined as the minimum number of coordinates needed to specify any point within it. Thus a line has a _____ of one because only one coordinate is needed to specify a point on it for example, the point at 5 on a number line. A surface such as a plane or the surface of a cylinder or sphere has a _____ of two because two coordinates are needed to specify a point on it for example, both a latitude and longitude are required to locate a point on the surface of a sphere. The inside of a cube, a cylinder or a sphere is three-_____ al because three coordinates are needed to locate a point within these spaces.

Exam Probability: **Low**

7. *Answer choices:*

(see index for correct answer)

- a. Experience design
- b. Kenco Singles
- c. Dimension
- d. Scentography

Guidance: level 1

:: Metal forming ::

_____ is a type of motion that combines rotation and translation of that object with respect to a surface, such that, if ideal conditions exist, the two are in contact with each other without sliding.

Exam Probability: **Low**

8. *Answer choices:*

(see index for correct answer)

- a. Hubbing
- b. Cryogenic treatment
- c. Skelp
- d. Liquid Impact Forming

Guidance: level 1

:: Casting (manufacturing) ::

> A _____ is a regularity in the world, man-made design, or abstract ideas. As such, the elements of a _____ repeat in a predictable manner. A geometric _____ is a kind of _____ formed of geometric shapes and typically repeated like a wallpaper design.

Exam Probability: **Low**

9. *Answer choices:*

(see index for correct answer)

- a. Coquille
- b. Casting defect
- c. Dross

- d. Permeability

Guidance: level 1

:: Gas technologies ::

A _____ is a rotary mechanical device that extracts energy from a fluid flow and converts it into useful work. The work produced by a _____ can be used for generating electrical power when combined with a generator. A _____ is a turbomachine with at least one moving part called a rotor assembly, which is a shaft or drum with blades attached. Moving fluid acts on the blades so that they move and impart rotational energy to the rotor. Early _____ examples are windmills and waterwheels.

Exam Probability: **Medium**

10. *Answer choices:*

(see index for correct answer)

- a. Guided rotor compressor
- b. Gas meter
- c. HEPA
- d. Bartlett Street Lamps

Guidance: level 1

:: ::

_____ refers to the confirmation of certain characteristics of an object, person, or organization. This confirmation is often, but not always, provided by some form of external review, education, assessment, or audit. Accreditation is a specific organization's process of _____ . According to the National Council on Measurement in Education, a _____ test is a credentialing test used to determine whether individuals are knowledgeable enough in a given occupational area to be labeled "competent to practice" in that area.

Exam Probability: **Medium**

11. *Answer choices:*

(see index for correct answer)

- a. levels of analysis
- b. co-culture
- c. information systems assessment
- d. Certification

Guidance: level 1

:: Production and manufacturing ::

_____ is a set of techniques and tools for process improvement. Though as a shortened form it may be found written as 6S, it should not be confused with the methodology known as 6S.

Exam Probability: **High**

12. Answer choices:

(see index for correct answer)

- a. Total quality management
- b. WorkPLAN
- c. Food processing
- d. Six Sigma

Guidance: level 1

:: Management ::

Business _____ is a discipline in operations management in which people use various methods to discover, model, analyze, measure, improve, optimize, and automate business processes. BPM focuses on improving corporate performance by managing business processes. Any combination of methods used to manage a company's business processes is BPM. Processes can be structured and repeatable or unstructured and variable. Though not required, enabling technologies are often used with BPM.

Exam Probability: **Low**

13. Answer choices:

(see index for correct answer)

- a. Process management
- b. Kata
- c. Line management

- d. Economic production quantity

Guidance: level 1

:: Quality assurance ::

The _____ is a United States-based nonprofit tax-exempt 501 organization that accredits more than 21,000 US health care organizations and programs. The international branch accredits medical services from around the world. A majority of US state governments recognize _____ accreditation as a condition of licensure for the receipt of Medicaid and Medicare reimbursements.

Exam Probability: **Low**

14. *Answer choices:*
(see index for correct answer)

- a. Technical Control Department
- b. Joint Commission
- c. Software quality assurance
- d. Swiss quality label for further education institutions

Guidance: level 1

:: Natural materials ::

_____ is a finely-grained natural rock or soil material that combines one or more _____ minerals with possible traces of quartz, metal oxides and organic matter. Geologic _____ deposits are mostly composed of phyllosilicate minerals containing variable amounts of water trapped in the mineral structure. _____s are plastic due to particle size and geometry as well as water content, and become hard, brittle and non–plastic upon drying or firing. Depending on the soil's content in which it is found, _____ can appear in various colours from white to dull grey or brown to deep orange-red.

Exam Probability: **High**

15. *Answer choices:*

(see index for correct answer)

- a. Pebble
- b. Thatching
- c. Perovskite
- d. Clay

Guidance: level 1

:: Project management ::

A _____ is a professional in the field of project management. _____ s have the responsibility of the planning, procurement and execution of a project, in any undertaking that has a defined scope, defined start and a defined finish; regardless of industry. _____ s are first point of contact for any issues or discrepancies arising from within the heads of various departments in an organization before the problem escalates to higher authorities. Project management is the responsibility of a _____ . This individual seldom participates directly in the activities that produce the end result, but rather strives to maintain the progress, mutual interaction and tasks of various parties in such a way that reduces the risk of overall failure, maximizes benefits, and minimizes costs.

Exam Probability: **Low**

16. *Answer choices:*

(see index for correct answer)

- a. Project manager
- b. Test and evaluation master plan
- c. Vertical slice
- d. Project team

Guidance: level 1

:: Insulators ::

A _____ is a piece of soft cloth large enough either to cover or to enfold a great portion of the user's body, usually when sleeping or otherwise at rest, thereby trapping radiant bodily heat that otherwise would be lost through convection, and so keeping the body warm.

Exam Probability: **Low**

17. *Answer choices:*

(see index for correct answer)

- a. Multi-layer insulation
- b. Blanket
- c. Mechanical insulation
- d. Dynamic insulation

Guidance: level 1

:: Supply chain management ::

_____ is a core supply chain function and includes supply chain planning and supply chain execution capabilities. Specifically, _____ is the capability firms use to plan total material requirements. The material requirements are communicated to procurement and other functions for sourcing. _____ is also responsible for determining the amount of material to be deployed at each stocking location across the supply chain, establishing material replenishment plans, determining inventory levels to hold for each type of inventory, and communicating information regarding material needs throughout the extended supply chain.

Exam Probability: **Medium**

18. *Answer choices:*

(see index for correct answer)

- a. Materials management
- b. ClearOrbit
- c. Design for logistics
- d. XIO Strategies

Guidance: level 1

:: Debt ::

_____ is the trust which allows one party to provide money or resources to another party wherein the second party does not reimburse the first party immediately , but promises either to repay or return those resources at a later date. In other words, _____ is a method of making reciprocity formal, legally enforceable, and extensible to a large group of unrelated people.

Exam Probability: **Medium**

19. *Answer choices:*

(see index for correct answer)

- a. Debt crisis
- b. Legal liability

- c. Debt management plan
- d. Floating charge

Guidance: level 1

:: Goods ::

In most contexts, the concept of _____ denotes the conduct that should be preferred when posed with a choice between possible actions. _____ is generally considered to be the opposite of evil, and is of interest in the study of morality, ethics, religion and philosophy. The specific meaning and etymology of the term and its associated translations among ancient and contemporary languages show substantial variation in its inflection and meaning depending on circumstances of place, history, religious, or philosophical context.

Exam Probability: **High**

20. *Answer choices:*

(see index for correct answer)

- a. Superior good
- b. Public good
- c. Good
- d. Global public good

Guidance: level 1

:: ::

_____ refers to a business or organization attempting to acquire goods or services to accomplish its goals. Although there are several organizations that attempt to set standards in the _____ process, processes can vary greatly between organizations. Typically the word " _____ " is not used interchangeably with the word "procurement", since procurement typically includes expediting, supplier quality, and transportation and logistics in addition to _____ .

Exam Probability: **Medium**

21. *Answer choices:*

(see index for correct answer)

- a. hierarchical perspective
- b. Purchasing
- c. deep-level diversity
- d. surface-level diversity

Guidance: level 1

:: Industrial engineering ::

_____ , in its contemporary conceptualisation, is a comparison of perceived expectations of a service with perceived performance , giving rise to the equation SQ=P-E. This conceptualistion of _____ has its origins in the expectancy-disconfirmation paradigm.

Exam Probability: **Low**

22. *Answer choices:*

(see index for correct answer)

- a. Service quality
- b. Defect concentration diagram
- c. H. Milton Stewart School of Industrial and Systems Engineering
- d. Pilot plant

Guidance: level 1

:: Information technology management ::

_____ is a collective term for all approaches to prepare, support and help individuals, teams, and organizations in making organizational change. The most common change drivers include: technological evolution, process reviews, crisis, and consumer habit changes; pressure from new business entrants, acquisitions, mergers, and organizational restructuring. It includes methods that redirect or redefine the use of resources, business process, budget allocations, or other modes of operation that significantly change a company or organization. Organizational _____ considers the full organization and what needs to change, while _____ may be used solely to refer to how people and teams are affected by such organizational transition. It deals with many different disciplines, from behavioral and social sciences to information technology and business solutions.

Exam Probability: **Medium**

23. *Answer choices:*

(see index for correct answer)

- a. Computerized maintenance management system
- b. Electronic document and records management system
- c. HP Open Extensibility Platform
- d. Change management

Guidance: level 1

:: Project management ::

> _____s can take many forms depending on the type of project being implemented and the nature of the organization. The _____ details the project deliverables and describes the major objectives. The objectives should include measurable success criteria for the project.

Exam Probability: **High**

24. *Answer choices:*

(see index for correct answer)

- a. Sunk costs
- b. Scope statement
- c. Project network
- d. Project initiation document

Guidance: level 1

:: Costs ::

In process improvement efforts, _____ or cost of quality is a means to quantify the total cost of quality-related efforts and deficiencies. It was first described by Armand V. Feigenbaum in a 1956 Harvard Business Review article.

Exam Probability: **High**

25. *Answer choices:*

(see index for correct answer)

- a. Average variable cost
- b. Joint cost
- c. Psychic cost
- d. Quality costs

Guidance: level 1

:: Business ::

The seller, or the provider of the goods or services, completes a sale in response to an acquisition, appropriation, requisition or a direct interaction with the buyer at the point of sale. There is a passing of title of the item, and the settlement of a price, in which agreement is reached on a price for which transfer of ownership of the item will occur. The seller, not the purchaser typically executes the sale and it may be completed prior to the obligation of payment. In the case of indirect interaction, a person who sells goods or service on behalf of the owner is known as a _____ man or _____ woman or _____ person, but this often refers to someone selling goods in a store/shop, in which case other terms are also common, including _____ clerk, shop assistant, and retail clerk.

Exam Probability: **High**

26. *Answer choices:*

(see index for correct answer)

- a. Corporate social media
- b. Door-to-door
- c. Absentee business owner
- d. Sales

Guidance: level 1

:: Teams ::

A _____ usually refers to a group of individuals who work together from different geographic locations and rely on communication technology such as email, FAX, and video or voice conferencing services in order to collaborate. The term can also refer to groups or teams that work together asynchronously or across organizational levels. Powell, Piccoli and Ives define _____ s as "groups of geographically, organizationally and/or time dispersed workers brought together by information and telecommunication technologies to accomplish one or more organizational tasks." According to Ale Ebrahim et. al. , _____ s can also be defined as "small temporary groups of geographically, organizationally and/or time dispersed knowledge workers who coordinate their work predominantly with electronic information and communication technologies in order to accomplish one or more organization tasks."

Exam Probability: **High**

27. *Answer choices:*

(see index for correct answer)

- a. team composition
- b. Team-building

Guidance: level 1

:: ::

An _____ is a company that produces parts and equipment that may be marketed by another manufacturer. For example, Foxconn, a Taiwanese electronics contract manufacturing company, which produces a variety of parts and equipment for companies such as Apple Inc., Dell, Google, Huawei, Nintendo, etc., is the largest OEM company in the world by both scale and revenue.

Exam Probability: **Low**

28. *Answer choices:*

(see index for correct answer)

- a. imperative
- b. Character
- c. Original equipment manufacturer
- d. process perspective

Guidance: level 1

:: Supply chain management ::

A _____ is a type of auction in which the traditional roles of buyer and seller are reversed. Thus, there is one buyer and many potential sellers. In an ordinary auction, buyers compete to obtain goods or services by offering increasingly higher prices. In contrast, in a _____, the sellers compete to obtain business from the buyer and prices will typically decrease as the sellers underbid each other.

Exam Probability: **High**

29. *Answer choices:*

(see index for correct answer)

- a. Universal Product Code
- b. Reverse auction
- c. ERP system
- d. Supply chain cyber security

Guidance: level 1

:: Management ::

A supply-chain network is an evolution of the basic supply chain. Due to rapid technological advancement, organisations with a basic supply chain can develop this chain into a more complex structure involving a higher level of interdependence and connectivity between more organisations, this constitutes a supply-chain network.

Exam Probability: **High**

30. *Answer choices:*

(see index for correct answer)

- a. Supply chain network
- b. Marketing science
- c. Risk management
- d. Adhocracy

Guidance: level 1

:: ::

A _____ consists of an orchestrated and repeatable pattern of business activity enabled by the systematic organization of resources into processes that transform materials, provide services, or process information. It can be depicted as a sequence of operations, the work of a person or group, the work of an organization of staff, or one or more simple or complex mechanisms.

Exam Probability: **Low**

31. *Answer choices:*

(see index for correct answer)

- a. levels of analysis
- b. Workflow
- c. empathy
- d. imperative

Guidance: level 1

:: Production and manufacturing ::

An _____ is a manufacturing process in which parts are added as the semi-finished assembly moves from workstation to workstation where the parts are added in sequence until the final assembly is produced. By mechanically moving the parts to the assembly work and moving the semi-finished assembly from work station to work station, a finished product can be assembled faster and with less labor than by having workers carry parts to a stationary piece for assembly.

Exam Probability: **Low**

32. *Answer choices:*

(see index for correct answer)

- a. Process layout
- b. Assembly line
- c. Production plan
- d. Advanced product quality planning

Guidance: level 1

:: Project management ::

A _____ is the approximation of the cost of a program, project, or operation. The _____ is the product of the cost estimating process. The _____ has a single total value and may have identifiable component values. A problem with a cost overrun can be avoided with a credible, reliable, and accurate _____. A cost estimator is the professional who prepares _____s. There are different types of cost estimators, whose title may be preceded by a modifier, such as building estimator, or electrical estimator, or chief estimator. Other professionals such as quantity surveyors and cost engineers may also prepare _____s or contribute to _____s. In the US, according to the Bureau of Labor Statistics, there were 185,400 cost estimators in 2010. There are around 75,000 professional quantity surveyors working in the UK.

Exam Probability: **High**

33. *Answer choices:*
(see index for correct answer)

- a. Outcomes theory
- b. Project appraisal
- c. Problem domain analysis
- d. Cost estimate

Guidance: level 1

:: Project management ::

Contemporary business and science treat as a _____ any undertaking, carried out individually or collaboratively and possibly involving research or design, that is carefully planned to achieve a particular aim.

Exam Probability: **High**

34. *Answer choices:*

(see index for correct answer)

- a. Master of Science in Project Management
- b. Project plan
- c. Project
- d. Theme-centered interaction

Guidance: level 1

:: Packaging materials ::

_____ is a thin material produced by pressing together moist fibres of cellulose pulp derived from wood, rags or grasses, and drying them into flexible sheets. It is a versatile material with many uses, including writing, printing, packaging, cleaning, decorating, and a number of industrial and construction processes. _____s are essential in legal or non-legal documentation.

Exam Probability: **Low**

35. *Answer choices:*

(see index for correct answer)

- a. Paper
- b. Greensulate
- c. Paperboard
- d. Nonwoven fabric

Guidance: level 1

:: ::

In production, research, retail, and accounting, a _____ is the value of money that has been used up to produce something or deliver a service, and hence is not available for use anymore. In business, the _____ may be one of acquisition, in which case the amount of money expended to acquire it is counted as _____ . In this case, money is the input that is gone in order to acquire the thing. This acquisition _____ may be the sum of the _____ of production as incurred by the original producer, and further _____ s of transaction as incurred by the acquirer over and above the price paid to the producer. Usually, the price also includes a mark-up for profit over the _____ of production.

Exam Probability: **High**

36. *Answer choices:*

(see index for correct answer)

- a. hierarchical

- b. imperative
- c. co-culture
- d. empathy

Guidance: level 1

:: ::

_____ is a kind of action that occur as two or more objects have an effect upon one another. The idea of a two-way effect is essential in the concept of _____ , as opposed to a one-way causal effect. A closely related term is interconnectivity, which deals with the _____ s of _____ s within systems: combinations of many simple _____ s can lead to surprising emergent phenomena. _____ has different tailored meanings in various sciences. Changes can also involve _____ .

Exam Probability: **Medium**

37. *Answer choices:*

(see index for correct answer)

- a. Character
- b. functional perspective
- c. process perspective
- d. information systems assessment

Guidance: level 1

:: Retailing ::

_____ is the process of selling consumer goods or services to customers through multiple channels of distribution to earn a profit. _____ers satisfy demand identified through a supply chain. The term "_____er" is typically applied where a service provider fills the small orders of a large number of individuals, who are end-users, rather than large orders of a small number of wholesale, corporate or government clientele. Shopping generally refers to the act of buying products. Sometimes this is done to obtain final goods, including necessities such as food and clothing; sometimes it takes place as a recreational activity. Recreational shopping often involves window shopping and browsing: it does not always result in a purchase.

Exam Probability: **Medium**

38. *Answer choices:*

(see index for correct answer)

- a. Anchor store
- b. Consignment
- c. Gondola
- d. Used bookstore

Guidance: level 1

:: Lean manufacturing ::

_____ is a scheduling system for lean manufacturing and just-in-time manufacturing. Taiichi Ohno, an industrial engineer at Toyota, developed _____ to improve manufacturing efficiency. _____ is one method to achieve JIT. The system takes its name from the cards that track production within a factory. For many in the automotive sector, _____ is known as the "Toyota nameplate system" and as such the term is not used by some other automakers.

Exam Probability: **Low**

39. *Answer choices:*

(see index for correct answer)

- a. Kanban
- b. Oobeya
- c. Manufacturing supermarket
- d. Heijunka box

Guidance: level 1

:: Promotion and marketing communications ::

The _____ of American Manufacturers, now ThomasNet, is an online platform for supplier discovery and product sourcing in the US and Canada. It was once known as the "big green books" and "Thomas Registry", and was a multi-volume directory of industrial product information covering 650,000 distributors, manufacturers and service companies within 67,000-plus industrial categories that is now published on ThomasNet.

Exam Probability: **Medium**

40. *Answer choices:*

(see index for correct answer)

- a. Valpak
- b. Puffery
- c. Thomas Register
- d. Event television

Guidance: level 1

:: Quality ::

The _____ , formerly the _____ Control , is a knowledge-based global community of quality professionals, with nearly 80,000 members dedicated to promoting and advancing quality tools, principles, and practices in their workplaces and communities.

Exam Probability: **High**

41. *Answer choices:*

(see index for correct answer)

- a. Ringtest
- b. Secure Stations Scheme
- c. Market Driven Quality

- d. Process architecture

Guidance: level 1

:: Outsourcing ::

_____ is the practice of sourcing from the global market for goods and services across geopolitical boundaries. _____ often aims to exploit global efficiencies in the delivery of a product or service. These efficiencies include low cost skilled labor, low cost raw material and other economic factors like tax breaks and low trade tariffs. A large number of Information Technology projects and Services, including IS Applications and Mobile Apps and database services are outsourced globally to countries like Pakistan and India for more economical pricing.

Exam Probability: **Low**

42. *Answer choices:*
(see index for correct answer)

- a. PFSweb
- b. Managed security service
- c. Legal outsourcing
- d. Global sourcing

Guidance: level 1

:: Metrics ::

_____ is a computer model developed by the University of Idaho, that uses Landsat satellite data to compute and map evapotranspiration . _____ calculates ET as a residual of the surface energy balance, where ET is estimated by keeping account of total net short wave and long wave radiation at the vegetation or soil surface, the amount of heat conducted into soil, and the amount of heat convected into the air above the surface. The difference in these three terms represents the amount of energy absorbed during the conversion of liquid water to vapor, which is ET. _____ expresses near-surface temperature gradients used in heat convection as indexed functions of radio _____ surface temperature, thereby eliminating the need for absolutely accurate surface temperature and the need for air-temperature measurements.

Exam Probability: **High**

43. *Answer choices:*

(see index for correct answer)

- a. String metric
- b. Software Metrics Metamodel
- c. METRIC
- d. Full-time equivalent

Guidance: level 1

:: Commercial item transport and distribution ::

In commerce, supply-chain management, the management of the flow of goods and services, involves the movement and storage of raw materials, of work-in-process inventory, and of finished goods from point of origin to point of consumption. Interconnected or interlinked networks, channels and node businesses combine in the provision of products and services required by end customers in a supply chain. Supply-chain management has been defined as the "design, planning, execution, control, and monitoring of supply-chain activities with the objective of creating net value, building a competitive infrastructure, leveraging worldwide logistics, synchronizing supply with demand and measuring performance globally."SCM practice draws heavily from the areas of industrial engineering, systems engineering, operations management, logistics, procurement, information technology, and marketing and strives for an integrated approach. Marketing channels play an important role in supply-chain management. Current research in supply-chain management is concerned with topics related to sustainability and risk management, among others. Some suggest that the "people dimension" of SCM, ethical issues, internal integration, transparency/visibility, and human capital/talent management are topics that have, so far, been underrepresented on the research agenda.

Exam Probability: **Low**

44. *Answer choices:*

(see index for correct answer)

- a. Bonded warehouse
- b. Freight exchange
- c. DCT Industrial Trust
- d. Delivery order

Guidance: level 1

:: Production economics ::

In economics and related disciplines, a _____ is a cost in making any economic trade when participating in a market.

Exam Probability: **High**

45. *Answer choices:*

(see index for correct answer)

- a. short run
- b. Productive capacity
- c. Economies of scale
- d. Marginal product of labor

Guidance: level 1

:: Risk analysis ::

Supply-chain risk management is "the implementation of strategies to manage both everyday and exceptional risks along the supply chain based on continuous risk assessment with the objective of reducing vulnerability and ensuring continuity".

Exam Probability: **High**

46. *Answer choices:*

(see index for correct answer)

- a. Probabilistic risk assessment
- b. Collateral consequence
- c. Accident
- d. Factor analysis of information risk

Guidance: level 1

:: Help desk ::

Data center management is the collection of tasks performed by those responsible for managing ongoing operation of a data center This includes Business service management and planning for the future.

Exam Probability: **Low**

47. *Answer choices:*

(see index for correct answer)

- a. SysAid Technologies
- b. Technical support
- c. KnowledgeBase Manager Pro
- d. GLPI

Guidance: level 1

:: Management ::

In organizational studies, _____ is the efficient and effective development of an organization's resources when they are needed. Such resources may include financial resources, inventory, human skills, production resources, or information technology and natural resources.

Exam Probability: **High**

48. *Answer choices:*

(see index for correct answer)

- a. Social risk management
- b. Executive compensation
- c. Iterative and incremental development
- d. Resource management

Guidance: level 1

:: Management ::

In inventory management, _____ is the order quantity that minimizes the total holding costs and ordering costs. It is one of the oldest classical production scheduling models. The model was developed by Ford W. Harris in 1913, but R. H. Wilson, a consultant who applied it extensively, and K. Andler are given credit for their in-depth analysis.

Exam Probability: **Medium**

49. *Answer choices:*

(see index for correct answer)

- a. Supply chain sustainability
- b. Association management company
- c. Middle management
- d. Semiconductor consolidation

Guidance: level 1

:: Project management ::

A _____ is a team whose members usually belong to different groups, functions and are assigned to activities for the same project. A team can be divided into sub-teams according to need. Usually _____ s are only used for a defined period of time. They are disbanded after the project is deemed complete. Due to the nature of the specific formation and disbandment, _____ s are usually in organizations.

Exam Probability: **Low**

50. *Answer choices:*

(see index for correct answer)

- a. Authority
- b. Australian Institute of Project Management

- c. Integrated product team
- d. Project team

Guidance: level 1

:: Production economics ::

> _____ is the creation of a whole that is greater than the simple sum of its parts. The term _____ comes from the Attic Greek word sea synergia from synergos, , meaning "working together".

Exam Probability: **High**

51. *Answer choices:*

(see index for correct answer)

- a. Choice of techniques
- b. Marginal product of labor
- c. Capitalist mode of production
- d. Synergy

Guidance: level 1

:: Monopoly (economics) ::

_____ are "efficiencies formed by variety, not volume". For example, a gas station that sells gasoline can sell soda, milk, baked goods, etc through their customer service representatives and thus achieve gasoline companies _____ .

Exam Probability: **Low**

52. *Answer choices:*

(see index for correct answer)

- a. Economies of scope
- b. Tesco Town
- c. Legal monopoly
- d. Private finance initiative

Guidance: level 1

:: Management ::

_____ , also known as natural process limits, are horizontal lines drawn on a statistical process control chart, usually at a distance of ±3 standard deviations of the plotted statistic from the statistic's mean.

Exam Probability: **High**

53. *Answer choices:*

(see index for correct answer)

- a. Event chain diagram
- b. Control limits
- c. Enterprise decision management
- d. Line of business

Guidance: level 1

:: Project management ::

In economics and business decision-making, a sunk cost is a cost that has already been incurred and cannot be recovered.

Exam Probability: **Low**

54. *Answer choices:*
(see index for correct answer)

- a. Advanced Integrated Practice
- b. Risk register
- c. Risk management plan
- d. Task

Guidance: level 1

:: Information technology management ::

The term _____ is used to refer to periods when a system is unavailable. _____ or outage duration refers to a period of time that a system fails to provide or perform its primary function. Reliability, availability, recovery, and unavailability are related concepts. The unavailability is the proportion of a time-span that a system is unavailable or offline. This is usually a result of the system failing to function because of an unplanned event, or because of routine maintenance.

Exam Probability: **Low**

55. *Answer choices:*

(see index for correct answer)

- a. Production support
- b. ERP for IT
- c. ServiceNow
- d. Downtime

Guidance: level 1

:: Waste ::

_____ are unwanted or unusable materials. _____ is any substance which is discarded after primary use, or is worthless, defective and of no use. A by-product by contrast is a joint product of relatively minor economic value. A _____ product may become a by-product, joint product or resource through an invention that raises a _____ product's value above zero.

Exam Probability: **Low**

56. *Answer choices:*
(see index for correct answer)

- a. Waste
- b. Tailings
- c. Metabolic waste
- d. Demolition waste

Guidance: level 1

:: Management accounting ::

"_____ s are the structural determinants of the cost of an activity, reflecting any linkages or interrelationships that affect it". Therefore we could assume that the _____ s determine the cost behavior within the activities, reflecting the links that these have with other activities and relationships that affect them.

Exam Probability: **Medium**

57. Answer choices:

(see index for correct answer)

- a. Relevant cost
- b. Environmental full-cost accounting
- c. Cost driver
- d. Operating profit margin

Guidance: level 1

:: Procurement ::

Purchasing is the formal process of buying goods and services. The _____ can vary from one organization to another, but there are some common key elements.

Exam Probability: **High**

58. Answer choices:

(see index for correct answer)

- a. Procure-to-pay
- b. Proposal theme statement
- c. Request price quotation
- d. Purchasing process

Guidance: level 1

:: Production and manufacturing ::

> _____ was a management-led program to eliminate defects in industrial production that enjoyed brief popularity in American industry from 1964 to the early 1970s. Quality expert Philip Crosby later incorporated it into his "Absolutes of Quality Management" and it enjoyed a renaissance in the American automobile industry—as a performance goal more than as a program—in the 1990s. Although applicable to any type of enterprise, it has been primarily adopted within supply chains wherever large volumes of components are being purchased.

Exam Probability: **High**

59. *Answer choices:*

(see index for correct answer)

- a. Fiberglass molding
- b. Original design manufacturer
- c. Zero Defects
- d. Computer-integrated manufacturing

Guidance: level 1

Commerce

Commerce relates to "the exchange of goods and services, especially on a large scale." It includes legal, economic, political, social, cultural and technological systems that operate in any country or internationally.

:: E-commerce ::

_____ Inc. was an electronic money corporation founded by David Chaum in 1989. _____ transactions were unique in that they were anonymous due to a number of cryptographic protocols developed by its founder. _____ declared bankruptcy in 1998, and subsequently sold its assets to eCash Technologies, another digital currency company, which was acquired by InfoSpace on Feb. 19, 2002.

Exam Probability: **High**

1. *Answer choices:*

(see index for correct answer)

- a. Helpling
- b. SAScon
- c. Internet booking engine
- d. DigiCash

Guidance: level 1

_____ is a qualitative measure used to relate the quality of motor vehicle traffic service. LOS is used to analyze roadways and intersections by categorizing traffic flow and assigning quality levels of traffic based on performance measure like vehicle speed, density, congestion, etc.

Exam Probability: **Medium**

2. *Answer choices:*

(see index for correct answer)

- a. Level of service
- b. similarity-attraction theory
- c. functional perspective

- d. cultural

Guidance: level 1

:: ::

_____, or auditory perception, is the ability to perceive sounds by detecting vibrations, changes in the pressure of the surrounding medium through time, through an organ such as the ear. The academic field concerned with _____ is auditory science.

Exam Probability: **Low**

3. *Answer choices:*

(see index for correct answer)

- a. levels of analysis
- b. process perspective
- c. personal values
- d. Hearing

Guidance: level 1

:: Trading posts of the Hanseatic League ::

_____ is a city and unitary authority area in North _____ shire, England, with a population of 208,200 as of 2017. Located at the confluence of the Rivers Ouse and Foss, it is the county town of the historic county of _____ shire and was the home of the House of _____ throughout its existence. The city is known for its famous historical landmarks such as _____ Minster and the city walls, as well as a variety of cultural and sporting activities, which makes it a popular tourist destination in England. The local authority is the City of _____ Council, a single tier governing body responsible for providing all local services and facilities throughout the city. The City of _____ local government district includes rural areas beyond the old city boundaries.

Exam Probability: **Medium**

4. *Answer choices:*

(see index for correct answer)

- a. York
- b. Kontor
- c. Staraya Ladoga
- d. Kaunas

Guidance: level 1

:: Hospitality industry ::

_____ refers to the relationship between a guest and a host, wherein the host receives the guest with goodwill, including the reception and entertainment of guests, visitors, or strangers. Louis, chevalier de Jaucourt describes _____ in the Encyclopédie as the virtue of a great soul that cares for the whole universe through the ties of humanity.

Exam Probability: **Low**

5. *Answer choices:*

(see index for correct answer)

- a. Hospitality law
- b. Travel insurance
- c. Restaurant rating
- d. Restaurant ware

Guidance: level 1

:: Management ::

In business, a _____ is the attribute that allows an organization to outperform its competitors. A _____ may include access to natural resources, such as high-grade ores or a low-cost power source, highly skilled labor, geographic location, high entry barriers, and access to new technology.

Exam Probability: **Medium**

6. *Answer choices:*

(see index for correct answer)

- a. Business rule
- b. Resource management
- c. Competitive advantage
- d. Nonconformity

Guidance: level 1

:: Stochastic processes ::

_____ in its modern meaning is a "new idea, creative thoughts, new imaginations in form of device or method". _____ is often also viewed as the application of better solutions that meet new requirements, unarticulated needs, or existing market needs. Such _____ takes place through the provision of more-effective products, processes, services, technologies, or business models that are made available to markets, governments and society. An _____ is something original and more effective and, as a consequence, new, that "breaks into" the market or society. _____ is related to, but not the same as, invention, as _____ is more apt to involve the practical implementation of an invention to make a meaningful impact in the market or society, and not all _____ s require an invention. _____ often manifests itself via the engineering process, when the problem being solved is of a technical or scientific nature. The opposite of _____ is exnovation.

Exam Probability: **Low**

7. *Answer choices:*

(see index for correct answer)

- a. Lumpability
- b. Additive Markov chain
- c. Stochastic quantization
- d. Innovation

Guidance: level 1

:: Manufacturing ::

A _____ is a building for storing goods. _____ s are used by manufacturers, importers, exporters, wholesalers, transport businesses, customs, etc. They are usually large plain buildings in industrial parks on the outskirts of cities, towns or villages.

Exam Probability: **Medium**

8. *Answer choices:*

(see index for correct answer)

- a. Standard Motor Products
- b. Production Systems Engineering
- c. Point cloud
- d. Warehouse

Guidance: level 1

:: Business terms ::

_____ ning is an organization's process of defining its strategy, or direction, and making decisions on allocating its resources to pursue this strategy. It may also extend to control mechanisms for guiding the implementation of the strategy. _____ ning became prominent in corporations during the 1960s and remains an important aspect of strategic management. It is executed by _____ ners or strategists, who involve many parties and research sources in their analysis of the organization and its relationship to the environment in which it competes.

Exam Probability: **Medium**

9. *Answer choices:*

(see index for correct answer)

- a. churn rate
- b. front office
- c. back office
- d. noncommercial

Guidance: level 1

:: Supply chain management terms ::

In business and finance, _____ is a system of organizations, people, activities, information, and resources involved in moving a product or service from supplier to customer. _____ activities involve the transformation of natural resources, raw materials, and components into a finished product that is delivered to the end customer. In sophisticated _____ systems, used products may re-enter the _____ at any point where residual value is recyclable. _____ s link value chains.

Exam Probability: **Low**

10. *Answer choices:*

(see index for correct answer)

- a. Work in process
- b. Direct shipment
- c. Widget
- d. Supply chain

Guidance: level 1

:: Management ::

_____ is the identification, evaluation, and prioritization of risks followed by coordinated and economical application of resources to minimize, monitor, and control the probability or impact of unfortunate events or to maximize the realization of opportunities.

Exam Probability: **High**

11. *Answer choices:*

(see index for correct answer)

- a. Duality
- b. Fredmund Malik
- c. Risk management
- d. Business workflow analysis

Guidance: level 1

:: Marketing ::

> _____ or stock is the goods and materials that a business holds for the ultimate goal of resale.

Exam Probability: **High**

12. *Answer choices:*

(see index for correct answer)

- a. Inventory
- b. Porter hypothesis
- c. Commercial planning
- d. Adobe Media Optimizer

Guidance: level 1

A federation is a political entity characterized by a union of partially self-governing provinces, states, or other regions under a central _____ . In a federation, the self-governing status of the component states, as well as the division of power between them and the central government, is typically constitutionally entrenched and may not be altered by a unilateral decision of either party, the states or the federal political body. Alternatively, federation is a form of government in which sovereign power is formally divided between a central authority and a number of constituent regions so that each region retains some degree of control over its internal affairs. It is often argued that federal states where the central government has the constitutional authority to suspend a constituent state's government by invoking gross mismanagement or civil unrest, or to adopt national legislation that overrides or infringe on the constituent states' powers by invoking the central government's constitutional authority to ensure "peace and good government" or to implement obligations contracted under an international treaty, are not truly federal states.

Exam Probability: **Medium**

13. *Answer choices:*

(see index for correct answer)

- a. open system
- b. Federal government
- c. corporate values
- d. information systems assessment

Guidance: level 1

_____ s is the linguistic and philosophical study of meaning, in language, programming languages, formal logics, and semiotics. It is concerned with the relationship between signifiers—like words, phrases, signs, and symbols—and what they stand for in reality, their denotation.

Exam Probability: **High**

14. *Answer choices:*

(see index for correct answer)

- a. functional perspective
- b. corporate values
- c. hierarchical perspective
- d. Character

Guidance: level 1

The _____ is a political and economic union of 28 member states that are located primarily in Europe. It has an area of 4,475,757 km2 and an estimated population of about 513 million. The EU has developed an internal single market through a standardised system of laws that apply in all member states in those matters, and only those matters, where members have agreed to act as one. EU policies aim to ensure the free movement of people, goods, services and capital within the internal market, enact legislation in justice and home affairs and maintain common policies on trade, agriculture, fisheries and regional development. For travel within the Schengen Area, passport controls have been abolished. A monetary union was established in 1999 and came into full force in 2002 and is composed of 19 EU member states which use the euro currency.

Exam Probability: **Medium**

15. *Answer choices:*

(see index for correct answer)

- a. corporate values
- b. personal values
- c. co-culture
- d. European Union

Guidance: level 1

:: ::

Walter Elias Disney was an American entrepreneur, animator, voice actor and film producer. A pioneer of the American animation industry, he introduced several developments in the production of cartoons. As a film producer, Disney holds the record for most Academy Awards earned by an individual, having won 22 Oscars from 59 nominations. He was presented with two Golden Globe Special Achievement Awards and an Emmy Award, among other honors. Several of his films are included in the National Film Registry by the Library of Congress.

Exam Probability: **Medium**

16. *Answer choices:*

(see index for correct answer)

- a. cultural
- b. Sarbanes-Oxley act of 2002
- c. process perspective
- d. Walt Disney

Guidance: level 1

:: Commerce ::

_____, also known as duty _____ is defined by the United States Customs and Border Protection as the refund of certain duties, internal and revenue taxes and certain fees collected upon the importation of goods. Such refunds are only allowed upon the exportation or destruction of goods under U.S. Customs and Border Protection supervision. Duty _____ is an export promotions program sanctioned by the World Trade Organization and allows the refund of certain duties taxes and fees paid upon importation which was established in 1789 in order to promote U.S. innovation and manufacturing across the global market.

Exam Probability: **Medium**

17. *Answer choices:*

(see index for correct answer)

- a. Too cheap to meter
- b. Reseller
- c. GT Nexus
- d. Haul video

Guidance: level 1

:: Supply chain management ::

_____ is a variable pricing strategy, based on understanding, anticipating and influencing consumer behavior in order to maximize revenue or profits from a fixed, time-limited resource. As a specific, inventory-focused branch of revenue management, _____ involves strategic control of inventory to sell the right product to the right customer at the right time for the right price. This process can result in price discrimination, in which customers consuming identical goods or services are charged different prices. _____ is a large revenue generator for several major industries; Robert Crandall, former Chairman and CEO of American Airlines, gave _____ its name and has called it "the single most important technical development in transportation management since we entered deregulation."

Exam Probability: **High**

18. *Answer choices:*

(see index for correct answer)

- a. Astra Resources Plc
- b. Yield management
- c. Symphony EYC
- d. ICON-SCM

Guidance: level 1

:: Securities (finance) ::

A _____ is a container that is traditionally constructed from stiff fibers, and can be made from a range of materials, including wood splints, runners, and cane. While most _____ s are made from plant materials, other materials such as horsehair, baleen, or metal wire can be used. _____ s are generally woven by hand. Some _____ s are fitted with a lid, while others are left open on top.

Exam Probability: **Medium**

19. *Answer choices:*

(see index for correct answer)

- a. Basket
- b. ADS Securities
- c. Exempt market securities
- d. Bought out deal

Guidance: level 1

:: ::

The _____ is a U.S. business-focused, English-language international daily newspaper based in New York City. The Journal, along with its Asian and European editions, is published six days a week by Dow Jones & Company, a division of News Corp. The newspaper is published in the broadsheet format and online. The Journal has been printed continuously since its inception on July 8, 1889, by Charles Dow, Edward Jones, and Charles Bergstresser.

Exam Probability: **High**

20. *Answer choices:*

(see index for correct answer)

- a. corporate values
- b. Wall Street Journal
- c. hierarchical
- d. information systems assessment

Guidance: level 1

:: E-commerce ::

A _____ is a hosted service offering that acts as an intermediary between business partners sharing standards based or proprietary data via shared business processes. The offered service is referred to as " _____ services".

Exam Probability: **High**

21. *Answer choices:*

(see index for correct answer)

- a. UsedSoft
- b. Confinity
- c. Paid content

- d. Value-added network

Guidance: level 1

:: Theories ::

A _____ union is a type of multinational political union where negotiated power is delegated to an authority by governments of member states.

Exam Probability: **Low**

22. *Answer choices:*
(see index for correct answer)

- a. Taylorism
- b. Supranational

Guidance: level 1

:: Evaluation ::

_____ is a way of preventing mistakes and defects in manufactured products and avoiding problems when delivering products or services to customers; which ISO 9000 defines as "part of quality management focused on providing confidence that quality requirements will be fulfilled". This defect prevention in _____ differs subtly from defect detection and rejection in quality control and has been referred to as a shift left since it focuses on quality earlier in the process.

Exam Probability: **High**

23. *Answer choices:*

(see index for correct answer)

- a. Narrative evaluation
- b. Goddard College
- c. Quality assurance
- d. American Evaluation Association

Guidance: level 1

:: Commercial item transport and distribution ::

In commerce, supply-chain management, the management of the flow of goods and services, involves the movement and storage of raw materials, of work-in-process inventory, and of finished goods from point of origin to point of consumption. Interconnected or interlinked networks, channels and node businesses combine in the provision of products and services required by end customers in a supply chain. Supply-chain management has been defined as the "design, planning, execution, control, and monitoring of supply-chain activities with the objective of creating net value, building a competitive infrastructure, leveraging worldwide logistics, synchronizing supply with demand and measuring performance globally."SCM practice draws heavily from the areas of industrial engineering, systems engineering, operations management, logistics, procurement, information technology, and marketing and strives for an integrated approach. Marketing channels play an important role in supply-chain management. Current research in supply-chain management is concerned with topics related to sustainability and risk management, among others. Some suggest that the "people dimension" of SCM, ethical issues, internal integration, transparency/visibility, and human capital/talent management are topics that have, so far, been underrepresented on the research agenda.

Exam Probability: **Low**

24. *Answer choices:*

(see index for correct answer)

- a. MC Freight Systems
- b. Sidelifter
- c. Interchange
- d. Pipeline transport

Guidance: level 1

:: ::

_____ is a marketing communication that employs an openly sponsored, non-personal message to promote or sell a product, service or idea. Sponsors of _____ are typically businesses wishing to promote their products or services. _____ is differentiated from public relations in that an advertiser pays for and has control over the message. It differs from personal selling in that the message is non-personal, i.e., not directed to a particular individual. _____ is communicated through various mass media, including traditional media such as newspapers, magazines, television, radio, outdoor _____ or direct mail; and new media such as search results, blogs, social media, websites or text messages. The actual presentation of the message in a medium is referred to as an advertisement, or "ad" or advert for short.

Exam Probability: **Low**

25. *Answer choices:*

(see index for correct answer)

- a. information systems assessment
- b. interpersonal communication
- c. Advertising
- d. cultural

Guidance: level 1

:: Computer access control ::

_____ is the act of confirming the truth of an attribute of a single piece of data claimed true by an entity. In contrast with identification, which refers to the act of stating or otherwise indicating a claim purportedly attesting to a person or thing's identity, _____ is the process of actually confirming that identity. It might involve confirming the identity of a person by validating their identity documents, verifying the authenticity of a website with a digital certificate, determining the age of an artifact by carbon dating, or ensuring that a product is what its packaging and labeling claim to be. In other words, _____ often involves verifying the validity of at least one form of identification.

Exam Probability: **Low**

26. *Answer choices:*

(see index for correct answer)

- a. Role hierarchy
- b. Cryptographic log on
- c. Authentication
- d. Universal controls

Guidance: level 1

:: ::

In law, a _____ is a coming together of parties to a dispute, to present information in a tribunal, a formal setting with the authority to adjudicate claims or disputes. One form of tribunal is a court. The tribunal, which may occur before a judge, jury, or other designated trier of fact, aims to achieve a resolution to their dispute.

Exam Probability: **Low**

27. *Answer choices:*

(see index for correct answer)

- a. personal values
- b. information systems assessment
- c. levels of analysis
- d. Trial

Guidance: level 1

:: ::

_____ refers to the overall process of attracting, shortlisting, selecting and appointing suitable candidates for jobs within an organization. _____ can also refer to processes involved in choosing individuals for unpaid roles. Managers, human resource generalists and _____ specialists may be tasked with carrying out _____, but in some cases public-sector employment agencies, commercial _____ agencies, or specialist search consultancies are used to undertake parts of the process. Internet-based technologies which support all aspects of _____ have become widespread.

Exam Probability: **Medium**

28. *Answer choices:*

(see index for correct answer)

- a. personal values
- b. process perspective
- c. Recruitment
- d. imperative

Guidance: level 1

:: International trade ::

A _____ is a document issued by a carrier to acknowledge receipt of cargo for shipment. Although the term historically related only to carriage by sea, a _____ may today be used for any type of carriage of goods.

Exam Probability: **Low**

29. *Answer choices:*

(see index for correct answer)

- a. Denied trade screening
- b. Pauper labor argument
- c. ATR.1 certificate
- d. Bill of lading

Guidance: level 1

:: Project management ::

> Contemporary business and science treat as a _____ any undertaking, carried out individually or collaboratively and possibly involving research or design, that is carefully planned to achieve a particular aim.

Exam Probability: **Medium**

30. *Answer choices:*

(see index for correct answer)

- a. Alexander Laufer
- b. Project
- c. Front-end loading
- d. Agile management

Guidance: level 1

:: E-commerce ::

_____ is a method of e-commerce where shoppers' friends become involved in the shopping experience. _____ attempts to use technology to mimic the social interactions found in physical malls and stores. With the rise of mobile devices, _____ is now extending beyond the online world and into the offline world of shopping.

Exam Probability: **Medium**

31. *Answer choices:*

(see index for correct answer)

- a. Lyoness
- b. SAF-T
- c. Privalia
- d. Instant payment notification

Guidance: level 1

:: Industrial Revolution ::

The _____, now also known as the First _____, was the transition to new manufacturing processes in Europe and the US, in the period from about 1760 to sometime between 1820 and 1840. This transition included going from hand production methods to machines, new chemical manufacturing and iron production processes, the increasing use of steam power and water power, the development of machine tools and the rise of the mechanized factory system. The _____ also led to an unprecedented rise in the rate of population growth.

Exam Probability: **Low**

32. *Answer choices:*

(see index for correct answer)

- a. Grubb Family Iron Dynasty
- b. Cottonopolis
- c. American Woolen Company
- d. Industrial Revolution

Guidance: level 1

:: Human resource management ::

_____ are the people who make up the workforce of an organization, business sector, or economy. "Human capital" is sometimes used synonymously with " _____ ", although human capital typically refers to a narrower effect. Likewise, other terms sometimes used include manpower, talent, labor, personnel, or simply people.

Exam Probability: **Low**

33. *Answer choices:*

(see index for correct answer)

- a. Health human resources
- b. Multiculturalism

- c. Human resources
- d. Domestic inquiry

Guidance: level 1

:: Information technology management ::

B2B is often contrasted with business-to-consumer. In B2B commerce, it is often the case that the parties to the relationship have comparable negotiating power, and even when they do not, each party typically involves professional staff and legal counsel in the negotiation of terms, whereas B2C is shaped to a far greater degree by economic implications of information asymmetry. However, within a B2B context, large companies may have many commercial, resource and information advantages over smaller businesses. The United Kingdom government, for example, created the post of Small Business Commissioner under the Enterprise Act 2016 to "enable small businesses to resolve disputes" and "consider complaints by small business suppliers about payment issues with larger businesses that they supply."

Exam Probability: **Low**

34. *Answer choices:*

(see index for correct answer)

- a. GESMES/TS
- b. Battle command knowledge system
- c. Business-to-business
- d. Lean IT

Guidance: level 1

In law, an _____ is the process in which cases are reviewed, where parties request a formal change to an official decision. _____ s function both as a process for error correction as well as a process of clarifying and interpreting law. Although appellate courts have existed for thousands of years, common law countries did not incorporate an affirmative right to _____ into their jurisprudence until the 19th century.

Exam Probability: **High**

35. *Answer choices:*

(see index for correct answer)

- a. cultural
- b. hierarchical perspective
- c. Appeal
- d. information systems assessment

Guidance: level 1

The _____ or just chief executive, is the most senior corporate, executive, or administrative officer in charge of managing an organization especially an independent legal entity such as a company or nonprofit institution. CEOs lead a range of organizations, including public and private corporations, non-profit organizations and even some government organizations. The CEO of a corporation or company typically reports to the board of directors and is charged with maximizing the value of the entity, which may include maximizing the share price, market share, revenues or another element. In the non-profit and government sector, CEOs typically aim at achieving outcomes related to the organization's mission, such as reducing poverty, increasing literacy, etc.

Exam Probability: **Medium**

36. *Answer choices:*

(see index for correct answer)

- a. empathy
- b. Chief executive officer
- c. hierarchical perspective
- d. co-culture

Guidance: level 1

In marketing jargon, product lining is offering several related products for sale individually. Unlike product bundling, where several products are combined into one group, which is then offered for sale as a units, product lining involves offering the products for sale separately. A line can comprise related products of various sizes, types, colors, qualities, or prices. Line depth refers to the number of subcategories a category has. Line consistency refers to how closely related the products that make up the line are. Line vulnerability refers to the percentage of sales or profits that are derived from only a few products in the line.

Exam Probability: **High**

37. *Answer choices:*

(see index for correct answer)

- a. Product mix
- b. personal values
- c. imperative
- d. interpersonal communication

Guidance: level 1

:: ::

_____ is the social science that studies the production, distribution, and consumption of goods and services.

Exam Probability: **Low**

38. *Answer choices:*

(see index for correct answer)

- a. Character
- b. Economics
- c. surface-level diversity
- d. levels of analysis

Guidance: level 1

:: ::

A _____ is a person or firm who arranges transactions between a buyer and a seller for a commission when the deal is executed. A _____ who also acts as a seller or as a buyer becomes a principal party to the deal. Neither role should be confused with that of an agent—one who acts on behalf of a principal party in a deal.

Exam Probability: **Low**

39. *Answer choices:*

(see index for correct answer)

- a. empathy
- b. functional perspective
- c. personal values
- d. corporate values

Guidance: level 1

:: E-commerce ::

_____ is a United States-based payment gateway service provider allowing merchants to accept credit card and electronic check payments through their website and over an Internet Protocol connection. Founded in 1996, _____ is now a subsidiary of Visa Inc. Its service permits customers to enter credit card and shipping information directly onto a web page, in contrast to some alternatives that require the customer to sign up for a payment service before performing a transaction.

Exam Probability: **Low**

40. *Answer choices:*

(see index for correct answer)

- a. Plantify
- b. Authorize.Net
- c. Types of E-commerce
- d. ChamberSign

Guidance: level 1

:: Credit cards ::

The _____ Company, also known as Amex, is an American multinational financial services corporation headquartered in Three World Financial Center in New York City. The company was founded in 1850 and is one of the 30 components of the Dow Jones Industrial Average. The company is best known for its charge card, credit card, and traveler's cheque businesses.

Exam Probability: **High**

41. *Answer choices:*

(see index for correct answer)

- a. TaiwanMoney Card
- b. Gravity Payments
- c. OnePulse
- d. Ingenico

Guidance: level 1

:: Commerce ::

_____ relates to "the exchange of goods and services, especially on a large scale". It includes legal, economic, political, social, cultural and technological systems that operate in a country or in international trade.

Exam Probability: **High**

42. *Answer choices:*

(see index for correct answer)

- a. Going concern
- b. Quickbrowse
- c. Commerce
- d. Deal transaction

Guidance: level 1

:: Production economics ::

In microeconomics, _____ are the cost advantages that enterprises obtain due to their scale of operation, with cost per unit of output decreasing with increasing scale.

Exam Probability: **Medium**

43. *Answer choices:*
(see index for correct answer)

- a. Productivity world
- b. Marginal product
- c. Choice of techniques
- d. Sectoral output

Guidance: level 1

:: Retailing ::

A _____ or trolley, also known by a variety of other names, is a cart supplied by a shop, especially supermarkets, for use by customers inside the shop for transport of merchandise to the checkout counter during shopping. In many cases customers can then also use the cart to transport their purchased goods to their vehicles, but some carts are designed to prevent them from leaving the shop.

Exam Probability: **High**

44. *Answer choices:*

(see index for correct answer)

- a. Second-hand shop
- b. Buy Here Pay Here
- c. Shopping cart
- d. Hobby shop

Guidance: level 1

:: ::

A trade union is an association of workers forming a legal unit or legal personhood, usually called a "bargaining unit", which acts as bargaining agent and legal representative for a unit of employees in all matters of law or right arising from or in the administration of a collective agreement. Labour unions typically fund the formal organisation, head office, and legal team functions of the labour union through regular fees or union dues. The delegate staff of the labour union representation in the workforce are made up of workplace volunteers who are appointed by members in democratic elections.

Exam Probability: **High**

45. *Answer choices:*

(see index for correct answer)

- a. levels of analysis
- b. Labor union
- c. open system
- d. corporate values

Guidance: level 1

:: Cash flow ::

_____ s are narrowly interconnected with the concepts of value, interest rate and liquidity. A _____ that shall happen on a future day tN can be transformed into a _____ of the same value in t0.

Exam Probability: **Medium**

46. *Answer choices:*

(see index for correct answer)

- a. Cash flow forecasting
- b. Discounted cash flow
- c. Factoring
- d. Cash flow

Guidance: level 1

:: Payments ::

A _____ or government incentive is a form of financial aid or support extended to an economic sector generally with the aim of promoting economic and social policy. Although commonly extended from government, the term _____ can relate to any type of support – for example from NGOs or as implicit subsidies. Subsidies come in various forms including: direct and indirect.

Exam Probability: **Medium**

47. *Answer choices:*

(see index for correct answer)

- a. Market transition payments
- b. County payments
- c. KlickEx
- d. Payment

Guidance: level 1

:: Auctioneering ::

An _____ is a process of buying and selling goods or services by offering them up for bid, taking bids, and then selling the item to the highest bidder. The open ascending price _____ is arguably the most common form of _____ in use today. Participants bid openly against one another, with each subsequent bid required to be higher than the previous bid. An _____ eer may announce prices, bidders may call out their bids themselves, or bids may be submitted electronically with the highest current bid publicly displayed. In a Dutch _____, the _____ eer begins with a high asking price for some quantity of like items; the price is lowered until a participant is willing to accept the _____ eer's price for some quantity of the goods in the lot or until the seller's reserve price is met. While _____ s are most associated in the public imagination with the sale of antiques, paintings, rare collectibles and expensive wines, _____ s are also used for commodities, livestock, radio spectrum and used cars. In economic theory, an _____ may refer to any mechanism or set of trading rules for exchange.

Exam Probability: **High**

48. *Answer choices:*

(see index for correct answer)

- a. Unique bid auction
- b. Auction
- c. English auction
- d. Camden auction

Guidance: level 1

:: ::

_____ characterises the behaviour of a system or model whose components interact in multiple ways and follow local rules, meaning there is no reasonable higher instruction to define the various possible interactions.

Exam Probability: **Low**

49. *Answer choices:*

(see index for correct answer)

- a. Complexity
- b. surface-level diversity
- c. hierarchical
- d. levels of analysis

Guidance: level 1

:: Insolvency ::

_____ is a legal process through which people or other entities who cannot repay debts to creditors may seek relief from some or all of their debts. In most jurisdictions, _____ is imposed by a court order, often initiated by the debtor.

Exam Probability: **Medium**

50. *Answer choices:*

(see index for correct answer)

- a. Conservatorship
- b. Liquidation
- c. Bankruptcy
- d. Official Committee of Equity Security Holders

Guidance: level 1

:: Banking ::

A _____ is a financial institution that accepts deposits from the public and creates credit. Lending activities can be performed either directly or indirectly through capital markets. Due to their importance in the financial stability of a country, _____ s are highly regulated in most countries. Most nations have institutionalized a system known as fractional reserve _____ ing under which _____ s hold liquid assets equal to only a portion of their current liabilities. In addition to other regulations intended to ensure liquidity, _____ s are generally subject to minimum capital requirements based on an international set of capital standards, known as the Basel Accords.

Exam Probability: **High**

51. *Answer choices:*

(see index for correct answer)

- a. Service release premium
- b. Bank
- c. Bank secrecy
- d. Giropay

Guidance: level 1

:: ::

_____ is the production of products for use or sale using labour and machines, tools, chemical and biological processing, or formulation. The term may refer to a range of human activity, from handicraft to high tech, but is most commonly applied to industrial design, in which raw materials are transformed into finished goods on a large scale. Such finished goods may be sold to other manufacturers for the production of other, more complex products, such as aircraft, household appliances, furniture, sports equipment or automobiles, or sold to wholesalers, who in turn sell them to retailers, who then sell them to end users and consumers.

Exam Probability: **Low**

52. *Answer choices:*

(see index for correct answer)

- a. hierarchical perspective
- b. Manufacturing
- c. information systems assessment
- d. functional perspective

Guidance: level 1

:: Management ::

Logistics is generally the detailed organization and implementation of a complex operation. In a general business sense, logistics is the management of the flow of things between the point of origin and the point of consumption in order to meet requirements of customers or corporations. The resources managed in logistics may include tangible goods such as materials, equipment, and supplies, as well as food and other consumable items. The logistics of physical items usually involves the integration of information flow, materials handling, production, packaging, inventory, transportation, warehousing, and often security.

Exam Probability: **Medium**

53. *Answer choices:*
(see index for correct answer)

- a. Cross ownership
- b. Perth leadership outcome model
- c. Logistics Management
- d. Identity formation

Guidance: level 1

:: Management ::

The term _____ refers to measures designed to increase the degree of autonomy and self-determination in people and in communities in order to enable them to represent their interests in a responsible and self-determined way, acting on their own authority. It is the process of becoming stronger and more confident, especially in controlling one's life and claiming one's rights. _____ as action refers both to the process of self-_____ and to professional support of people, which enables them to overcome their sense of powerlessness and lack of influence, and to recognize and use their resources. To do work with power.

Exam Probability: **Low**

54. *Answer choices:*
(see index for correct answer)

- a. Product differentiation
- b. Empowerment
- c. Corporate recovery
- d. Innovation management

Guidance: level 1

:: Payment systems ::

Amazon Pay is an online payments processing service that is owned by Amazon. Launched in 2007, Amazon Pay uses the consumer base of Amazon.com and focuses on giving users the option to pay with their Amazon accounts on external merchant websites. As of January 2019 the service is available in Austria, Belgium, Cyprus, Germany, Denmark, Spain, France, Hungary, Luxembourg, Republic of Ireland, India, Italy, Japan, Netherlands, Portugal, Sweden, United Kingdom, United States.

Exam Probability: **Medium**

55. *Answer choices:*

(see index for correct answer)

- a. Cheque guarantee card
- b. Electronic Benefit Transfer
- c. Uniform Customs and Practice for Documentary Credits
- d. Amazon Payments

Guidance: level 1

:: Commercial item transport and distribution ::

A _____ in common law countries is a person or company that transports goods or people for any person or company and that is responsible for any possible loss of the goods during transport. A _____ offers its services to the general public under license or authority provided by a regulatory body. The regulatory body has usually been granted "ministerial authority" by the legislation that created it. The regulatory body may create, interpret, and enforce its regulations upon the _____ with independence and finality, as long as it acts within the bounds of the enabling legislation.

Exam Probability: **Low**

56. *Answer choices:*

(see index for correct answer)

- a. Stillage
- b. Drop shipping
- c. Common carrier
- d. USA Truck

Guidance: level 1

_____ or accountancy is the measurement, processing, and communication of financial information about economic entities such as businesses and corporations. The modern field was established by the Italian mathematician Luca Pacioli in 1494. _____, which has been called the "language of business", measures the results of an organization's economic activities and conveys this information to a variety of users, including investors, creditors, management, and regulators. Practitioners of _____ are known as accountants. The terms "_____" and "financial reporting" are often used as synonyms.

Exam Probability: **Medium**

57. *Answer choices:*

(see index for correct answer)

- a. functional perspective
- b. Sarbanes-Oxley act of 2002
- c. Accounting
- d. information systems assessment

Guidance: level 1

:: Warrants issued in Hong Kong Stock Exchange ::

_____ is a chemical element with symbol Ag and atomic number 47. A soft, white, lustrous transition metal, it exhibits the highest electrical conductivity, thermal conductivity, and reflectivity of any metal. The metal is found in the Earth's crust in the pure, free elemental form, as an alloy with gold and other metals, and in minerals such as argentite and chlorargyrite. Most _____ is produced as a byproduct of copper, gold, lead, and zinc refining.

Exam Probability: **High**

58. *Answer choices:*

(see index for correct answer)

- a. Xtep
- b. BOC Hong Kong
- c. Silver
- d. Shui On Land

Guidance: level 1

_____ is "property consisting of land and the buildings on it, along with its natural resources such as crops, minerals or water; immovable property of this nature; an interest vested in this an item of real property, buildings or housing in general. Also: the business of _____; the profession of buying, selling, or renting land, buildings, or housing." It is a legal term used in jurisdictions whose legal system is derived from English common law, such as India, England, Wales, Northern Ireland, United States, Canada, Pakistan, Australia, and New Zealand.

Exam Probability: **High**

59. *Answer choices:*

(see index for correct answer)

- a. hierarchical
- b. open system
- c. Sarbanes-Oxley act of 2002
- d. interpersonal communication

Guidance: level 1

Business ethics

Business ethics (also known as corporate ethics) is a form of applied ethics or professional ethics, that examines ethical principles and moral or ethical problems that can arise in a business environment. It applies to all aspects of business conduct and is relevant to the conduct of individuals and entire organizations. These ethics originate from individuals, organizational statements or from the legal system. These norms, values, ethical, and unethical practices are what is used to guide business. They help those businesses maintain a better connection with their stakeholders.

:: Parental leave ::

_____, or family leave, is an employee benefit available in almost all countries. The term "_____" may include maternity, paternity, and adoption leave; or may be used distinctively from "maternity leave" and "paternity leave" to describe separate family leave available to either parent to care for small children. In some countries and jurisdictions, "family leave" also includes leave provided to care for ill family members. Often, the minimum benefits and eligibility requirements are stipulated by law.

Exam Probability: **Medium**

1. *Answer choices:*

(see index for correct answer)

- a. Parental leave
- b. Geduldig v. Aiello
- c. Additional Paternity Leave Regulations 2010
- d. Pregnancy discrimination

Guidance: level 1

:: ::

_____ Ltd. is the world's 2nd largest offshore drilling contractor and is based in Vernier, Switzerland. The company has offices in 20 countries, including Switzerland, Canada, United States, Norway, Scotland, India, Brazil, Singapore, Indonesia and Malaysia.

Exam Probability: **Low**

2. *Answer choices:*

(see index for correct answer)

- a. surface-level diversity
- b. Transocean
- c. co-culture
- d. hierarchical

Guidance: level 1

:: Culture ::

_____ is a society which is characterized by individualism, which is the prioritization or emphasis, of the individual over the entire group. _____ s are oriented around the self, being independent instead of identifying with a group mentality. They see each other as only loosely linked, and value personal goals over group interests. _____ s tend to have a more diverse population and are characterized with emphasis on personal achievements, and a rational assessment of both the beneficial and detrimental aspects of relationships with others. _____ s have such unique aspects of communication as being a low power-distance culture and having a low-context communication style. The United States, Australia, Great Britain, Canada, the Netherlands, and New Zealand have been identified as highly _____ s.

Exam Probability: **Medium**

3. *Answer choices:*

(see index for correct answer)

- a. Intracultural
- b. Low-context
- c. Low-context culture
- d. cultural framework

Guidance: level 1

:: ::

_____ is "property consisting of land and the buildings on it, along with its natural resources such as crops, minerals or water; immovable property of this nature; an interest vested in this an item of real property, buildings or housing in general. Also: the business of _____ ; the profession of buying, selling, or renting land, buildings, or housing." It is a legal term used in jurisdictions whose legal system is derived from English common law, such as India, England, Wales, Northern Ireland, United States, Canada, Pakistan, Australia, and New Zealand.

Exam Probability: **Medium**

4. *Answer choices:*
(see index for correct answer)

- a. Character
- b. interpersonal communication
- c. hierarchical
- d. Real estate

Guidance: level 1

:: ::

The Federal National Mortgage Association, commonly known as _____, is a United States government-sponsored enterprise and, since 1968, a publicly traded company. Founded in 1938 during the Great Depression as part of the New Deal, the corporation's purpose is to expand the secondary mortgage market by securitizing mortgage loans in the form of mortgage-backed securities, allowing lenders to reinvest their assets into more lending and in effect increasing the number of lenders in the mortgage market by reducing the reliance on locally based savings and loan associations. Its brother organization is the Federal Home Loan Mortgage Corporation, better known as Freddie Mac. As of 2018, _____ is ranked #21 on the Fortune 500 rankings of the largest United States corporations by total revenue.

Exam Probability: **Low**

5. *Answer choices:*

(see index for correct answer)

- a. functional perspective
- b. cultural
- c. interpersonal communication
- d. Sarbanes-Oxley act of 2002

Guidance: level 1

:: Mortgage ::

In finance, _____ means making loans to people who may have difficulty maintaining the repayment schedule, sometimes reflecting setbacks, such as unemployment, divorce, medical emergencies, etc. Historically, subprime borrowers were defined as having FICO scores below 600, although "this has varied over time and circumstances."

Exam Probability: **High**

6. *Answer choices:*

(see index for correct answer)

- a. Bank walkaway
- b. Subprime lending
- c. Mortgage calculator
- d. Russian mortgage certificate

Guidance: level 1

:: ::

The _____, the Calvinist work ethic or the Puritan work ethic is a work ethic concept in theology, sociology, economics and history that emphasizes that hard work, discipline and frugality are a result of a person's subscription to the values espoused by the Protestant faith, particularly Calvinism. The phrase was initially coined in 1904–1905 by Max Weber in his book The Protestant Ethic and the Spirit of Capitalism.

Exam Probability: **Medium**

7. *Answer choices:*

(see index for correct answer)

- a. hierarchical
- b. Protestant work ethic
- c. hierarchical perspective
- d. information systems assessment

Guidance: level 1

:: Production and manufacturing ::

_____ is a set of techniques and tools for process improvement. Though as a shortened form it may be found written as 6S, it should not be confused with the methodology known as 6S.

Exam Probability: **Low**

8. *Answer choices:*

(see index for correct answer)

- a. Six Sigma
- b. Experience curve
- c. SafetyBUS p
- d. EFQM Excellence Model

Guidance: level 1

:: ::

_____ is the practice of deliberately managing the spread of information between an individual or an organization and the public. _____ may include an organization or individual gaining exposure to their audiences using topics of public interest and news items that do not require direct payment. This differentiates it from advertising as a form of marketing communications. _____ is the idea of creating coverage for clients for free, rather than marketing or advertising. But now, advertising is also a part of greater PR Activities. An example of good _____ would be generating an article featuring a client, rather than paying for the client to be advertised next to the article. The aim of _____ is to inform the public, prospective customers, investors, partners, employees, and other stakeholders and ultimately persuade them to maintain a positive or favorable view about the organization, its leadership, products, or political decisions. _____ professionals typically work for PR and marketing firms, businesses and companies, government, and public officials as PIOs and nongovernmental organizations, and nonprofit organizations. Jobs central to _____ include account coordinator, account executive, account supervisor, and media relations manager.

Exam Probability: **High**

9. *Answer choices:*

(see index for correct answer)

- a. Public relations
- b. interpersonal communication
- c. cultural

- d. personal values

Guidance: level 1

:: Leadership ::

_____ is a theory of leadership where a leader works with teams to identify needed change, creating a vision to guide the change through inspiration, and executing the change in tandem with committed members of a group; it is an integral part of the Full Range Leadership Model. _____ serves to enhance the motivation, morale, and job performance of followers through a variety of mechanisms; these include connecting the follower's sense of identity and self to a project and to the collective identity of the organization; being a role model for followers in order to inspire them and to raise their interest in the project; challenging followers to take greater ownership for their work, and understanding the strengths and weaknesses of followers, allowing the leader to align followers with tasks that enhance their performance.

Exam Probability: **Low**

10. *Answer choices:*
(see index for correct answer)

- a. Situational leadership
- b. Transformational leadership
- c. Three levels of leadership model
- d. Complex adaptive leadership

Guidance: level 1

:: Market-based policy instruments ::

Cause marketing is defined as a type of corporate social responsibility, in which a company's promotional campaign has the dual purpose of increasing profitability while bettering society.

Exam Probability: **Medium**

11. *Answer choices:*
(see index for correct answer)

- a. Ecorates
- b. Tree credits
- c. Cobra effect
- d. Regional Clean Air Incentives Market

Guidance: level 1

:: Labour relations ::

_____ is a field of study that can have different meanings depending on the context in which it is used. In an international context, it is a subfield of labor history that studies the human relations with regard to work – in its broadest sense – and how this connects to questions of social inequality. It explicitly encompasses unregulated, historical, and non-Western forms of labor. Here, _____ define "for or with whom one works and under what rules. These rules determine the type of work, type and amount of remuneration, working hours, degrees of physical and psychological strain, as well as the degree of freedom and autonomy associated with the work."

Exam Probability: **Low**

12. *Answer choices:*

(see index for correct answer)

- a. Labor relations
- b. Lockout
- c. Eurocadres
- d. Union representative

Guidance: level 1

:: ::

The _____ is an institution of the European Union, responsible for proposing legislation, implementing decisions, upholding the EU treaties and managing the day-to-day business of the EU. Commissioners swear an oath at the European Court of Justice in Luxembourg City, pledging to respect the treaties and to be completely independent in carrying out their duties during their mandate. Unlike in the Council of the European Union, where members are directly and indirectly elected, and the European Parliament, where members are directly elected, the Commissioners are proposed by the Council of the European Union, on the basis of suggestions made by the national governments, and then appointed by the European Council after the approval of the European Parliament.

Exam Probability: **Medium**

13. *Answer choices:*

(see index for correct answer)

- a. Sarbanes-Oxley act of 2002
- b. hierarchical perspective
- c. information systems assessment
- d. functional perspective

Guidance: level 1

:: Anti-capitalism ::

_____ is a range of economic and social systems characterised by social ownership of the means of production and workers' self-management, as well as the political theories and movements associated with them. Social ownership can be public, collective or cooperative ownership, or citizen ownership of equity. There are many varieties of _____ and there is no single definition encapsulating all of them, with social ownership being the common element shared by its various forms.

Exam Probability: **Low**

14. *Answer choices:*

(see index for correct answer)

- a. Socialism
- b. Deep Green Resistance
- c. Invisible Party
- d. Free association

Guidance: level 1

:: ::

The _____ to Fight AIDS, Tuberculosis and Malaria is an international financing organization that aims to "attract, leverage and invest additional resources to end the epidemics of HIV/AIDS, tuberculosis and malaria to support attainment of the Sustainable Development Goals established by the United Nations." A public-private partnership, the organization maintains its secretariat in Geneva, Switzerland. The organization began operations in January 2002. Microsoft founder Bill Gates was one of the first private foundations among many bilateral donors to provide seed money for the partnership.

Exam Probability: **Medium**

15. *Answer choices:*

(see index for correct answer)

- a. cultural
- b. hierarchical perspective
- c. Global Fund
- d. personal values

Guidance: level 1

:: White-collar criminals ::

_____ refers to financially motivated, nonviolent crime committed by businesses and government professionals. It was first defined by the sociologist Edwin Sutherland in 1939 as "a crime committed by a person of respectability and high social status in the course of their occupation". Typical _____ s could include wage theft, fraud, bribery, Ponzi schemes, insider trading, labor racketeering, embezzlement, cybercrime, copyright infringement, money laundering, identity theft, and forgery. Lawyers can specialize in _____ .

Exam Probability: **High**

16. *Answer choices:*

(see index for correct answer)

- a. White-collar crime
- b. Du Jun

Guidance: level 1

:: ::

A _____ is a set of rules, often written, with regards to clothing. _____ s are created out of social perceptions and norms, and vary based on purpose, circumstances and occasions. Different societies and cultures are likely to have different _____ s.

Exam Probability: **High**

17. *Answer choices:*

(see index for correct answer)

- a. Character
- b. similarity-attraction theory
- c. interpersonal communication
- d. Dress code

Guidance: level 1

:: ::

_____ was a philosopher during the Classical period in Ancient Greece, the founder of the Lyceum and the Peripatetic school of philosophy and Aristotelian tradition. Along with his teacher Plato, he is considered the "Father of Western Philosophy". His writings cover many subjects – including physics, biology, zoology, metaphysics, logic, ethics, aesthetics, poetry, theatre, music, rhetoric, psychology, linguistics, economics, politics and government. _____ provided a complex synthesis of the various philosophies existing prior to him, and it was above all from his teachings that the West inherited its intellectual lexicon, as well as problems and methods of inquiry. As a result, his philosophy has exerted a unique influence on almost every form of knowledge in the West and it continues to be a subject of contemporary philosophical discussion.

Exam Probability: **Low**

18. *Answer choices:*

(see index for correct answer)

- a. functional perspective
- b. hierarchical perspective
- c. similarity-attraction theory
- d. Aristotle

Guidance: level 1

:: Social enterprise ::

Corporate social responsibility is a type of international private business self-regulation. While once it was possible to describe CSR as an internal organisational policy or a corporate ethic strategy, that time has passed as various international laws have been developed and various organisations have used their authority to push it beyond individual or even industry-wide initiatives. While it has been considered a form of corporate self-regulation for some time, over the last decade or so it has moved considerably from voluntary decisions at the level of individual organisations, to mandatory schemes at regional, national and even transnational levels.

Exam Probability: **High**

19. *Answer choices:*

(see index for correct answer)

- a. Social enterprise
- b. Social venture

Guidance: level 1

:: Business ethics ::

_____ is a type of harassment technique that relates to a sexual nature and the unwelcome or inappropriate promise of rewards in exchange for sexual favors. _____ includes a range of actions from mild transgressions to sexual abuse or assault. Harassment can occur in many different social settings such as the workplace, the home, school, churches, etc. Harassers or victims may be of any gender.

Exam Probability: **Medium**

20. *Answer choices:*

(see index for correct answer)

- a. Being Globally Responsible Conference
- b. Journal of Business Ethics
- c. Contingent work
- d. Corporate social responsibility

Guidance: level 1

:: Professional ethics ::

In the mental health field, a _____ is a situation where multiple roles exist between a therapist, or other mental health practitioner, and a client. _____ s are also referred to as multiple relationships, and these two terms are used interchangeably in the research literature. The American Psychological Association Ethical Principles of Psychologists and Code of Conduct is a resource that outlines ethical standards and principles to which practitioners are expected to adhere. Standard 3.05 of the APA ethics code outlines the definition of multiple relationships. Dual or multiple relationships occur when.

Exam Probability: **Low**

21. *Answer choices:*

(see index for correct answer)

- a. Dual relationship
- b. ethical code
- c. professional conduct

Guidance: level 1

:: ::

A _____ is a problem offering two possibilities, neither of which is unambiguously acceptable or preferable. The possibilities are termed the horns of the _____ , a clichéd usage, but distinguishing the _____ from other kinds of predicament as a matter of usage.

Exam Probability: **High**

22. *Answer choices:*

(see index for correct answer)

- a. hierarchical perspective
- b. process perspective
- c. interpersonal communication
- d. Dilemma

Guidance: level 1

:: ::

An _____ is the release of a liquid petroleum hydrocarbon into the environment, especially the marine ecosystem, due to human activity, and is a form of pollution. The term is usually given to marine _____ s, where oil is released into the ocean or coastal waters, but spills may also occur on land. _____ s may be due to releases of crude oil from tankers, offshore platforms, drilling rigs and wells, as well as spills of refined petroleum products and their by-products, heavier fuels used by large ships such as bunker fuel, or the spill of any oily refuse or waste oil.

Exam Probability: **High**

23. *Answer choices:*

(see index for correct answer)

- a. Oil spill
- b. interpersonal communication
- c. Sarbanes-Oxley act of 2002
- d. imperative

Guidance: level 1

:: Hazard analysis ::

Broadly speaking, a _____ is the combined effort of 1. identifying and analyzing potential events that may negatively impact individuals, assets, and/or the environment ; and 2. making judgments "on the tolerability of the risk on the basis of a risk analysis" while considering influencing factors . Put in simpler terms, a _____ analyzes what can go wrong, how likely it is to happen, what the potential consequences are, and how tolerable the identified risk is. As part of this process, the resulting determination of risk may be expressed in a quantitative or qualitative fashion. The _____ is an inherent part of an overall risk management strategy, which attempts to, after a _____ , "introduce control measures to eliminate or reduce" any potential risk-related consequences.

Exam Probability: **Low**

24. *Answer choices:*

(see index for correct answer)

- a. Hazard identification
- b. Swiss cheese model
- c. Hazardous Materials Identification System

Guidance: level 1

:: Waste ::

_____ is any unwanted material in all forms that can cause harm. Many of today's household products such as televisions, computers and phones contain toxic chemicals that can pollute the air and contaminate soil and water. Disposing of such waste is a major public health issue.

Exam Probability: **Low**

25. *Answer choices:*

(see index for correct answer)

- a. Marine debris
- b. Biodegradable waste
- c. Metabolic waste
- d. Zero waste agriculture

Guidance: level 1

:: Social philosophy ::

The "_____" is a method of determining the morality of issues. It asks a decision-maker to make a choice about a social or moral issue, and assumes that they have enough information to know the consequences of their possible decisions for everyone but would not know, or would not take into account, which person he or she is. The theory contends that not knowing one's ultimate position in society would lead to the creation of a just system, as the decision-maker would not want to make decisions which benefit a certain group at the expense of another, because the decision-maker could theoretically end up in either group. The idea has been present in moral philosophy at least since the eighteenth century. The _____ is part of a long tradition of thinking in terms of a social contract that includes the writings of Immanuel Kant, Thomas Hobbes, John Locke, Jean Jacques Rousseau, and Thomas Jefferson. Prominent modern names attached to it are John Harsanyi and John Rawls.

Exam Probability: **Low**

26. *Answer choices:*

(see index for correct answer)

- a. vacancy chain
- b. Societal attitudes towards abortion
- c. Veil of ignorance
- d. Invisible hand

Guidance: level 1

:: ::

A _____ is the ability to carry out a task with determined results often within a given amount of time, energy, or both. _____ s can often be divided into domain-general and domain-specific _____ s. For example, in the domain of work, some general _____ s would include time management, teamwork and leadership, self-motivation and others, whereas domain-specific _____ s would be used only for a certain job. _____ usually requires certain environmental stimuli and situations to assess the level of _____ being shown and used.

Exam Probability: **Medium**

27. *Answer choices:*

(see index for correct answer)

- a. Skill
- b. open system
- c. personal values
- d. surface-level diversity

Guidance: level 1

:: Auditing ::

_____ , as defined by accounting and auditing, is a process for assuring of an organization's objectives in operational effectiveness and efficiency, reliable financial reporting, and compliance with laws, regulations and policies. A broad concept, _____ involves everything that controls risks to an organization.

Exam Probability: **High**

28. *Answer choices:*

(see index for correct answer)

- a. International Register of Certificated Auditors
- b. Assurance services
- c. Internal control
- d. Clinical audit

Guidance: level 1

:: Pyramid and Ponzi schemes ::

_____ was an Italian swindler and con artist in the U.S. and Canada. His aliases include Charles Ponci, Carlo, and Charles P. Bianchi. Born and raised in Italy, he became known in the early 1920s as a swindler in North America for his money-making scheme. He promised clients a 50% profit within 45 days or 100% profit within 90 days, by buying discounted postal reply coupons in other countries and redeeming them at face value in the United States as a form of arbitrage. In reality, Ponzi was paying earlier investors using the investments of later investors. While this type of fraudulent investment scheme was not originally invented by Ponzi, it became so identified with him that it now is referred to as a "Ponzi scheme". His scheme ran for over a year before it collapsed, costing his "investors" $20 million.

Exam Probability: **High**

29. *Answer choices:*

(see index for correct answer)

- a. Holiday Magic
- b. Angelo Haligiannis
- c. Charles Ponzi
- d. Scott W. Rothstein

Guidance: level 1

:: Water law ::

The _____ is the primary federal law in the United States governing water pollution. Its objective is to restore and maintain the chemical, physical, and biological integrity of the nation's waters; recognizing the responsibilities of the states in addressing pollution and providing assistance to states to do so, including funding for publicly owned treatment works for the improvement of wastewater treatment; and maintaining the integrity of wetlands. It is one of the United States' first and most influential modern environmental laws. As with many other major U.S. federal environmental statutes, it is administered by the U.S. Environmental Protection Agency, in coordination with state governments. Its implementing regulations are codified at 40 C.F.R. Subchapters D, N, and O.

Exam Probability: **Low**

30. *Answer choices:*

(see index for correct answer)

- a. Water law

- b. Permanent water rights
- c. Return flow
- d. Clean Water Act

Guidance: level 1

:: ::

The _____ Group is a global financial investment management and insurance company headquartered in Des Moines, Iowa.

Exam Probability: **Low**

31. *Answer choices:*

(see index for correct answer)

- a. interpersonal communication
- b. levels of analysis
- c. process perspective
- d. imperative

Guidance: level 1

:: Workplace ::

In business management, _____ is a management style whereby a manager closely observes and/or controls the work of his/her subordinates or employees.

Exam Probability: **Medium**

32. *Answer choices:*

(see index for correct answer)

- a. Toxic workplace
- b. performance review
- c. Workplace harassment
- d. Micromanagement

Guidance: level 1

:: Power (social and political) ::

_____ is a form of reverence gained by a leader who has strong interpersonal relationship skills. _____, as an aspect of personal power, becomes particularly important as organizational leadership becomes increasingly about collaboration and influence, rather than command and control.

Exam Probability: **High**

33. *Answer choices:*

(see index for correct answer)

- a. Referent power
- b. Hard power
- c. need for power

Guidance: level 1

:: Nepotism ::

_____ is the granting of favour to relatives in various fields, including business, politics, entertainment, sports, religion and other activities. The term originated with the assignment of nephews to important positions by Catholic popes and bishops. Trading parliamentary employment for favors is a modern-day example of _____ . Criticism of _____, however, can be found in ancient Indian texts such as the Kural literature.

Exam Probability: **Low**

34. *Answer choices:*

(see index for correct answer)

- a. Nepotism
- b. Cardinal-nephew
- c. Monklandsgate
- d. Wasta

Guidance: level 1

:: Renewable energy ::

_____ is the conversion of energy from sunlight into electricity, either directly using photovoltaics, indirectly using concentrated _____, or a combination. Concentrated _____ systems use lenses or mirrors and tracking systems to focus a large area of sunlight into a small beam. Photovoltaic cells convert light into an electric current using the photovoltaic effect.

Exam Probability: **Low**

35. *Answer choices:*

(see index for correct answer)

- a. Solar power
- b. Crosswind kite power
- c. Carbon Recycling International
- d. Biofuel

Guidance: level 1

:: Private equity ::

In finance, a high-yield bond is a bond that is rated below investment grade. These bonds have a higher risk of default or other adverse credit events, but typically pay higher yields than better quality bonds in order to make them attractive to investors.

Exam Probability: **Low**

36. *Answer choices:*

(see index for correct answer)

- a. Venture capital
- b. Junk bond
- c. co-investment
- d. Airwide Solutions

Guidance: level 1

:: ::

In regulatory jurisdictions that provide for it, _____ is a group of laws and organizations designed to ensure the rights of consumers as well as fair trade, competition and accurate information in the marketplace. The laws are designed to prevent the businesses that engage in fraud or specified unfair practices from gaining an advantage over competitors. They may also provides additional protection for those most vulnerable in society. _____ laws are a form of government regulation that aim to protect the rights of consumers. For example, a government may require businesses to disclose detailed information about products—particularly in areas where safety or public health is an issue, such as food.

Exam Probability: **High**

37. *Answer choices:*

(see index for correct answer)

- a. Consumer Protection
- b. deep-level diversity
- c. levels of analysis
- d. open system

Guidance: level 1

:: Human resource management ::

> _____ encompasses values and behaviors that contribute to the unique social and psychological environment of a business. The _____ influences the way people interact, the context within which knowledge is created, the resistance they will have towards certain changes, and ultimately the way they share knowledge. _____ represents the collective values, beliefs and principles of organizational members and is a product of factors such as history, product, market, technology, strategy, type of employees, management style, and national culture; culture includes the organization's vision, values, norms, systems, symbols, language, assumptions, environment, location, beliefs and habits.

Exam Probability: **High**

38. *Answer choices:*

(see index for correct answer)

- a. Recruitment process outsourcing
- b. Adecco Group North America
- c. Organizational culture
- d. Autonomous work group

Guidance: level 1

:: Carbon finance ::

The _____ is an international treaty which extends the 1992 United Nations Framework Convention on Climate Change that commits state parties to reduce greenhouse gas emissions, based on the scientific consensus that global warming is occurring and it is extremely likely that human-made CO2 emissions have predominantly caused it. The _____ was adopted in Kyoto, Japan on 11 December 1997 and entered into force on 16 February 2005. There are currently 192 parties to the Protocol.

Exam Probability: **Medium**

39. *Answer choices:*
(see index for correct answer)

- a. Western Climate Initiative
- b. Kyoto Protocol
- c. Ecosecurities
- d. FirstCarbon Solutions

Guidance: level 1

:: Business ethics ::

_____ is an area of applied ethics which deals with the moral principles behind the operation and regulation of marketing. Some areas of _____ overlap with media ethics.

Exam Probability: **High**

40. *Answer choices:*

(see index for correct answer)

- a. Walmarting
- b. Marketing ethics
- c. The Crooked E: The Unshredded Truth About Enron
- d. Corporate sustainable profitability

Guidance: level 1

:: Majority–minority relations ::

It was established as axiomatic in anthropological research by Franz Boas in the first few decades of the 20th century and later popularized by his students. Boas first articulated the idea in 1887: "civilization is not something absolute, but ... is relative, and ... our ideas and conceptions are true only so far as our civilization goes". However, Boas did not coin the term.

Exam Probability: **Medium**

41. *Answer choices:*

(see index for correct answer)

- a. cultural dissonance
- b. Cultural relativism
- c. positive discrimination

Guidance: level 1

:: Law ::

_____ is a body of law which defines the role, powers, and structure of different entities within a state, namely, the executive, the parliament or legislature, and the judiciary; as well as the basic rights of citizens and, in federal countries such as the United States and Canada, the relationship between the central government and state, provincial, or territorial governments.

Exam Probability: **Medium**

42. *Answer choices:*

(see index for correct answer)

- a. Comparative law
- b. Constitutional law

Guidance: level 1

:: Price fixing convictions ::

> _____ AG is a German multinational conglomerate company headquartered in Berlin and Munich and the largest industrial manufacturing company in Europe with branch offices abroad.

Exam Probability: **Medium**

43. *Answer choices:*

(see index for correct answer)

- a. JJB Sports
- b. AGC Glass Europe
- c. Siemens
- d. Grolsch Brewery

Guidance: level 1

:: ::

_____ Corporation was an American energy, commodities, and services company based in Houston, Texas. It was founded in 1985 as a merger between Houston Natural Gas and InterNorth, both relatively small regional companies. Before its bankruptcy on December 3, 2001, _____ employed approximately 29,000 staff and was a major electricity, natural gas, communications and pulp and paper company, with claimed revenues of nearly $101 billion during 2000. Fortune named _____ "America's Most Innovative Company" for six consecutive years.

Exam Probability: **Medium**

44. *Answer choices:*

(see index for correct answer)

- a. imperative
- b. interpersonal communication
- c. Enron
- d. empathy

Guidance: level 1

_____ or accountancy is the measurement, processing, and communication of financial information about economic entities such as businesses and corporations. The modern field was established by the Italian mathematician Luca Pacioli in 1494. _____ , which has been called the "language of business", measures the results of an organization's economic activities and conveys this information to a variety of users, including investors, creditors, management, and regulators. Practitioners of _____ are known as accountants. The terms "_____" and "financial reporting" are often used as synonyms.

Exam Probability: **Medium**

45. *Answer choices:*

(see index for correct answer)

- a. cultural
- b. deep-level diversity
- c. Character
- d. open system

Guidance: level 1

:: Separation of investment and commercial banking ::

The _____ refers to § 619 of the Dodd–Frank Wall Street Reform and Consumer Protection Act. The rule was originally proposed by American economist and former United States Federal Reserve Chairman Paul Volcker to restrict United States banks from making certain kinds of speculative investments that do not benefit their customers. Volcker argued that such speculative activity played a key role in the financial crisis of 2007–2008. The rule is often referred to as a ban on proprietary trading by commercial banks, whereby deposits are used to trade on the bank's own accounts, although a number of exceptions to this ban were included in the Dodd-Frank law.

Exam Probability: **Low**

46. *Answer choices:*

(see index for correct answer)

- a. Independent Commission on Banking
- b. Commercial bank
- c. Bank Holding Company Act
- d. Bancassurance

Guidance: level 1

:: Product certification ::

_____ is food produced by methods that comply with the standards of organic farming. Standards vary worldwide, but organic farming features practices that cycle resources, promote ecological balance, and conserve biodiversity. Organizations regulating organic products may restrict the use of certain pesticides and fertilizers in the farming methods used to produce such products. _____ s typically are not processed using irradiation, industrial solvents, or synthetic food additives.

Exam Probability: **High**

47. *Answer choices:*

(see index for correct answer)

- a. SGS S.A.
- b. ECOCERT
- c. Organic food
- d. Farm assurance

Guidance: level 1

:: Utilitarianism ::

_____ is a school of thought that argues that the pursuit of pleasure and intrinsic goods are the primary or most important goals of human life. A hedonist strives to maximize net pleasure. However upon finally gaining said pleasure, happiness may remain stationary.

Exam Probability: **Low**

48. Answer choices:

(see index for correct answer)

- a. The Methods of Ethics
- b. Preference utilitarianism
- c. Paradox of hedonism
- d. Mere addition paradox

Guidance: level 1

:: Cognitive biases ::

In personality psychology, _____ is the degree to which people believe that they have control over the outcome of events in their lives, as opposed to external forces beyond their control. Understanding of the concept was developed by Julian B. Rotter in 1954, and has since become an aspect of personality studies. A person's "locus" is conceptualized as internal or external.

Exam Probability: **Medium**

49. Answer choices:

(see index for correct answer)

- a. Hawthorne effect
- b. Negativity bias
- c. Locus of control
- d. Illusion of external agency

Guidance: level 1

:: Marketing ::

_____ is the marketing of products that are presumed to be environmentally safe. It incorporates a broad range of activities, including product modification, changes to the production process, sustainable packaging, as well as modifying advertising. Yet defining _____ is not a simple task where several meanings intersect and contradict each other; an example of this will be the existence of varying social, environmental and retail definitions attached to this term. Other similar terms used are environmental marketing and ecological marketing.

Exam Probability: **Low**

50. *Answer choices:*
(see index for correct answer)

- a. societal marketing
- b. Official statistics
- c. Green marketing
- d. Product lining

Guidance: level 1

:: Electronic feedback ::

_____ occurs when outputs of a system are routed back as inputs as part of a chain of cause-and-effect that forms a circuit or loop. The system can then be said to feed back into itself. The notion of cause-and-effect has to be handled carefully when applied to _____ systems.

Exam Probability: **Medium**

51. *Answer choices:*

(see index for correct answer)

- a. Positive feedback
- b. feedback loop

Guidance: level 1

:: Agricultural labor ::

The _____ of America, or more commonly just _____, is a labor union for farmworkers in the United States. It originated from the merger of two workers' rights organizations, the Agricultural Workers Organizing Committee led by organizer Larry Itliong, and the National Farm Workers Association led by César Chávez and Dolores Huerta. They became allied and transformed from workers' rights organizations into a union as a result of a series of strikes in 1965, when the mostly Filipino farmworkers of the AWOC in Delano, California initiated a grape strike, and the NFWA went on strike in support. As a result of the commonality in goals and methods, the NFWA and the AWOC formed the _____ Organizing Committee on August 22, 1966. This organization was accepted into the AFL-CIO in 1972 and changed its name to the _____ Union.

Exam Probability: **Low**

52. *Answer choices:*

(see index for correct answer)

- a. Kibbutz
- b. United Farm Workers
- c. Picking Cotton
- d. Prendeur

Guidance: level 1

:: Statutory law ::

_____ or statute law is written law set down by a body of legislature or by a singular legislator. This is as opposed to oral or customary law; or regulatory law promulgated by the executive or common law of the judiciary. Statutes may originate with national, state legislatures or local municipalities.

Exam Probability: **Low**

53. *Answer choices:*

(see index for correct answer)

- a. incorporation by reference
- b. ratification

- c. Statute of repose
- d. Statutory law

Guidance: level 1

:: Euthenics ::

_____ is an ethical framework and suggests that an entity, be it an organization or individual, has an obligation to act for the benefit of society at large. _____ is a duty every individual has to perform so as to maintain a balance between the economy and the ecosystems. A trade-off may exist between economic development, in the material sense, and the welfare of the society and environment, though this has been challenged by many reports over the past decade. _____ means sustaining the equilibrium between the two. It pertains not only to business organizations but also to everyone whose any action impacts the environment. This responsibility can be passive, by avoiding engaging in socially harmful acts, or active, by performing activities that directly advance social goals. _____ must be intergenerational since the actions of one generation have consequences on those following.

Exam Probability: **Low**

54. *Answer choices:*

(see index for correct answer)

- a. Family and consumer science
- b. Euthenics
- c. Home economics
- d. Minnie Cumnock Blodgett

Guidance: level 1

:: Business ethics ::

> _____ is a type of international private business self-regulation. While once it was possible to describe CSR as an internal organisational policy or a corporate ethic strategy, that time has passed as various international laws have been developed and various organisations have used their authority to push it beyond individual or even industry-wide initiatives. While it has been considered a form of corporate self-regulation for some time, over the last decade or so it has moved considerably from voluntary decisions at the level of individual organisations, to mandatory schemes at regional, national and even transnational levels.

Exam Probability: **Medium**

55. *Answer choices:*

(see index for correct answer)

- a. University of Illinois clout scandal
- b. Evolution of corporate social responsibility in India
- c. Corporate social responsibility
- d. Bribery Act 2010

Guidance: level 1

:: Social philosophy ::

The _____ describes the unintended social benefits of an individual's self-interested actions. Adam Smith first introduced the concept in The Theory of Moral Sentiments, written in 1759, invoking it in reference to income distribution. In this work, however, the idea of the market is not discussed, and the word "capitalism" is never used.

Exam Probability: **Medium**

56. *Answer choices:*

(see index for correct answer)

- a. Freedom to contract
- b. Societal attitudes towards abortion
- c. vacancy chain
- d. Invisible hand

Guidance: level 1

:: ::

Bernard Lawrence _____ is an American former market maker, investment advisor, financier, fraudster, and convicted felon, who is currently serving a federal prison sentence for offenses related to a massive Ponzi scheme. He is the former non-executive chairman of the NASDAQ stock market, the confessed operator of the largest Ponzi scheme in world history, and the largest financial fraud in U.S. history. Prosecutors estimated the fraud to be worth $64.8 billion based on the amounts in the accounts of _____ 's 4,800 clients as of November 30, 2008.

Exam Probability: **Low**

57. *Answer choices:*

(see index for correct answer)

- a. Sarbanes-Oxley act of 2002
- b. cultural
- c. functional perspective
- d. hierarchical

Guidance: level 1

:: Corporate scandals ::

The _____ was a privately held international group of financial services companies controlled by Allen Stanford, until it was seized by United States authorities in early 2009. Headquartered in the Galleria Tower II in Uptown Houston, Texas, it had 50 offices in several countries, mainly in the Americas, included the Stanford International Bank, and said it managed US$8.5 billion of assets for more than 30,000 clients in 136 countries on six continents. On February 17, 2009, U.S. Federal agents placed the company into receivership due to charges of fraud. Ten days later, the U.S. Securities and Exchange Commission amended its complaint to accuse Stanford of turning the company into a "massive Ponzi scheme".

Exam Probability: **Medium**

58. *Answer choices:*

(see index for correct answer)

- a. Terra Securities scandal
- b. Central Energy Italian Gas Holding
- c. Stanford Financial Group
- d. YoungStartup Ventures

Guidance: level 1

:: ::

A _____ is a proceeding by a party or parties against another in the civil court of law. The archaic term "suit in law" is found in only a small number of laws still in effect today. The term "_____" is used in reference to a civil action brought in a court of law in which a plaintiff, a party who claims to have incurred loss as a result of a defendant's actions, demands a legal or equitable remedy. The defendant is required to respond to the plaintiff's complaint. If the plaintiff is successful, judgment is in the plaintiff's favor, and a variety of court orders may be issued to enforce a right, award damages, or impose a temporary or permanent injunction to prevent an act or compel an act. A declaratory judgment may be issued to prevent future legal disputes.

Exam Probability: **High**

59. *Answer choices:*

(see index for correct answer)

- a. corporate values
- b. deep-level diversity
- c. process perspective

- d. personal values

Guidance: level 1

Accounting

Accounting or accountancy is the measurement, processing, and communication of financial information about economic entities such as businesses and corporations. The modern field was established by the Italian mathematician Luca Pacioli in 1494. Accounting, which has been called the "language of business", measures the results of an organization's economic activities and conveys this information to a variety of users, including investors, creditors, management, and regulators.

:: Options (finance) ::

A _____ bond is a type of bond that allows the issuer of the bond to retain the privilege of redeeming the bond at some point before the bond reaches its date of maturity. In other words, on the call date, the issuer has the right, but not the obligation, to buy back the bonds from the bond holders at a defined call price. Technically speaking, the bonds are not really bought and held by the issuer but are instead cancelled immediately.

Exam Probability: **Low**

1. *Answer choices:*

(see index for correct answer)

- a. Ascot
- b. Callable
- c. Timer Call
- d. Compound option

Guidance: level 1

:: Management accounting ::

_____ is an accountancy practice, the aim of which is to provide an offset to the mark-to-market movement of the derivative in the profit and loss account. There are two types of hedge recognized. For a fair value hedge the offset is achieved either by marking-to-market an asset or a liability which offsets the P&L movement of the derivative. For a cash flow hedge some of the derivative volatility into a separate component of the entity's equity called the cash flow hedge reserve. Where a hedge relationship is effective, most of the mark-to-market derivative volatility will be offset in the profit and loss account. _____ entails much compliance - involving documenting the hedge relationship and both prospectively and retrospectively proving that the hedge relationship is effective.

Exam Probability: **Low**

2. *Answer choices:*

(see index for correct answer)

- a. Institute of Management Accountants
- b. Corporate travel management
- c. Chartered Institute of Management Accountants
- d. Hedge accounting

Guidance: level 1

:: Production and manufacturing ::

_____ consists of organization-wide efforts to "install and make permanent climate where employees continuously improve their ability to provide on demand products and services that customers will find of particular value." "Total" emphasizes that departments in addition to production are obligated to improve their operations; "management" emphasizes that executives are obligated to actively manage quality through funding, training, staffing, and goal setting. While there is no widely agreed-upon approach, TQM efforts typically draw heavily on the previously developed tools and techniques of quality control. TQM enjoyed widespread attention during the late 1980s and early 1990s before being overshadowed by ISO 9000, Lean manufacturing, and Six Sigma.

Exam Probability: **High**

3. *Answer choices:*

(see index for correct answer)

- a. Reverse engineering
- b. Total quality management
- c. Highly accelerated stress audit
- d. Division of labour

Guidance: level 1

:: Insurance terms ::

A _____ in the broadest sense is a natural person or other legal entity who receives money or other benefits from a benefactor. For example, the _____ of a life insurance policy is the person who receives the payment of the amount of insurance after the death of the insured.

Exam Probability: **High**

4. *Answer choices:*

(see index for correct answer)

- a. Certified marine insurance professional
- b. Beneficiary
- c. Certified Insurance Counselor
- d. Copayment

Guidance: level 1

:: United States Generally Accepted Accounting Principles ::

In the United States, the _____ , Subpart F of the OMB Uniform Guidance, is a rigorous, organization-wide audit or examination of an entity that expends $750,000 or more of federal assistance received for its operations. Usually performed annually, the _____ 's objective is to provide assurance to the US federal government as to the management and use of such funds by recipients such as states, cities, universities, non-profit organizations, and Indian Tribes. The audit is typically performed by an independent certified public accountant and encompasses both financial and compliance components. The _____ s must be submitted to the Federal Audit Clearinghouse along with a data collection form, Form SF-SAC.

Exam Probability: **High**

5. *Answer choices:*

(see index for correct answer)

- a. GASB 45
- b. FIN 46
- c. Working Group on Financial Markets
- d. Single Audit

Guidance: level 1

:: Real property law ::

_____ is the judicial process whereby a will is "proved" in a court of law and accepted as a valid public document that is the true last testament of the deceased, or whereby the estate is settled according to the laws of intestacy in the state of residence [or real property] of the deceased at time of death in the absence of a legal will.

Exam Probability: **Low**

6. *Answer choices:*
(see index for correct answer)

- a. Locus in quo
- b. Property abstract
- c. Probate
- d. Land registration

Guidance: level 1

:: ::

_____ is the process of making predictions of the future based on past and present data and most commonly by analysis of trends. A commonplace example might be estimation of some variable of interest at some specified future date. Prediction is a similar, but more general term. Both might refer to formal statistical methods employing time series, cross-sectional or longitudinal data, or alternatively to less formal judgmental methods. Usage can differ between areas of application: for example, in hydrology the terms "forecast" and "_____" are sometimes reserved for estimates of values at certain specific future times, while the term "prediction" is used for more general estimates, such as the number of times floods will occur over a long period.

Exam Probability: **High**

7. *Answer choices:*

(see index for correct answer)

- a. interpersonal communication
- b. Sarbanes-Oxley act of 2002
- c. Forecasting
- d. similarity-attraction theory

Guidance: level 1

:: Competition (economics) ::

In taxation and accounting, _____ refers to the rules and methods for pricing transactions within and between enterprises under common ownership or control. Because of the potential for cross-border controlled transactions to distort taxable income, tax authorities in many countries can adjust intragroup transfer prices that differ from what would have been charged by unrelated enterprises dealing at arm's length. The OECD and World Bank recommend intragroup pricing rules based on the arm's-length principle, and 19 of the 20 members of the G20 have adopted similar measures through bilateral treaties and domestic legislation, regulations, or administrative practice. Countries with _____ legislation generally follow the OECD _____ Guidelines for Multinational Enterprises and Tax Administrations in most respects, although their rules can differ on some important details.

Exam Probability: **Low**

8. *Answer choices:*

(see index for correct answer)

- a. Regulatory competition
- b. Competition
- c. Level playing field
- d. School choice

Guidance: level 1

:: Management accounting ::

_____ are costs that are not directly accountable to a cost object. _____ may be either fixed or variable. _____ include administration, personnel and security costs. These are those costs which are not directly related to production. Some _____ may be overhead. But some overhead costs can be directly attributed to a project and are direct costs.

Exam Probability: **Low**

9. *Answer choices:*

(see index for correct answer)

- a. Certified Management Accountant
- b. Institute of Management Accountants
- c. Indirect costs
- d. Management control system

Guidance: level 1

:: Corporations law ::

_____, also referred to as the certificate of incorporation or the corporate charter, are a document or charter that establishes the existence of a corporation in the United States and Canada. They generally are filed with the Secretary of State or other company registrar.

Exam Probability: **Medium**

10. *Answer choices:*

(see index for correct answer)

- a. Corporate lawyer
- b. Drag-along right
- c. Articles of incorporation
- d. Director primacy

Guidance: level 1

:: Financial accounting ::

A _____ is an ownership interest in a corporation with enough voting stock shares to prevail in any stockholders' motion. A majority of voting shares is always a _____. When a party holds less than the majority of the voting shares, other present circumstances can be considered to determine whether that party is still considered to hold a controlling ownership interest.

Exam Probability: **High**

11. *Answer choices:*

(see index for correct answer)

- a. Controlling interest
- b. Book value
- c. Finance charge
- d. Certified Public Accountants Association

Guidance: level 1

:: Organizational structure ::

An _____ defines how activities such as task allocation, coordination, and supervision are directed toward the achievement of organizational aims.

Exam Probability: **Medium**

12. *Answer choices:*

(see index for correct answer)

- a. Organizational structure
- b. Blessed Unrest
- c. Unorganisation
- d. Followership

Guidance: level 1

:: Management accounting ::

In business, a _____ is a division that gains revenue from product sales or service provided. The manager in _____ is accountable for revenue only.

Exam Probability: **Low**

13. *Answer choices:*

(see index for correct answer)

- a. Notional profit
- b. Indirect costs
- c. Revenue center
- d. Variable Costing

Guidance: level 1

:: Management ::

Business _____ is a discipline in operations management in which people use various methods to discover, model, analyze, measure, improve, optimize, and automate business processes. BPM focuses on improving corporate performance by managing business processes. Any combination of methods used to manage a company's business processes is BPM. Processes can be structured and repeatable or unstructured and variable. Though not required, enabling technologies are often used with BPM.

Exam Probability: **High**

14. *Answer choices:*

(see index for correct answer)

- a. Relational view

- b. Automated decision support
- c. Topple rate
- d. Project team builder

Guidance: level 1

:: Management accounting ::

An _____ is a classification used for business units within an enterprise. The essential element of an _____ is that it is treated as a unit which is measured against its use of capital, as opposed to a cost or profit center, which are measured against raw costs or profits.

Exam Probability: **Medium**

15. *Answer choices:*

(see index for correct answer)

- a. Owner earnings
- b. Cost accounting
- c. Resource consumption accounting
- d. Investment center

Guidance: level 1

:: Banking ::

A _____ is a financial account maintained by a bank for a customer. A _____ can be a deposit account, a credit card account, a current account, or any other type of account offered by a financial institution, and represents the funds that a customer has entrusted to the financial institution and from which the customer can make withdrawals. Alternatively, accounts may be loan accounts in which case the customer owes money to the financial institution.

Exam Probability: **Medium**

16. *Answer choices:*

(see index for correct answer)

- a. Bought deal
- b. Village banking
- c. Bank account
- d. Demand deposit

Guidance: level 1

A _____ is the period used by governments for accounting and budget purposes, which varies between countries. It is also used for financial reporting by business and other organizations. Laws in many jurisdictions require company financial reports to be prepared and published on an annual basis, but generally do not require the reporting period to align with the calendar year. Taxation laws generally require accounting records to be maintained and taxes calculated on an annual basis, which usually corresponds to the _____ used for government purposes. The calculation of tax on an annual basis is especially relevant for direct taxation, such as income tax. Many annual government fees—such as Council rates, licence fees, etc.—are also levied on a _____ basis, while others are charged on an anniversary basis.

Exam Probability: **Low**

17. *Answer choices:*

(see index for correct answer)

- a. corporate values
- b. Fiscal year
- c. hierarchical perspective
- d. functional perspective

Guidance: level 1

:: Accounting in the United States ::

_____ refers to a Memorandum of Understanding signed in September 2002 between the Financial Accounting Standards Board, the US standard setter, and the International Accounting Standards Board. The agreement is so called as it was reached in Norwalk.

Exam Probability: **Medium**

18. *Answer choices:*

(see index for correct answer)

- a. National Association of State Boards of Accountancy
- b. Plug
- c. Financial Accounting Foundation
- d. Joseph Eve, Certified Public Accountants

Guidance: level 1

:: Loans ::

In finance, a _____ is the lending of money by one or more individuals, organizations, or other entities to other individuals, organizations etc. The recipient incurs a debt, and is usually liable to pay interest on that debt until it is repaid, and also to repay the principal amount borrowed.

Exam Probability: **Low**

19. *Answer choices:*

(see index for correct answer)

- a. BankBazaar
- b. Loan credit default swap index
- c. Title loan
- d. Loan

Guidance: level 1

:: Asset ::

In financial accounting, an _____ is any resource owned by the business. Anything tangible or intangible that can be owned or controlled to produce value and that is held by a company to produce positive economic value is an _____ . Simply stated, _____ s represent value of ownership that can be converted into cash . The balance sheet of a firm records the monetary value of the _____ s owned by that firm. It covers money and other valuables belonging to an individual or to a business.

Exam Probability: **Low**

20. *Answer choices:*

(see index for correct answer)

- a. Current asset
- b. Asset

Guidance: level 1

:: Accounting in the United States ::

The _____ is located in Norwalk, Connecticut, United States. It was organized in 1972 as a non-stock, Delaware Corporation. It is an independent organization in the private sector, operating with the goal of ensuring objectivity and integrity in financial reporting standards.

Exam Probability: **Low**

21. *Answer choices:*
(see index for correct answer)

- a. Financial Accounting Foundation
- b. Norwalk Agreement
- c. Trueblood Committee
- d. Accounting Principles Board

Guidance: level 1

:: Management accounting ::

_____ is a professional certification credential in the management accounting and financial management fields. The certification signifies that the person possesses knowledge in the areas of financial planning, analysis, control, decision support, and professional ethics. The CMA is a U.S.-based, globally recognized certification offered by the Institute of Management Accountants.

Exam Probability: **Low**

22. *Answer choices:*

(see index for correct answer)

- a. Process costing
- b. Hedge accounting
- c. Certified Management Accountant
- d. Corporate travel management

Guidance: level 1

:: Accounting terminology ::

A _____ contains all the accounts for recording transactions relating to a company's assets, liabilities, owners' equity, revenue, and expenses. In modern accounting software or ERP, the _____ works as a central repository for accounting data transferred from all subledgers or modules like accounts payable, accounts receivable, cash management, fixed assets, purchasing and projects. The _____ is the backbone of any accounting system which holds financial and non-financial data for an organization. The collection of all accounts is known as the _____. Each account is known as a ledger account. In a manual or non-computerized system this may be a large book. The statement of financial position and the statement of income and comprehensive income are both derived from the _____. Each account in the _____ consists of one or more pages. The _____ is where posting to the accounts occurs. Posting is the process of recording amounts as credits, and amounts as debits, in the pages of the _____. Additional columns to the right hold a running activity total.

Exam Probability: **Medium**

23. *Answer choices:*

(see index for correct answer)

- a. Impairment cost
- b. General ledger
- c. Accounts receivable
- d. Record to report

Guidance: level 1

:: Management accounting ::

_____s are costs that change as the quantity of the good or service that a business produces changes. _____s are the sum of marginal costs over all units produced. They can also be considered normal costs. Fixed costs and _____s make up the two components of total cost. Direct costs are costs that can easily be associated with a particular cost object. However, not all _____s are direct costs. For example, variable manufacturing overhead costs are _____s that are indirect costs, not direct costs. _____s are sometimes called unit-level costs as they vary with the number of units produced.

Exam Probability: **Medium**

24. *Answer choices:*

(see index for correct answer)

- a. Indirect costs
- b. Institute of Management Accountants
- c. Variable cost
- d. Semi-variable cost

Guidance: level 1

:: Commerce ::

Continuation of an entity as a _____ is presumed as the basis for financial reporting unless and until the entity's liquidation becomes imminent. Preparation of financial statements under this presumption is commonly referred to as the _____ basis of accounting. If and when an entity's liquidation becomes imminent, financial statements are prepared under the liquidation basis of accounting.

Exam Probability: **Medium**

25. *Answer choices:*

(see index for correct answer)

- a. Emerging Markets Index
- b. Going concern
- c. Coincidence of wants
- d. Mail order

Guidance: level 1

:: Commerce ::

A _____, is a document acknowledging that a person has received money or property in payment following a sale or other transfer of goods or provision of a service. All _____ s must have the date of purchase on them. If the recipient of the payment is legally required to collect sales tax or VAT from the customer, the amount would be added to the _____ and the collection would be deemed to have been on behalf of the relevant tax authority. In many countries, a retailer is required to include the sales tax or VAT in the displayed price of goods sold, from which the tax amount would be calculated at point of sale and remitted to the tax authorities in due course. Similarly, amounts may be deducted from amounts payable, as in the case of wage withholding taxes. On the other hand, tips or other gratuities given by a customer, for example in a restaurant, would not form part of the payment amount or appear on the _____ .

Exam Probability: **High**

26. *Answer choices:*

(see index for correct answer)

- a. Receipt
- b. The Staple
- c. Linestanding
- d. European Retail Round Table

Guidance: level 1

:: Corporate crime ::

_____ LLP, based in Chicago, was an American holding company. Formerly one of the "Big Five" accounting firms, the firm had provided auditing, tax, and consulting services to large corporations. By 2001, it had become one of the world's largest multinational companies.

Exam Probability: **Low**

27. *Answer choices:*

(see index for correct answer)

- a. Corporate Manslaughter and Corporate Homicide Act 2007
- b. General Development Corporation
- c. Arthur Andersen
- d. NatWest Three

Guidance: level 1

:: Accounting in the United States ::

The _____ is the source of generally accepted accounting principles used by state and local governments in the United States. As with most of the entities involved in creating GAAP in the United States, it is a private, non-governmental organization.

Exam Probability: **Medium**

28. *Answer choices:*

(see index for correct answer)

- a. Trueblood Committee
- b. Uniform Certified Public Accountant Examination
- c. Public Company Accounting Oversight Board
- d. Governmental Accounting Standards Board

Guidance: level 1

:: International taxation ::

A _____ tax, or a retention tax, is an income tax to be paid to the government by the payer of the income rather than by the recipient of the income. The tax is thus withheld or deducted from the income due to the recipient. In most jurisdictions, _____ tax applies to employment income. Many jurisdictions also require _____ tax on payments of interest or dividends. In most jurisdictions, there are additional _____ tax obligations if the recipient of the income is resident in a different jurisdiction, and in those circumstances _____ tax sometimes applies to royalties, rent or even the sale of real estate. Governments use _____ tax as a means to combat tax evasion, and sometimes impose additional _____ tax requirements if the recipient has been delinquent in filing tax returns, or in industries where tax evasion is perceived to be common.

Exam Probability: **High**

29. *Answer choices:*

(see index for correct answer)

- a. Foreign personal holding company

- b. World taxation system
- c. Currency transaction tax
- d. Tax harmonization

Guidance: level 1

:: Management ::

The _____ is a strategy performance management tool – a semi-standard structured report, that can be used by managers to keep track of the execution of activities by the staff within their control and to monitor the consequences arising from these actions.

Exam Probability: **Low**

30. *Answer choices:*

(see index for correct answer)

- a. Balanced scorecard
- b. Remedial action
- c. Dominant design
- d. Design leadership

Guidance: level 1

:: Basic financial concepts ::

In finance, maturity or _____ refers to the final payment date of a loan or other financial instrument, at which point the principal is due to be paid.

Exam Probability: **Medium**

31. *Answer choices:*

(see index for correct answer)

- a. Maturity date
- b. Deflation
- c. Lodgement
- d. Base effect

Guidance: level 1

:: Management accounting ::

_____ is a professional business study of Accounts and management in which we learn importance of accounts in our management system.

Exam Probability: **Low**

32. *Answer choices:*

(see index for correct answer)

- a. Chartered Institute of Management Accountants
- b. Resource consumption accounting
- c. Managerial risk accounting
- d. Accounting management

Guidance: level 1

:: Financial markets ::

_____ s are monetary contracts between parties. They can be created, traded, modified and settled. They can be cash , evidence of an ownership interest in an entity , or a contractual right to receive or deliver cash .

Exam Probability: **Medium**

33. *Answer choices:*
(see index for correct answer)

- a. Floor broker
- b. Money market in India
- c. Trading strategy
- d. Financial instrument

Guidance: level 1

:: Finance ::

_____, in finance and accounting, means stated value or face value. From this come the expressions at par, over par and under par.

Exam Probability: **High**

34. *Answer choices:*

(see index for correct answer)

- a. Anaplan
- b. Political arbitrage
- c. Par value
- d. Total return swap

Guidance: level 1

:: Financial ratios ::

_____ or interest coverage ratio is a measure of a company's ability to honor its debt payments. It may be calculated as either EBIT or EBITDA divided by the total interest payable.

Exam Probability: **Medium**

35. *Answer choices:*

(see index for correct answer)

- a. Times interest earned
- b. Sortino ratio
- c. Average collection period
- d. Price/cash flow ratio

Guidance: level 1

:: Management accounting ::

In economics, _____ s, indirect costs or overheads are business expenses that are not dependent on the level of goods or services produced by the business. They tend to be time-related, such as interest or rents being paid per month, and are often referred to as overhead costs. This is in contrast to variable costs, which are volume-related and unknown at the beginning of the accounting year. For a simple example, such as a bakery, the monthly rent for the baking facilities, and the monthly payments for the security system and basic phone line are _____ s, as they do not change according to how much bread the bakery produces and sells. On the other hand, the wage costs of the bakery are variable, as the bakery will have to hire more workers if the production of bread increases. Economists reckon _____ as a entry barrier for new entrepreneurs.

Exam Probability: **Medium**

36. *Answer choices:*

(see index for correct answer)

- a. Fixed cost
- b. Direct material price variance

- c. Spend management
- d. Variable Costing

Guidance: level 1

:: Business law ::

A _____, also known as the sole trader, individual entrepreneurship or proprietorship, is a type of enterprise that is owned and run by one person and in which there is no legal distinction between the owner and the business entity. A sole trader does not necessarily work `alone`—it is possible for the sole trader to employ other people.

Exam Probability: **Low**

37. *Answer choices:*

(see index for correct answer)

- a. Duty of fair representation
- b. Oppression remedy
- c. Ease of doing business index
- d. Uniform Commercial Code

Guidance: level 1

:: Management accounting ::

In _____ or managerial accounting, managers use the provisions of accounting information in order to better inform themselves before they decide matters within their organizations, which aids their management and performance of control functions.

Exam Probability: **Low**

38. *Answer choices:*

(see index for correct answer)

- a. Target costing
- b. Management accounting
- c. Dual overhead rate
- d. Grenzplankostenrechnung

Guidance: level 1

:: Financial statements ::

In financial accounting, a _____ or statement of financial position or statement of financial condition is a summary of the financial balances of an individual or organization, whether it be a sole proprietorship, a business partnership, a corporation, private limited company or other organization such as Government or not-for-profit entity. Assets, liabilities and ownership equity are listed as of a specific date, such as the end of its financial year. A _____ is often described as a "snapshot of a company's financial condition". Of the four basic financial statements, the _____ is the only statement which applies to a single point in time of a business' calendar year.

Exam Probability: **High**

39. *Answer choices:*

(see index for correct answer)

- a. Emphasis of matter
- b. PnL Explained
- c. Statement on Auditing Standards No. 55
- d. Balance sheet

Guidance: level 1

:: ::

_____ is the consumption and saving opportunity gained by an entity within a specified timeframe, which is generally expressed in monetary terms. For households and individuals, " _____ is the sum of all the wages, salaries, profits, interest payments, rents, and other forms of earnings received in a given period of time."

Exam Probability: **Low**

40. *Answer choices:*

(see index for correct answer)

- a. empathy
- b. co-culture

- c. process perspective
- d. Income

Guidance: level 1

:: ::

An _____ is an asset that lacks physical substance. It is defined in opposition to physical assets such as machinery and buildings. An _____ is usually very hard to evaluate. Patents, copyrights, franchises, goodwill, trademarks, and trade names. The general interpretation also includes software and other intangible computer based assets are all examples of _____ s. _____ s generally—though not necessarily—suffer from typical market failures of non-rivalry and non-excludability.

Exam Probability: **Low**

41. *Answer choices:*

(see index for correct answer)

- a. information systems assessment
- b. functional perspective
- c. Intangible asset
- d. hierarchical

Guidance: level 1

:: Mathematical finance ::

In economics and finance, _____, also known as present discounted value, is the value of an expected income stream determined as of the date of valuation. The _____ is always less than or equal to the future value because money has interest-earning potential, a characteristic referred to as the time value of money, except during times of negative interest rates, when the _____ will be more than the future value. Time value can be described with the simplified phrase, "A dollar today is worth more than a dollar tomorrow". Here, `worth more` means that its value is greater. A dollar today is worth more than a dollar tomorrow because the dollar can be invested and earn a day`s worth of interest, making the total accumulate to a value more than a dollar by tomorrow. Interest can be compared to rent. Just as rent is paid to a landlord by a tenant without the ownership of the asset being transferred, interest is paid to a lender by a borrower who gains access to the money for a time before paying it back. By letting the borrower have access to the money, the lender has sacrificed the exchange value of this money, and is compensated for it in the form of interest. The initial amount of the borrowed funds is less than the total amount of money paid to the lender.

Exam Probability: **Medium**

42. *Answer choices:*

(see index for correct answer)

- a. Stochastic investment model
- b. Mathematical finance
- c. Present value
- d. Volatility smile

Guidance: level 1

:: Business models ::

A _____ is a company that owns enough voting stock in another firm to control management and operation by influencing or electing its board of directors. The company is deemed a subsidiary of the _____ .

Exam Probability: **Low**

43. *Answer choices:*
(see index for correct answer)

- a. Business networking
- b. Brainsworking
- c. Data as a service
- d. Artel

Guidance: level 1

:: Shareholders ::

A _____ is a payment made by a corporation to its shareholders, usually as a distribution of profits. When a corporation earns a profit or surplus, the corporation is able to re-invest the profit in the business and pay a proportion of the profit as a _____ to shareholders. Distribution to shareholders may be in cash or, if the corporation has a _____ reinvestment plan, the amount can be paid by the issue of further shares or share repurchase. When _____s are paid, shareholders typically must pay income taxes, and the corporation does not receive a corporate income tax deduction for the _____ payments.

Exam Probability: **High**

44. *Answer choices:*

(see index for correct answer)

- a. Shareholder Rights Directive
- b. UK Individual Shareholders Society
- c. Shareholder primacy
- d. Dividend

Guidance: level 1

:: Stock market ::

A _____, equity market or share market is the aggregation of buyers and sellers of stocks, which represent ownership claims on businesses; these may include securities listed on a public stock exchange, as well as stock that is only traded privately. Examples of the latter include shares of private companies which are sold to investors through equity crowdfunding platforms. Stock exchanges list shares of common equity as well as other security types, e.g. corporate bonds and convertible bonds.

Exam Probability: **Medium**

45. *Answer choices:*

(see index for correct answer)

- a. Instinet
- b. Ada TV
- c. Wealth management
- d. Short-term trading

Guidance: level 1

:: Financial ratios ::

_____ is the difference between revenue and cost of goods sold divided by revenue. _____ is expressed as a percentage. Generally, it is calculated as the selling price of an item, less the cost of goods sold .
_____ is often used interchangeably with Gross Profit, but the terms are different. When speaking about a monetary amount, it is technically correct to use the term Gross Profit; when referring to a percentage or ratio, it is correct to use _____ . In other words, _____ is a percentage value, while Gross Profit is a monetary value.

Exam Probability: **Low**

46. *Answer choices:*

(see index for correct answer)

- a. Cash conversion cycle
- b. Gross margin
- c. P/B ratio
- d. Jaws ratio

Guidance: level 1

:: Generally Accepted Accounting Principles ::

The term _____ is most often used to describe a practice or document that is provided as a courtesy or satisfies minimum requirements, conforms to a norm or doctrine, tends to be performed perfunctorily or is considered a formality.

Exam Probability: **Medium**

47. *Answer choices:*

(see index for correct answer)

- a. Reserve
- b. Gross profit
- c. AICPA Statements of Position
- d. Pro forma

Guidance: level 1

:: Management accounting ::

> _____ is accounting which tracks the costs and revenues by "job" and enables standardized reporting of profitability by job. For an accounting system to support _____, it must allow job numbers to be assigned to individual items of expenses and revenues. A job can be defined to be a specific project done for one customer, or a single unit of product manufactured, or a batch of units of the same type that are produced together.

Exam Probability: **High**

48. *Answer choices:*

(see index for correct answer)

- a. Financial statement analysis
- b. Job costing

- c. Fixed cost
- d. Direct material usage variance

Guidance: level 1

:: Investment ::

In economics, _____ is spending which increases the availability of fixed capital goods or means of production and goods inventories. It is the total spending on newly produced physical capital and on inventories —that is, gross investment—minus replacement investment, which simply replaces depreciated capital goods. It is productive capital formation plus net additions to the stock of housing and the stock of inventories.

Exam Probability: **High**

49. *Answer choices:*

(see index for correct answer)

- a. Private equity
- b. Amateur investor
- c. Net investment
- d. capital Budget

Guidance: level 1

:: Inventory ::

_____ is a system of inventory in which updates are made on a periodic basis. This differs from perpetual inventory systems, where updates are made as seen fit.

Exam Probability: **Medium**

50. *Answer choices:*

(see index for correct answer)

- a. Phantom inventory
- b. Cost of goods sold
- c. Reorder point
- d. Periodic inventory

Guidance: level 1

:: United States Generally Accepted Accounting Principles ::

A _____ is a set of U.S. government financial statements comprising the financial report of a state, municipal or other governmental entity that complies with the accounting requirements promulgated by the Governmental Accounting Standards Board. GASB provides standards for the content of a CAFR in its annually updated publication Codification of Governmental Accounting and Financial Reporting Standards. The U.S. Federal Government adheres to standards determined by the Federal Accounting Standards Advisory Board.

Exam Probability: **High**

51. Answer choices:

(see index for correct answer)

- a. Working Group on Financial Markets
- b. Comprehensive annual financial report
- c. Available for sale
- d. Accounting for leases in the United States

Guidance: level 1

:: Real estate valuation ::

_____ or OMV is the price at which an asset would trade in a competitive auction setting. _____ is often used interchangeably with open _____, fair value or fair _____, although these terms have distinct definitions in different standards, and may or may not differ in some circumstances.

Exam Probability: **Low**

52. Answer choices:

(see index for correct answer)

- a. Highest and best use
- b. Market value
- c. Real estate benchmarking
- d. cap rate

Guidance: level 1

:: Accounting terminology ::

> _____ is an independent, objective assurance and consulting activity designed to add value to and improve an organization's operations. It helps an organization accomplish its objectives by bringing a systematic, disciplined approach to evaluate and improve the effectiveness of risk management, control and governance processes. _____ achieves this by providing insight and recommendations based on analyses and assessments of data and business processes. With commitment to integrity and accountability, _____ provides value to governing bodies and senior management as an objective source of independent advice. Professionals called internal auditors are employed by organizations to perform the _____ activity.

Exam Probability: **Medium**

53. *Answer choices:*
(see index for correct answer)

- a. double-entry bookkeeping
- b. outstanding balance
- c. managerial accounting
- d. Internal auditing

Guidance: level 1

:: Financial ratios ::

The _____ is a financial ratio indicating the relative proportion of equity used to finance a company's assets. The two components are often taken from the firm's balance sheet or statement of financial position, but the ratio may also be calculated using market values for both, if the company's equities are publicly traded.

Exam Probability: **Medium**

54. *Answer choices:*

(see index for correct answer)

- a. interest margin
- b. Return on event
- c. Equity ratio
- d. Rate of return on a portfolio

Guidance: level 1

:: Generally Accepted Accounting Principles ::

A _____ or reacquired stock is stock which is bought back by the issuing company, reducing the amount of outstanding stock on the open market.

Exam Probability: **High**

55. *Answer choices:*

(see index for correct answer)

- a. Depreciation
- b. Treasury stock
- c. Gross sales
- d. Operating income

Guidance: level 1

:: Generally Accepted Accounting Principles ::

The _____ principle is a cornerstone of accrual accounting together with the matching principle. They both determine the accounting period in which revenues and expenses are recognized. According to the principle, revenues are recognized when they are realized or realizable, and are earned , no matter when cash is received. In cash accounting – in contrast – revenues are recognized when cash is received no matter when goods or services are sold.

Exam Probability: **Medium**

56. *Answer choices:*
(see index for correct answer)

- a. Cost pool
- b. Shares outstanding
- c. Net realizable value
- d. Cost principle

Guidance: level 1

:: ::

An inheritance or _____ is a tax paid by a person who inherits money or property or a levy on the estate of a person who has died.

Exam Probability: **Medium**

57. *Answer choices:*

(see index for correct answer)

- a. Estate tax
- b. hierarchical perspective
- c. personal values
- d. open system

Guidance: level 1

:: ::

_____ science is the application of science to criminal and civil laws, mainly—on the criminal side—during criminal investigation, as governed by the legal standards of admissible evidence and criminal procedure.

Exam Probability: **Medium**

58. *Answer choices:*

(see index for correct answer)

- a. process perspective
- b. interpersonal communication
- c. Character
- d. empathy

Guidance: level 1

:: Generally Accepted Accounting Principles ::

In accounting, _____, gross margin, sales profit, or credit sales is the difference between revenue and the cost of making a product or providing a service, before deducting overheads, payroll, taxation, and interest payments. This is different from operating profit. Gross margin is the term normally used in the U.S., while _____ is the more common usage in the UK and Australia.

Exam Probability: **High**

59. *Answer choices:*

(see index for correct answer)

- a. Generally Accepted Accounting Practice
- b. Earnings before interest, taxes, depreciation, and amortization
- c. Consolidation
- d. Construction in progress

Guidance: level 1

INDEX: Correct Answers

Foundations of Business

1. a: Land

2. b: Finance

3. b: Evaluation

4. c: Comparative advantage

5. : Limited liability

6. d: Preference

7. c: Explanation

8. a: Credit

9. : Restructuring

10. : E-commerce

11. b: Small business

12. a: Efficiency

13. b: Schedule

14. c: Sales

15. d: Alliance

16. c: Balanced scorecard

17. : Advertising

18. a: Fraud

19. d: Solution

20. d: Question

21. b: Recession

22. : Debt

23. : Income statement

24. a: Dimension

25. d: Money

26. d: Economy

27. d: Crisis

28. b: Arbitration

29. b: Pattern

30. b: Resource management

31. b: Benchmarking

32. a: Cooperation

33. b: Capitalism

34. b: Energies

35. c: Planning

36. a: Stock market

37. : Focus group

38. c: Market segmentation

39. c: Goal

40. a: Internal Revenue Service

41. c: Entrepreneur

42. : Risk

43. d: Present value

44. a: Bias

45. c: Expense

46. d: Diagram

47. a: Dividend

48. a: SWOT analysis

49. a: Working capital

50. a: Affirmative action

51. : Market value

52. a: Availability

53. : Career

54. c: Brainstorming

55. a: Foreign direct investment

56. c: Internal control

57. d: Accounting

58. : Training

59. d: Sony

Management

1. a: Inspection

2. a: Purchasing

3. c: Problem solving

4. c: Resource allocation

5. d: Job enlargement

6. c: Employee stock

7. : Authority

8. a: Resource management

9. c: Cooperative

10. a: Span of control

11. c: Industrial Revolution

12. : Income

13. b: Goal setting

14. b: Problem

15. b: Size

16. a: Information

17. d: Learning organization

18. c: Productivity

19. : Case study

20. b: Sexual harassment

21. a: Choice

22. : Scheduling

23. c: E-commerce

24. : Human capital

25. a: Firm

26. b: Emotional intelligence

27. b: Referent power

28. b: Management system

29. a: Feedback

30. c: Governance

31. d: Labor relations

32. : Balanced scorecard

33. c: Scientific management

34. : Chief executive

35. d: Logistics

36. a: Procurement

37. a: Free trade

38. : Job rotation

39. b: Bottom line

40. d: Property

41. b: Management by objectives

42. b: Question

43. c: Analysis

44. : Management

45. c: Product life cycle

46. c: Competitive advantage

47. c: Meeting

48. d: Customer

49. c: Forecasting

50. d: Quality circle

51. d: Organization chart

52. d: Subsidiary

53. c: Business model

54. : Bias

55. d: Quality assurance

56. b: Telecommuting

57. b: Explanation

58. : Goal

59. c: Checklist

Business law

1. c: Product liability

2. b: Criminal law

3. d: Treaty

4. : Marketing

5. c: Securities and Exchange Commission

6. : Common carrier

7. : Lien

8. : Bankruptcy

9. d: Money laundering

10. c: Economy

11. a: World Trade Organization

12. a: Competitor

13. b: Eminent domain

14. b: Appeal

15. a: Cyberspace

16. : Dividend

17. b: Warranty

18. a: Affidavit

19. b: Broker

20. : Committee

21. : Presentment

22. : Negotiation

23. b: Mens rea

24. c: Labor relations

25. d: Preference

26. : Amendment

27. d: Prohibition

28. a: White-collar crime

29. a: Issuer

30. : Output contract

31. d: Independent contractor

32. c: Bailee

33. : Requirements contract

34. b: Firm

35. c: Sole proprietorship

36. c: Advertisement

37. : Condition precedent

38. : Rescind

39. a: Technology

40. a: Property

41. a: Jurisdiction

42. : Trespass

43. a: Scienter

44. : Management

45. d: Computer fraud

46. c: Employment discrimination

47. a: Merchant

48. d: Brand

49. c: Categorical imperative

50. : Consumer Good

51. b: Delegation

52. b: Implied warranty

53. d: Public policy

54. : Welfare

55. c: Subrogation

56. c: Purchasing

57. a: Resource

58. c: Fraud

59. c: Commerce

Finance

1. a: Residual value

2. c: Interest

3. b: Incentive

4. c: Wall Street

5. c: Net worth

6. d: Goldman Sachs

7. : Contract

8. : Shares

9. : Secondary market

10. c: Average Cost

11. : Book value

12. d: Expense

13. : Corporate governance

14. : Stock exchange

15. c: Expected return

16. d: Raw material

17. : Sinking fund

18. b: Operating lease

19. : Property

20. a: Initial public offering

21. b: Debt-to-equity ratio

22. b: Stock

23. b: Finance

24. a: Adjusting entries

25. a: Accountant

26. d: Stock price

27. b: Accounting

28. d: Securities and Exchange Commission

29. a: Managerial accounting

30. b: Opportunity cost

31. a: Income statement

32. : Competition

33. b: Inflation

34. c: Cost of goods sold

35. c: Indenture

36. : Standard deviation

37. c: Stockholder

38. a: Inventory turnover

39. b: Current asset

40. b: Time value of money

41. c: Call option

42. a: Accounting method

43. b: Preferred stock

44. : Put option

45. c: Return on assets

46. b: Matching principle

47. a: Debt ratio

48. b: Credit

49. d: General ledger

50. d: Chief financial officer

51. : Risk premium

52. c: Earnings per share

53. d: Cost allocation

54. d: Risk assessment

55. : Bank reconciliation

56. a: Return on investment

57. : Absorption costing

58. b: Cost

59. d: Write-off

Human resource management

1. a: Layoff

2. c: Restricted stock

3. d: Expert power

4. c: Nepotism

5. c: Job description

6. d: Psychological contract

7. d: Interdependence

8. d: Structured interview

9. c: Golden parachute

10. b: Individualism

11. a: Person Analysis

12. : Eustress

13. b: Industrial relations

14. b: Talent management

15. a: Outplacement

16. b: Independent contractor

17. a: Deferred compensation

18. b: Congress

19. : Occupational Safety and Health Act

20. b: Disability insurance

21. b: Xerox Corporation

22. b: Performance appraisal

23. b: Right-to-work law

24. c: Foreign worker

25. : Overlearning

26. a: Severance package

27. c: Drug test

28. d: Price Waterhouse v. Hopkins

29. a: Sexual orientation

30. a: Works council

31. c: Equal Employment Opportunity Commission

32. b: Retirement

33. : Profit sharing

34. a: Labor force

35. c: Best practice

36. b: Living wage

37. a: Social media

38. b: Action learning

39. b: Employee Free Choice Act

40. b: Hazard analysis

41. a: Distance learning

42. d: Progressive discipline

43. c: Job performance

44. : Onboarding

45. c: Bottom line

46. b: Employee Polygraph Protection Act

47. : Seniority

48. a: Brainstorming

49. : Family violence

50. b: Predictive validity

51. : Mining

52. d: Public administration

53. a: Job sharing

54. b: Compensation and benefits

55. c: Performance measurement

56. c: Substance abuse

57. b: Merit pay

58. : Learning organization

59. c: Applicant tracking system

Information systems

1. a: Interactivity

2. d: Web page

3. b: Virtual world

4. d: Picasa

5. b: Google Maps

6. : Disaster recovery plan

7. c: Non-repudiation

8. c: Consumerization

9. c: Click-through rate

10. b: Census

11. b: Sensitivity analysis

12. d: Common Criteria

13. d: Geocoding

14. a: Mouse

15. b: Folksonomy

16. a: Structured query language

17. a: PayPal

18. b: Unstructured data

19. c: Blogger

20. d: Avatar

21. c: Supply chain management

22. c: Accessibility

23. b: Diagram

24. : Information flow

25. a: Data security

26. c: Kinect

27. a: Encryption

28. d: Interaction

29. b: Facebook

30. c: Information ethics

31. : Information overload

32. a: Monopoly

33. d: Data field

34. a: Data cleansing

35. c: Data governance

36. b: Radio-frequency identification

37. a: Information

38. d: Decision-making

39. b: Extensible Markup Language

40. c: Manifesto

41. : Balanced scorecard

42. : YouTube

43. d: Epicor

44. c: Data element

45. b: Extranet

46. : Random access

47. : Management information system

48. d: Statistics

49. c: Personalization

50. : Positioning system

51. d: Search engine optimization

52. c: Computer-aided manufacturing

53. d: Cookie

54. d: Relational database

55. a: Identity theft

56. : Interoperability

57. a: Automated teller machine

58. c: Help desk

59. a: Infrastructure

Marketing

1. a: Frequency

2. c: Consultant

3. d: Mass customization

4. d: Department store

5. d: Globalization

6. b: Electronic data interchange

7. : Planning

8. c: Franchising

9. : American Express

10. a: Standing

11. d: Price war

12. b: Marketing mix

13. b: Product line

14. b: Google

15. c: Appeal

16. a: E-commerce

17. b: Merchant

18. c: Product development

19. b: Competition

20. : Direct mail

21. a: Budget

22. a: Research and development

23. d: Mobile marketing

24. : Brand extension

25. c: Copyright

26. d: Telemarketing

27. : Contract

28. a: Publicity

29. : Advertising campaign

30. b: Dimension

31. c: Marketing

32. b: Perception

33. d: New product development

34. a: Exchange rate

35. d: Market segmentation

36. b: Business model

37. b: Sherman Antitrust Act

38. a: Personnel

39. d: Warranty

40. c: Mass marketing

41. b: Secondary data

42. c: Consumer Protection

43. : Patent

44. b: Social marketing

45. d: Household

46. d: Public relations

47. : Negotiation

48. c: Coupon

49. d: Subsidiary

50. d: Intellectual property

51. b: Brand

52. d: Pricing

53. b: Shares

54. : INDEX

55. c: Sales promotion

56. : Penetration pricing

57. a: Customer

58. d: Brainstorming

59. : Technology

Manufacturing

1. b: Property

2. a: Expediting

3. a: Poka-yoke

4. a: Cost reduction

5. b: Inventory

6. c: Process engineering

7. c: Dimension

8. : Rolling

9. : Pattern

10. : Turbine

11. d: Certification

12. d: Six Sigma

13. a: Process management

14. b: Joint Commission

15. d: Clay

16. a: Project manager

17. b: Blanket

18. a: Materials management

19. : Credit

20. c: Good

21. b: Purchasing

22. a: Service quality

23. d: Change management

24. b: Scope statement

25. d: Quality costs

26. d: Sales

27. c: Virtual team

28. c: Original equipment manufacturer

29. b: Reverse auction

30. a: Supply chain network

31. b: Workflow

32. b: Assembly line

33. d: Cost estimate

34. c: Project

35. a: Paper

36. : Cost

37. : Interaction

38. : Retail

39. a: Kanban

40. c: Thomas Register

41. : American Society for Quality

42. d: Global sourcing

43. c: METRIC

44. : Supply chain management

45. : Transaction cost

46. : Supply chain risk management

47. b: Technical support

48. d: Resource management

49. : Economic order quantity

50. d: Project team

51. d: Synergy

52. a: Economies of scope

53. b: Control limits

54. : Sunk costs

55. d: Downtime

56. a: Waste

57. c: Cost driver

58. d: Purchasing process

59. c: Zero Defects

Commerce

1. d: DigiCash

2. a: Level of service

3. d: Hearing

4. a: York

5. : Hospitality

6. c: Competitive advantage

7. d: Innovation

8. d: Warehouse

9. : Strategic plan

10. d: Supply chain

11. c: Risk management

12. a: Inventory

13. b: Federal government

14. : Semantic

15. d: European Union

16. d: Walt Disney

17. : Drawback

18. b: Yield management

19. a: Basket

20. b: Wall Street Journal

21. d: Value-added network

22. b: Supranational

23. c: Quality assurance

24. : Supply chain management

25. c: Advertising

26. c: Authentication

27. d: Trial

28. c: Recruitment

29. d: Bill of lading

30. b: Project

31. : Social shopping

32. d: Industrial Revolution

33. c: Human resources

34. c: Business-to-business

35. c: Appeal

36. b: Chief executive officer

37. a: Product mix

38. b: Economics

39. : Broker

40. b: Authorize.Net

41. : American Express

42. c: Commerce

43. : Economies of scale

44. c: Shopping cart

45. b: Labor union

46. d: Cash flow

47. : Subsidy

48. b: Auction

49. a: Complexity

50. c: Bankruptcy

51. b: Bank

52. b: Manufacturing

53. c: Logistics Management

54. b: Empowerment

55. d: Amazon Payments

56. c: Common carrier

57. c: Accounting

58. c: Silver

59. : Real estate

Business ethics

1. a: Parental leave

2. b: Transocean

3. : Individualistic culture

4. d: Real estate

5. : Fannie Mae

6. b: Subprime lending

7. b: Protestant work ethic

8. a: Six Sigma

9. a: Public relations

10. b: Transformational leadership

11. : Cause-related marketing

12. a: Labor relations

13. : European Commission

14. a: Socialism

15. c: Global Fund

16. a: White-collar crime

17. d: Dress code

18. d: Aristotle

19. c: Corporate citizenship

20. : Sexual harassment

21. a: Dual relationship

22. d: Dilemma

23. a: Oil spill

24. d: Risk assessment

25. : Toxic waste

26. c: Veil of ignorance

27. a: Skill

28. c: Internal control

29. c: Charles Ponzi

30. d: Clean Water Act

31. : Principal Financial

32. d: Micromanagement

33. a: Referent power

34. a: Nepotism

35. a: Solar power

36. b: Junk bond

37. a: Consumer Protection

38. c: Organizational culture

39. b: Kyoto Protocol

40. b: Marketing ethics

41. b: Cultural relativism

42. b: Constitutional law

43. c: Siemens

44. c: Enron

45. : Accounting

46. : Volcker Rule

47. c: Organic food

48. : Hedonism

49. c: Locus of control

50. c: Green marketing

51. c: Feedback

52. b: United Farm Workers

53. d: Statutory law

54. : Social responsibility

55. c: Corporate social responsibility

56. d: Invisible hand

57. : Madoff

58. c: Stanford Financial Group

59. : Lawsuit

Accounting

1. b: Callable

2. d: Hedge accounting

3. b: Total quality management

4. b: Beneficiary

5. d: Single Audit

6. c: Probate

7. c: Forecasting

8. : Transfer pricing

9. c: Indirect costs

10. c: Articles of incorporation

11. a: Controlling interest

12. a: Organizational structure

13. c: Revenue center

14. : Process Management

15. d: Investment center

16. c: Bank account

17. b: Fiscal year

18. : Norwalk Agreement

19. d: Loan

20. b: Asset

21. a: Financial Accounting Foundation

22. c: Certified Management Accountant

23. b: General ledger

24. c: Variable cost

25. b: Going concern

26. a: Receipt

27. c: Arthur Andersen

28. d: Governmental Accounting Standards Board

29. : Withholding

30. a: Balanced scorecard

31. a: Maturity date

32. d: Accounting management

33. d: Financial instrument

34. c: Par value

35. a: Times interest earned

36. a: Fixed cost

37. : Sole proprietorship

38. b: Management accounting

39. d: Balance sheet

40. d: Income

41. c: Intangible asset

42. c: Present value

43. : Parent company

44. d: Dividend

45. : Stock Market

46. b: Gross margin

47. d: Pro forma

48. b: Job costing

49. c: Net investment

50. d: Periodic inventory

51. b: Comprehensive annual financial report

52. b: Market value

53. d: Internal auditing

54. c: Equity ratio

55. b: Treasury stock

56. : Revenue recognition

57. a: Estate tax

58. : Forensic

59. : Gross profit

CPSIA information can be obtained
at www.ICGtesting.com
Printed in the USA
LVHW031107301019
635717LV00004B/379/P